The Emergence of the European Human Rights Law

The Emergence of the European Human Rights Law

An Essay on Judicial Creativity

Dragoljub Popović

eleven
international publishing

Published, sold and distributed by Eleven International Publishing
P.O. Box 85576
2508 CG Den Haag
Tel.: +31 70 330 7033
Fax: +31 70-330 7030
e-mail: verkoop@budh.nl
www.elevenpub.com

Sold and distributed in USA and Canada
International Specialized Book Services
920 NE 58th Avenue, Suite 300
Portland, OR 97213-3786, USA
Tel: 1-800-944-6190 (toll-free)
Fax: +1 503 280-8832
orders@isbs.com
www.isbs.com

Printed on acid-free paper.

ISBN: 978-94-90947-13-2

Printed in The Netherlands

For Maja, and for Jovana and Nadège

Table of Contents

Abbreviations

app.	application
Convention	The European Convention on Human Rights/ the Convention for the Protection of Human Rights and Fundamental Freedoms of 1950
Court	The European Court of Human Rights
ECHR	The European Court of Human Rights
HUDOC	HUDOC database <http://echr.coe.int>
judgments and decisions	Judgments and Decisions of the European Court of Human Rights
member state	member state of the Council of Europe
Reports	Reports of Judgments and Decisions of the European Court of Human Rights
Strasbourg	European Court of Human Rights
UCL	University Collge London

Preface

The rule of law guiding a particular case is always to be determined by written law, customary law, the general principles of law, judicial decisions, including publications by highly qualified scholars discussing their jurisprudence. This principle is also provided in Article 38 of the Statute of the International Court of Justice. Moreover, whenever a court is asked to implement a document – be it a constitution or an international treaty – which in practice is almost unchangeable, it is challenged with not only applying the document but to adapting it to the changing society and developing political reality. This is in particular the case of the European Court of Human Rights. With his essay on the *Emergence of the European Human Rights Law*, Dragoljub Popovic, Judge at the European Court of Human Rights in Strasbourg and Professor of History of Law and Constitutional Law, aims – as he writes – to contribute to the emerging European Human Rights Law. However, those who read this essay (which in fact is a well documented analysis) will learn that European Human Rights Law is not only emerging but, on the contrary, it is already well established. In our legal tradition seldom has an acting judge of an international court of such high standing and influence not only contributed to the jurisprudence of his court with his own participation in and opinions on the Court's rulings but also produced a creative and thorough analysis of the jurisprudence of his court. This dialogue with the history of the jurisprudence of the ECHR reveals the deep concern of this court about the effective protection of human rights. Moreover, it also reveals that the Court manages to bring and hold together judges coming from a great number of diverse legal and cultural traditions. They are not only able to be loyal to the previous precedents of the Court but they are even able to develop – guided by the highest value of the protection of human rights – convincingly basic principles of human rights law, and to balance innovation with consistency for the sake of coherent and conclusive jurisprudence. The analysis of most of the key issues, such as creativity, binding force of precedence and interpretation, opens to the attentive reader, who may not be familiar with the jurisprudence of the ECHR, a whole new world in which the complexity of the case-by-case international protection of human rights is highlighted. The latter part focuses on the fundamental approach and in particular the rise of positive obligations of states protecting human rights makes it plain that the traditional negative view of human rights at least in Europe is transcended and that the Court does not need the traditional state action doctrine so important in the tradition of the American Supreme Court. This analysis gives not only scholars but also practitioners in particular a memorable insight into a prudent but also innovative construct of opinions on the Court's jurisprudence. Having read this book, or while reading this book, one understands that the Court well followed the advice of its founders. Namely, that even the most disdained individual who has suffered a violation of his or her fundamental rights and freedoms must have access to the Court and benefit from the Court's justice. All human beings must be on an equal footing before the Court even when they have a complaint against the most powerful government. Any individual must have the possibility to defend his or her rights also against the democratic majority vote of citizens who disregard the fundamental principle that men should be guided by law and not by men. Would the founders who installed this court ever have expected that from such an international court composed of judges coming of very different legal cultures and traditions. Although they are embedded in the diversity of the legal cultures of the member states of the Council of Europe they were and are still able to establish and to develop a coherent jurisprudence guided by the spirit of the Convention in order to protect whenever possible individual freedoms and human rights. With his book, Judge Popovic answers convincingly the question of what spirit guides this court and enables it to develop its consistent jurisprudence and to overcome the overload of innumerable cases. It is the conviction of the ECHR that its legal reasoning must persistently be guided by the concern to give any human being an unquestionable protection of inalienable human rights.

Thomas Fleiner
Professor Emeritus of the University of Fribourg (Switzerland) and
Former President of the International Association for Constitutional Law

Foreword

Each morning when I come to my office at the European Court of Human Rights in Strasbourg, I find some 150 volumes waiting for me, tidily arranged on the shelves. They contain the jurisprudence of the ECHR as put together by selecting committees and editorial boards and published in series, which are not easily kept up-to-date (at this moment the volume of 2006 has not yet been completed). Even more abundant than this published collection is the Court's case-law, which can be found on the internet, on the site of the Council of Europe (HUDOC), where thousands of judgments and decisions of the ECHR are preserved. They represent the outcome of the Court's implementation of the European Convention on Human Rights.

"The European Convention on Human Rights has brought into being the most effective international system of human rights protection ever developed." Those were the words of the former president of the ECHR, judge Wildhaber, at the opening ceremony of the judicial year 2006.[1] The system he referred to is nowadays a coherent body of law, known as the European human rights law, namely the volumes described in the first passage of this foreword.

This rather huge body of law has emerged through a slow but constant process of rendering justice by the ECHR and is based on applying the provisions of the European Convention on Human Rights to the various cases the Court has had to deal with. The text of the Convention is however not extensive. On the contrary, it is rather short and modest in character. The text of the Convention with all its additional protocols that are in force today is no longer than sixty pages when published in a pocket format. The expressions used in the text which lay the foundations of the protection of human rights were overwhelming and according to president Wildhaber once again, "open to the future, to be unfolded and developed in the light of changing conditions".[2] By applying the provisions of the Convention and its broadly formulated provisions, the Court boldly faced the challenge of changing conditions and social developments in general.

The purpose of this book is to research how those legal provisions, which were few in the text of the Convention, emerged into the huge body of law which exists today?

The answer to such a question may be simple. It was the Court's case-law, which properly shaped the body of law mentioned above, by developing the Convention provisions.

1 L. Wildhaber, *The European Court of Human Rights 1998-2006 – History, Achievements, Reform*, Kehl – Strasbourg – Arlington 2006, 63.

2 Wildhaber (fn. 1), 66.

At this point other questions will inevitably arise: was it the Court that indeed created the law? Could the Court be considered to be a law-making body?[3] How did European human rights law emerge in the technical sense of the term and what were the general lines of its evolution like? How did it reach its present stage?

When trying to answer such questions we should bear in mind that the ECHR operates at the crossroads of two great legal systems – Common law and European continental law. These two systems basically have opposite standpoints towards the first two questions posed above, *i.e.* law-making by judges. Continental lawyers fear what the French call *gouvernement des juges*, whereas the lawyers trained in Common law adopt a more subtle approach to the idea of completing the law by jurisprudence. The attitudes of the two legal systems are however closer to one another than it seems at first glance. I have exposed the two extremes here only in order to create an image of the fundamental dilemma. Legal practices converge in the two great legal systems and continental lawyers are less and less opposed to the idea of *jurisprudence prétorienne*, to use a French expression again.

That is why I decided to research some basic questions and institutions concerning the role of judiciary in the operation of law, before trying to tackle the main subject of this book, which is the emergence of European human rights law.

Another colleague of mine, Judge Rozakis, Vice-President of the ECHR, has recently remarked that "Strasbourg undoubtedly operates rather more as a common-law court than as a continental European (civil law) court".[4] I must say I fully agree with judge Rozakis. As a matter of fact it was exactly that specific feature of the Court's work which attracted me and made me try to sail the uncharted seas. This consisted of researching the emergence of a specific body of law performed by an international institution, such as the Court. The process of emergence took place in the course of the implementation of an international treaty, namely the European Convention on Human Rights.

The Convention and its implementation are closely linked to one another and can not be separated. This is true to such an extent that – to borrow an expression from Monica Macovei – "the text of the Convention may not be read outside its case-law". The Convention she also says, "functions under the common law system".[5]

The remarks I have quoted well describe the scope and nature of the Court's activity, as well as the pattern of judicial creativity, on which its work is based. It was in the course of the practice of the Court in Strasbourg that the body of law, labelled as European human rights law, emerged. My task in this book will therefore be to explain how that process developed and what indeed the role of judicial creativity throughout its development was.

---

3 See Wildhaber, ibid, giving an answer in the affirmative.

4 Ch. Rozakis, "Is the Case-Law of the European Court of Human Rights a Procrustean Bed? Or is it a Contribution to the Creation of a European Public Order? A Modest Reply to Lord Hoffmann's Criticisms", *UCL Human Rights Review*, Vol. 2/2009, 53.

5 M. Macovei, *Freedom of Expression*, Strasbourg 2004, 5.

In my humble opinion it was neither an example of *gouvernement des juges*, nor exactly *la jurisprudence prétorienne.* It should be considered as a historical fact reflecting some basic features of the operation of law and its structure in general. The book is therefore supposed to be an essay on judicial creativity in the proper and substantial meaning of the term.

Strasbourg, November 2010

Dragoljub Popovic

Part 1
Judicial Creativity

Introduction

Judicial creativity is a somewhat puzzling expression. Neither lawyers nor the public at large are fully accustomed to it, for other words are more often used to apply to a rather similar or even identical substance.

The expression has however been quoted by many scholars. Mauro Cappelletti was one of its outstanding promoters. His main effort was not to give a proper definition to the concept, but rather to find out the degree of judicial creativity in the day-to-day work of the courts of law.[1] That is why Cappelletti used the expression judicial creativity in a general manner in order to refer to the same substance as the one covered by other expressions, such as for instance judicial discretion.

The meaning that will be given to the notion of judicial creativity in this book slightly differs from the one used by the Italian author. It is my intention to show that judicial creativity is a special feature of the process of the operation of law, which mostly characterizes legal interpretation. The two approaches are however close to one another, which is why it is necessary to distinguish one from the other.

Judicial creativity has also recently been referred to in some articles consecrated to the topics similar to those that are to be discussed further on in the present essay.[2] Whittaker uses the expression in a context very close to the one in which I shall try to situate it. The context mostly concerns the interpretation of law, as viewed from the standpoint of the lack of democratic legitimacy, for which judges are being reproached in respect of law-making.

Justice Kirby on the other hand is inclined to attach the use of the expression judicial creativity to those who are favourable to judicial activism and would probably like to avoid the latter expression. Such avoidance seems to be justified to some extent, but I prefer to avoid taking sides in the academic discussion, before we properly understand the notion of judicial creativity itself.

The aim of Part One of this book is therefore to explain and delineate the concept of judicial creativity. Its task is mainly to distinguish the concept from similar notions, such as judicial discretion or activism and the like.

Further on it will continue to the specific circumstances of judicial creativity in respect of the European Court of Human Rights. The origins of those specific circumstances are to be found in the Court's composition and its international character, but nonetheless in

1 M. Cappelletti, *Le pouvoir des juges*, Paris – Aix-en-Provence 1990, 32-35.

2 Cf. S. Whittaker, "Precedent in English Law: A View from the Citadel" and M. Kirby, "Precedent – Report on Australia", both in: E. Hondius (ed.), *Precedent and the law*, Bruxelles 2007. I am referring to p. 63 (Whittaker) and p. 80-83 (Kirby).

the current state of development of modern judiciary at the global level. The latter is reflected in various dialogues of judges and jurisdictions.

However, at the very beginning of this enterprise one cannot escape a parallel to an episode in a famous work of literature. As he was about to start his visit to the inferno and before meeting Vergilius, Dante encounters three creatures intimidating him tremendously: a panther, a lion and a wolf. The three beasts provoke fear, impede the poet's steps and make him move into the shadows and loose orientation.[3]

Like the three creatures obstructing his steps forward and imposing themselves to the lonely traveller, three theories emerge in respect of the concept of judicial creativity, which threaten to cause its annihilation.

One of these plainly says *there is no* judicial creativity at all. The other, although admitting there might be some, insists on the idea that *there should be no* judicial creativity. Finally the third one appears at first sight to be the least intimidating of the three. It admits that *there must be some* judicial creativity, but it doesn't succeed in giving either its definition or limits. These theories lie at the entrance to the dark and rather huge forest, not to say inferno, of the legal mind, to which we shall have to accede, trying to push through, go ahead and research the characteristic features of the concept of judicial creativity.

3 Dante, *Inferno* I 31-60.

I Concept Disputed and Defined

1.1 There is No Judicial Creativity

When judicial creativity is mentioned, the first and the simplest meaning of that notion is that it is a process of creation of legal rules *i.e.* of their formulation. What legal rules actually are is a matter of controversy between two great legal systems, namely European continental or Civil law and Common law.[1] Leaving the controversy aside, we might understand the legal rule as a phenomenon of a general nature. Legal rule is on certain occasions opposed to another concept. That concept is judgment. The former is considered to be general in character and the latter specific or particular. The former is to be found in legislation, the latter in the acts of the judiciary power. I shall try, below, to shed more light on this subject, which needs clarification.

The next step in this line of thinking is to say that the legal rules are propositions that are general in nature, applying to a number of individuals or situations that can not be determined in advance, whereas an act of the judiciary applies to the litigants who were before a court of law presenting their case and taking part in a lawsuit.

What has been said here so far clearly shows the idea, supported by the classical legal doctrine developed on the European continent, that the judiciary must be excluded from the possibility of creating or setting legal rules of universal applicability. Setting legal rules is an attribution vested with representative bodies, relying on sovereign power. It is therefore exclusively in acts of parliament that the source of law resides. A brief survey of the literature on the subject can be quite illustrative in this respect.

The doctrine in German language insists on the difference between a substantial and a formal notion of law (*Gesetz*). A law in the formal sense of the word is any act of the representative body, whereas a law in its substantial meaning is an act posing a legal rule, general in character.[2]

Another approach, close to the one just mentioned, tends to distinguish the material or substantial notion of legislative power from a formal one and defines the former as a power of posing general and abstract legal rules.[3] That power is vested with parliament.

1 More on this subject is to be found in my book published in my mother tongue; see D. Popović, *Uvod u uporedno pravo* (*Introduction to Comparative Law*), Belgrade 2007, 166-167.

2 A Swiss manual follows the classical German doctrine; see Th. Fleiner & L. Basta-Fleiner, *Allgemeine Staatslehre*, Oxford - New York 2004, 415-416.

3 W. Haller & A. Költz, *Allgemeines Staatsrecht*, Basel - Genf - München, 1999, 249.

French authors also insist on the same idea when giving definitions of law (*loi*), a rule which is general in nature. Therefore we find definitions such as the one that the law (*loi*) is a general and impersonal rule, adopted by the representatives of the people, freely and regularly elected.[4] And to take only two more examples, the French authors insist that a law, *i.e.* an act containing rules of general nature, must be adopted either by parliament or directly by the people and promulgated by the head of state.[5]

If determining general and impersonal legal rules is an exclusive power of the legislators then it must be clear that the courts of law can by no means set such rules. This is a conclusion that comes out of the very nature of the judiciary, if compared to the legislative power. It is quite obvious then that the courts of law are not susceptible to the creation of legal rules *i.e.* general and impersonal propositions applying to an undetermined number of individuals. Their acts apply to the parties of a given case and to no one else.

The trouble with this, I dare say, somewhat simplified way of reasoning is that it does not fully correspond to the reality. For instance it is a commonplace to say that the whole body of the administrative law in France is a product of the activity of the specialised administrative tribunals. There are authors who insist on the fact that the contribution of the judiciary to the development of French administrative law exists even in domains covered by the texts of legislative acts. Their precious intervention consisted of interpreting the texts.[6]

However, there are authors who, although admitting the important role of the judiciary in interpreting legal rules, are not ready to go so far as to consider equal that role in French law with the one it has in Common law. Thus Jestaz is of opinion that the contribution of the French jurisprudence to legal developments should not be exaggerated. He considers the role played by the jurisprudence and its significance as a source of law to be only moderate in his country and states that the jurisprudence can not claim the paternity of the positive law of France.[7] This opinion stands somehow halfway to the second of the three theories contesting judicial creativity, because of admitting its existence at least, but it basically denies the creative role of jurisprudence. At the same time by way of comparison it makes a bridge to the other great legal system, namely Common law.

---

4 M.A. Cohendet, *Droit constitutionnel*, Paris 2006, 231.

5 This is a definition aggregated from the rather similar opinions of two authors; see P. Ardent, *Institutions politiques et droit constitutionnel*, Paris 2003, 44 and P. Pactet, *Institutions politiques – Droit constitutionnel*, Paris 2002, 594.

6 Y. Gaudemet, *Droit administratif*, Paris 2005, 19. It is to be noted that the administrative tribunals of France belong to the administration itself and represent its part. A subject merits discussion from the standpoint of the notion of the separation of powers, which is not my task here. Cf. my article – D. Popović, "European Court of Human Rights and the Concept of Separation of Powers", in M. Prabhakar (ed.), *Separation of Powers – Global Perspectives*, Hyderabad 2008, 194-220.

7 Ph. Jestaz, *Les sources du droit*, Paris 2005, 68-69.

Common law is usually perceived as a structure of legal rules relying for the most part on the activity of the judiciary and consequently to be mostly the fruit of judicial creativity. In other words Common law is considered by many to be a sort of a judge-made law. This is however not universally accepted among common lawyers themselves. Let me quote Lord Esher M.R. as reported by Justice Kirby, who stated towards the end of the 19th century:

> "There is, in fact, no such thing as judge-made law, for the judges do not make the law, though they frequently have to apply existing law to circumstances as to which it has not previously been authoritatively laid down that such law is applicable."[8]

Lord Esher's attitude is quite clear in favour of the most annihilating theory on judicial creativity that has been discussed here. There is no creativity on the side of the courts of law. The law, as a set of rules and principles is eternal and although it does not necessarily reside in the written texts stemming from parliament the judiciary does not create the law *i.e.* legal rules. The principles of the law for a lawyer formed in Common law are believed to have been already in existence before anyone has discovered what they are.[9] Judges therefore only apply the law already in existence without any contribution to its emergence being performed by the courts of law and their proper work.

This proves that the theory denying judicial creativity exists in both legal systems that European countries belong to. Whether the law as such, as a set of legal rules, stems from a written text produced by legislators is not of crucial importance. The theory is only a bit more clearly visible if exposed on the basis of such assumptions.

To close this passage I shall use a fruitful example of that particular version of the theory. Probably the most prominent legal writer in Serbian language of all time, Slobodan Jovanović, expressed the theory of non-existence of judicial creativity in a way which is perfectly clear. It was almost one hundred years ago when he wrote:

> "A judgment issued by a court of law is already contained in a piece of legislation and the judge has only to distil it thereof."[10]

---

8 Lord Esher M.R. in *Willis v. Baddeley* [1892] 2 Q.B. 324, as quoted by M. Kirby, *Judicial Activism – Authority, Principle and Policy in the Judicial Method*, London 2004, 6.

9 J.H. Baker, *An Introduction to English Legal History*, London 1979, 170. The author remarks that this is a "convenient figure of speech" albeit widely spread.

10 The translation is mine. See, S. Jovanović, *O državi* (*On the State*), Beograd 1922, 237. The first edition of the book appeared before World War I.

This author says at the same time that a judge is not free to act on his own, because he only draws conclusions *i.e.* makes subsumptions of the cases he has to try within the rules of law already formulated by someone else. A judge, according to Jovanović, has to formulate the legislators' order and not to create his own. Therefore, there is no room left to judicial creativity. The whole of the judge's task and activity is merely making conclusions from the precepts posed by the legislation.

1.2 There Should Be no Judicial Creativity

The second of the three anti-creativity theories seems to be less rigid in considering the facts of life, although its consequences, if properly interpreted, are not at all favourable to the phenomenon of judicial creativity.

The first theory is descriptive. Its aim is in a certain way to understand the functioning of the judiciary. It does not want to admit any possibility whatsoever of the existence of a contribution on the part of judges to the creation of legal rules. These have been set out elsewhere and judges have to interpret them, implement them and make them effective, but it is by no means conceivable that judges can create legal rules. It is the attitude towards the substance of the activity of the judiciary, which is decisive in this opinion.

The second theory is more realistic, but it is no less dangerous to the phenomenon of judicial creativity than the first theory mentioned above. This attitude has a sense of social reality as its starting point. In reality, so it seems, judges are in a position to create legal rules, be it justified or not. Therefore the second theory is prescriptive. Its main goal is to combat certain practices developed by the courts of law. Its purpose is to put a halt to unjustified law making by judges. Its statements are not primarily results of an academic approach to the problem, based on research. They are rather statements of policy. The principal effort of the theory is to convince judges, as well as lawyers and the public at large, that its strict precepts should replace the imprudent, unjustified and ill founded practices of the courts of law.

There should be no judicial creativity, herald the supporters of this theory in order to suggest that if there had been any attempts or tendencies to develop law making by courts of law, these should be abandoned. This opinion is most clearly visible in the American debates on interpreting the Constitution of the United States, consisting of confrontations between the followers of activism and originalism. The debate marked the last quarter of the 20th century and the theory we are discussing here also took the name of Jurisprudence of Original Intention.[11]

11 S.G. Calabresi (ed.), *Originalism – A Quarter-Century Debate*, Washington DC 2007, 1 (Editor's Introduction).

It should be noted however that the policy combating judicial legislation can not be restricted to the area of debates in American law and especially not to originalism. There are tendencies within the broader mainstream of this line of thinking that include other approaches close to the main one. Intentionalism and textualism should be mentioned among such.[12] They fundamentally belong to the idea of originalism and the latter is often confronted with judicial activism, evolutive interpretation and similar phenomena.

Returning to the American legal debate, which is most illustrative in this respect, one can take as the starting point an opinion expressed in the 1980s by Attorney General Edwin Meese, III. Attorney General Meese stressed that in his view in many of the judgments rendered by the American courts of law, policy choices were to be found instead of articulations of the constitutional principles.[13]

That was worth reproach, for Attorney General Meese stated judges were, in his opinion, "expected to resist any political effort to depart from the literal provisions of the Constitution".[14]

This was well founded on the fact that the judges lacked legitimate power to create legal rules *i.e.* to legislate. The legislative power is vested with the representatives of the people. That is why the judges' task could only be to find the original intention of the legitimate law makers, which made Attorney General Meese conclude:

> "A jurisprudence seriously aimed at the explication of original intention would produce defensible principles of government that would not be tainted by ideological predilection. This belief in a jurisprudence of original intention also reflects a deeply rooted commitment to the idea of democracy."[15]

The so-called democratic deficit on their side prevents judges from formulating legal rules. Their office does not consist in making or formulating these rules, but exclusively in interpreting them. We shall see later on in this book what the problem of legal interpretation is and where it should be actually situated.

One of the champions of originalism, Justice Scalia, of the Supreme Court of the United States, clearly exposed the current state of affairs in respect of the theory advocating originalism in his foreword to Calabresi's book on the subject that has been cited here.[16]

Justice Scalia fairly admits that the opposite idea, the one he labels as "philosophy of the living Constitution" is today prevailing in the courts of law and in the law schools in

---

12 G. Letsas, *A Theory of Interpretation of the European Convention on Human Rights*, Oxford – New York 2007, 58-61; 68-72. The author is not favourable to these opinions.

13 E. Meese, III, "Speech Before the American Bar Association" on 9 July 1985; in S.G. Calabresi, 52.

14 Ibid. 48.

15 Ibid. 53.

16 A. Scalia, Foreword to Part I, in: S.G. Calabresi, 43-45.

the United States as well.[17] This is regretful to his mind and his main purpose is to suggest another approach, the only one justified in his opinion, consisting of fidelity to the text of the written constitution. He observed that originalism was gaining ground in law schools, as well as in the courts of law and declared him in favour of such developments, finding them encouraging.[18]

What Justice Scalia is particularly opposed to is the idea of "a document whose meaning changes to suit times", as he plainly put it, speaking of the United States Constitution.[19] The pattern could also apply to other documents similar in nature, such as the European Convention on Human Rights for instance. A judge should not try to be creative at all, says this opinion; his only task is to interpret the document, which represents the starting point and foundation of judges' work.

If compared to the first theory combating judicial creativity, the main difference in originalism concerns the substance itself. Originalism is prescriptive; it is a policy idea, explaining what judges should do, instead of trying to understand their activity in a way one thinks appropriate. It is accepted that there are deviations from the right track, as understood by the dedicated followers of originalism, and these should be amended by avoiding legislation performed by the judiciary. Therefore, even if there might be some judicial creativity it is nothing else than a regretful fact of life, which should be suppressed in future and finally, put to an end.

1.3 There Must Be Some Judicial Creativity

I have so far exposed two theories on judicial creativity that are completely opposed to it, either by denying its existence or by suggesting its abandonment. The third theory is milder than these two, because it admits the existence of judicial creativity and does not go so far as to suggest its total suppression. However, it also has a weak point, for it neither delineates the concept, nor does it clearly indicate the way it should apply before the courts of law.

In his Hamlyn trust lectures on judicial activism, Justice Kirby, after having exposed his views on judicial activism and its opponents, tried to make a synthesis at the end and gave the title of Concordat to his conclusive lecture on the subject.[20] He admitted he was unable to draw a line between the phenomenon he labelled as legitimate judicial development of the law on one hand and the refusal of that task in a particular case in favour of parliamentary legislation, on the other. One of his main conclusions was that a theory of

17 Ibid. 43.
18 Ibid. 44.
19 Ibid. 43.
20 M. Kirby, *Judicial Activism – Authority, Principle and Policy in the Judicial Method*, London 2004, 61-91.

permissible limits to what he called "judge lawmaking" should be developed in order to have a serious debate on judicial activism and its relation to the judicial self-restraint.[21]

Justice Kirby addressed the problem of judicial creativity in a way that could not be clearer, saying:

> "Judges must necessarily decide cases that involve unique facts. They must respond, as their vocation obliges, to the parties' arguments. It is the obligation to make a decision in a particular case, affecting real parties that concentrates the judicial mind on the duty to find, as accurately and efficiently as possible, the applicable rule of legal authority."[22]

One gets the impression that Justice Kirby tried in vain to situate his opinion expressed in the conclusive lecture for the Hamlyn trust in an area between judicial activism and self-restraint. He went beyond the classical dichotomy, stating that sources of guidance for a judge could be legal principle and legal policy, beside proper legal authority. He has put it clearly that the judicial task is an "inescapably creative activity".[23]

The problem with this theory consists primarily in the lack of definition of the concept of judicial creativity. This gives rise to the impossibility to find its respective limits. These seem to be the most striking deficiencies that the approach to the problem of judicial creativity tending to remain halfway between judicial activism and judicial self-restraint suffers from. The features of such an approach are visible in Justice Kirby's opinion. We need further studies of details and precisions if we are to understand what judicial creativity actually is. It does not suffice to say that it must be present in judicial practice.

Another example of this kind of approach to the problem is to be found in Morse, in an article of his published some time ago and which also seems to be rather illustrative. Morse's central concept is the rule of law, on which he reflects from the standpoint of judicial constraint.[24]

Morse is fully aware of the fact that judicial creativity exists. His object of research is the tax law of the United States of America. He describes its normative situation in the following way:

> "The Internal revenue Code occupies hundreds of pages of text and is supplemented by thousands of pages of regulations and other pronouncements."

---

21 Ibid. 64.

22 Ibid. 80.

23 Ibid. 83-86; citing R. Dworkin, *Taking Rights Seriously* and following his views.

24 E. Morse, "Reflections on the Rule of Law and 'Clear Reflection of Income': what constrains Discretion?", *Cornell Journal of Law and Public Policy*, 8 1998/9, especially pages 445-453.

All that rather abundant corpus of legal rules and regulations serve the purpose of providing guidance to taxpayers and government actors charged with administering tax law.[25]

What Morse labels as discretion originates according to him in the existing situation, which comprises a complicated network of various rules. He says:

> "Discretion arises from the practical impossibility of drafting rules to every situation governed by law".

To his mind, discretion produces uncertainty, which should by no means be allowed if good administration of justice is to be achieved.[26] In spite of this rather general attitude towards judicial creativity Morse puts it fairly clearly:

> "Some discretion, though clearly avoidable is nevertheless permitted in our legal system."[27]

What was said earlier on Justice Kirby's attitude towards the problem can be repeated if commenting on Morse's opinion. Its origin is rather descriptive; it also lacks definition and probably can not be sufficiently prescriptive because of its character tending to make a compromise between two opposed extremes.

To close this passage I should mention another opinion of the same kind. In a rather small and effective essay Nathalie Dongois asks the following question: "*Is Justice just?*"[28] One of the topics she discusses in such a curiously entitled essay is whether a law which is flexible, *i.e.* subject to development and, I should add, to judicial creativity as well, is preferable to a rather conservative and immutable legal system.

Nathalie Dongois says that jurisprudence, as well as legal doctrine, makes the law vivid. However, if there is a necessity for the law to be flexible this must not be achieved to the detriment of legal certainty. In her opinion legality and legal formalism are guarantees against arbitrary power, but at the same time she admits that, for the sake of the interests of parties to litigation, a judge, is on certain occasions, guided by equity.[29] It remains unclear where the limits of such an approach performed by judges reside. There is some judicial creativity, but we are left without response as to its boundaries, definition and last but not least, as to the way it actually operates in practice.

---

25 Ibid, 451.

26 Ibid, 449, citing R. Dworkin, *Taking Rights Seriously*, mostly unfavourable to his opinion.

27 Ibid, 450.

28 N. Dongois, *La justice est-elle juste?* Grolley 2006.

29 Ibid, 46. Allow me to let this author explain: "au nom de l'intérêt individuel des justiciables, le juge recourt parfois à son pouvoir d'appréciation en étant guidé par un souci d'équité."

1.4 The Concept of Judicial Creativity Defined

1.4.1 General Approach

I must put forward from the outset, that although opposing the three above-mentioned theories on judicial creativity, I do agree with some of the features of each and every one. For instance, the first theory is descriptive, which as a matter of fact goes in parallel to my task here to define what a certain phenomenon really is. My conclusions might be fully opposed to those of the first anti-creativity theory, but the similarity of the methods applied in reaching the conclusions will nonetheless remain.

The second theory admits the existence of judicial creativity, with which I agree, for it is a mere fact of life, in my mind. What I do not approve of is the prescriptive character of the theory which represents its core and tends to suggest the suppression of judicial creativity.

Finally, the third theory is for the most part an attempt to make a compromise between judicial activism and self-restraint. With this I basically agree, supporting my point of view with a line by Tennyson, for like the famous poet, I also believe in the "*falsehood of extremes*". My disagreement with the third theory is based on the fact that it neither offers a definition of the concept of judicial creativity, discussed here, nor can it present its respective limits and characteristic features.

Last but not least, I dare say that the main problem as regards judicial creativity, in the hands of the supporters of the three theories I have exposed above, lies in the fact that the whole concept of judicial creativity is not properly perceived. The concept has been confused with some other similar notions, such as, for instance judicial discretion or even judicial activism.

1.4.2 An Old Myth

In order to be able to define the concept of judicial creativity for the purposes of this essay I shall allow myself to begin with an old myth. It has various names and versions; it has been called "mechanical jurisprudence", or "judge as mechanic" and the like. The origin of the myth can be traced back to the French Revolution of 1789 and the firm belief in Reason, dominant in those times, which made the revolutionaries launch themselves in one of the most marvellous enterprises ever, being the codification of law. Let me hand you over to Kelly and let him explain the spirit of the age of codification:

> "The leading idea of the French codifiers had been to exclude uncertainty and arbitrariness in the administration of law, and for that purpose they wished to

> reduce as far as possible the interpretative and creative function of judges, which they distrusted. The judge was to be no more than a machine intelligently applying a body of clear and stable rules; and these were therefore to be a complete, smooth, seamless network, the measurement of any problem against which would automatically indicate its solution."[30]

This romantic myth glorified the legislation, perceiving it as a source of justice and legal certainty. The expectations from the codified law were enormous in those days; the ideal seemed to be irreproachable.

At the same time the old myth looked upon judges as dedicated followers of rules and mere administrators of the highest justice as once imagined and pronounced by legislators inspired by Reason, which could by no means be impaired. Judges were perceived as if they were deprived of their own will and their work was neglected to such an extent that one of the most prominent leaders of the Revolution, Robespierre himself, suggested that the word jurisprudence should no longer exist in the French language.[31]

However, this whole image is naïve, for the administration of justice is not so automatic, and neither is the entire operation of the law so unbelievably simple and deprived of subtlety.

1.4.3 Stages in the Operation of the Law

As the above-mentioned myth is designed to tell the story of how the law is supposed to operate it occurs to me that it is inevitable to start from the analysis of the phenomenon of the operation of the law in order to try to reach a definition of judicial creativity. If we try to draw a more detailed picture of the operation of the law we shall inevitably realise that it is made up of different stages.

The first stage is enactment. It consists of making propositions of general application that are to serve as a basis or source of law. In order to simplify my argument here, I shall limit the notion of enactment to enacting statutes. Let me however put a remark that enactment does not necessarily mean passing of statutes. In other words it can not always be exhausted in the concept of legislation neither in the technical nor in the constitutional sense of the term.[32]

---

30 J.M. Kelly, *A Short History of Western Legal Theory*, Oxford – New York 1999, 312.

31 Jestaz (fn. 7), 62.

32 Cf. R. Dworkin, *Taking Rights Seriously*, London 1987, 111. Dworkin insists on the fact that the interpretation of statutes is different from the interpretation of what he calls judicial enactments. French authors also make a distinction between enactment and a legal rule, *i.e.* between what they call *énoncé* and *norme*. Cf. M. Troper, *La philosophie du droit*, Paris 2008, 87.

The next stage in the operation of the law is interpretation. The common understanding of that notion is to find the exact meaning of an enactment. I would like to say at this point that the concept of interpretation is certainly broader than that. The main purpose of interpretation is passing to the subsequent stage in order to make the law operate.

As a matter of fact there can be many interpretations, as well as interpreters, of an enactment but the only one which counts is the one vested with authority and performed for the purpose of adjudication. An authoritative interpretation is the one to which the legal order attaches consequences.[33] Therefore, it should be pointed out that there can be no adjudication without an authoritative interpretation of an enactment.

The third stage in this list is adjudication. It consists of taking a decision on an individual's rights and obligations by way of an authoritative interpretation of an enactment. That is why we are usually tempted to consider these two stages (interpretation and adjudication) as being one and the same. They should however be distinguished. Adjudication primarily means pronouncing a judgment, whereas interpretation, preceding it, is by far more complex in character.

Finally, after adjudication, comes the stage of enforcement, being the last in the sequence of steps by which the law normally operates. This step is ultimately taken by some sort of administration and is organised to suit different situations and purposes.

An analysis of the four stages of the operation of the law, which I have just enumerated, takes into account the fact that they are performed by the authorities. It leads to the conclusion that, apart from enactment and enforcement, the other two stages fall within the competence of the judiciary. Those who interpret the law and adjudicate are judges.

Another question should be asked here, namely whether one or the other of the two stages belonging to operation of the law attributed to judges' activity could be considered to be closer to either of the two poles representing the beginning and the end of the whole process described.

The answer to this question should be in the affirmative. It seems to me that the interpretation is linked to the first stage, being the enactment, whereas the adjudication is more closely linked to the enforcement. In other words, adjudication is a basis or a pretext for enforcement and interpretation is somehow a continuation of enactment, or rather it specifies the enactment itself.

This point is crucial for my argumentation. Interpretation made by a court of law can not be easily distinguished from the substance of an enactment. It provides for its understanding; it makes the enactment comprehensible and without it neither a layman nor a lawyer can be sure of what the contents of a legal rule really are. Legal rule is broader than

33 At this particular point I am following Michel Troper, who follows Kelsen. Troper uses the expression authentic interpretation, instead of authoritative, which occurs to me to be better suited to my line of argument. Cf. Troper (fn. 32), 100.

an enactment; the former represents an explicative part of the latter. Or, to go along with Troper once again, the rule is a prescriptive signification of an enactment.[34]

1.4.4 *Interpretation as Part of the Legal Rule*

At this point the concept of the legal rule should be considered more exhaustively. The considerations firstly refer to discrepancies between the two great legal systems, Common law and Civil law, which are visible in this respect. Secondly, they concern differences in approach to the problem existing among classical pure theorists on one side and legal comparatists on the other. Those two aspects are indeed intermingled and reflect two facets of the same coin. Finally it should be noted that modern theorists are closer to the position of legal comparatists, rather than to the one of classical theorists.

Classical pure theorists followed for the most part the streamline of legal positivism. One of their main ideas was to confound the concept of legal rule with a statutory provision.[35] Legal positivists were unfavourable to the interpretation of statutes. Any sort of interpretation of enacted rules tending to exceed the positive law, or to include concern for values was considered to be unacceptable.[36] According to legal positivists the lawyers' only task should consist of learning what the positive law actually is. The positive law was to be purified of any reference to nature or values and it was viewed from an axiological standpoint to be perfectly neutral.[37]

This conception led to diminishing the role of interpretation of law, or rather of statutes and enactments, because the interpretation was perceived as a sort of second grade activity, serving the great cause of law in an almost slave-like manner. Its significance was limited, its techniques were reminiscent of those of craftsmen, fairly skilful at their work, but not highly positioned in the market and therefore without a profound attachment to their own products.

Classical ideas must not be understood as mere treasures of legal history. Their roots are deep, for they go back to the 18th and 19th centuries, but the legal positivists' approach to the phenomena discussed here are still strong and widely spread among lawyers and legal scholars.

An eminent French scholar has recently exposed a clear opinion on the subject. François Terré entitled one of his recent texts in a rather vivacious and polemic way: "*A judge creator of Law? No, thank you!*"[38]

---

34 Ibid. 105.

35 S. Goyard-Fabre, "Loi", in: Ph. Raynaud & S. Rials, *Dictionnaire de philosophie politique*, Paris 2003, 419.

36 Ibid.

37 Cf. M. Levinet, *Théorie générale des droits et libertés*, Bruxelles 2006, 239-242; presenting attitudes of Carré de Malberg and Kelsen.

38 F.Terré, "Un juge créateur de droit? Non merci!", *Archives de philosophie du droit*, tome 50/2007, 305-311.

Terré refers to the interpretation of statutes, although without stating it explicitly. His idea to deny judicial creativity is rooted in his specific understanding of certain concepts. Namely, if a judge is to find out a certain meaning of a statute, which has not been discovered so far, there is no creativity either in his effort, or in its outcome. Therefore, Terré proceeds to the next step in his line of argument, so as to declare that what has come out of the series of judgments rendered by courts of law is nothing else but a work of introducing coherence into the implementation, and as he also admits, in the evolution of the law.

The opinion exposed by the eminent French author tends to situate the creativity between contingencies of individual acts and social interaction. In a philosophic perception and with reference to Sartre, he insists on the phenomenon that an object of creation detaches from its creator in order to affirm its own existence, but being thus detached, it represents only nothingness (*le néant*). The jurisprudence is therefore unable to become anything else but a continuing application of the law. Judicial creation of law can never be in accordance with such a role and task of the judiciary. This leads the author to pose the ultimate question, as announced in the title of his text, and give it immediately a straightforward answer:

> "Le juge créateur de droit ; comme dans les pays de common law? Non merci!"[39]

The interpretation of statutes and its significance for functioning of the law are given a rather restricted role in this line of thought. The interpretation can not achieve the stage of creativity and remains in its ancillary position towards enactments. To some extent the meaning of this approach may seem formalistic. Namely, if there should be anything new in the jurisprudence, all novelties put forward by judges should be considered as already envisaged by the legislators. The impression remains that the author is unable to deny the existence of such novelties, which leads him to make an effort to understand them in a special way, in order to circumvent the real problem. It is to be noted that with such widely spread attitudes, the positivist approach survives to this day and it shows a tendency to be explained in a new and modern way, with the support of existentialism.

As a reference has been made to the distinction of the two great legal systems, this seems to be the right place to introduce reflections concerning attitudes of legal comparatists towards the issue of relations of enactments and their interpretation.

It is René David, one of the greatest legal comparatists of all time, whose work and attitudes I shall refer to in order to determine delimitations and scope of interference between enactments and interpretation. The reference will be made to the 11th edition of

39 Ibid. 311.

his classical masterpiece, the book on great legal systems of contemporary law, which was published together with Camille Jauffret-Spinosi as co-author.[40]

The problem discussed here does not have a unique answer in the two great legal systems which currently exist. Sources of law are treated differently in Civil law and in Common law. The fact has been fairly observed by Terré, as we have seen above and he rejected the idea of accepting for Civil law countries the system existing in Common law. Let me therefore give the word to David and Jauffret-Spinosi to explain the situation in Common law.

The starting point of the explanation is in underlining the difference between two basic notions. One of those belongs to the Civil law system and in French it is the concept of "*règle de droit*". That concept should be opposed to what is called *legal rule* in English. Inexperienced translators might be tempted to confuse the two, but the two notions are by no means to be identified.

The first point of this little analysis is that the *legal rule* as a concept is closely related to a certain set of facts, to which it is linked and somehow represents the outcome of those. That is why the two authors remark:

> "La *legal rule* anglaise se place en conséquence au niveau de l'espèce à l'occasion de laquelle, et pour trancher laquelle, elle a été dégagée."[41]

This is followed by an explanation, saying that the English do not place a legal rule above the facts of a case, which seems to be essential for the understanding of the functioning of the whole system of Common law. It concerns the rather close relationship existing between an enactment and its interpretation. Pursuing this path the authors describe the attitude of the English towards legal rules and legislative enactments:

> "[Les Anglais] n'adoptent vraiment les règles formulées par le législateur, pour peu qu'elles demandent une interprétation, que lorsqu'elles ont été effectivement interprétées par la jurisprudence."[42]

The purpose of this statement is to explain how the law operates within the Common law system. It underlines the reality of functioning of the law that is reflected among lawyers but also in the eyes of the public at large. In a Common law country one does not usually ask what is written in an act of parliament, but rather what the courts of law admit or pronounce in their judgments, applying respective acts of parliament. That is why to learn

---

40 R. David & C. Jauffret-Spinosi, *Les grands systèmes de droit contemporains*, Paris 2002.

41 Ibid. 266. Other comparatists also insist on the close relation of facts to the legal rule in the Common Law system; cf. G. Cuniberti, *Grands systèmes de droit contemporains*, Paris 2007, 89.

42 Ibid.

the law means to learn the position of the courts of law towards a certain issue. This leads the two authors to the conclusion that I consider essential for the topic discussed in this chapter:

> "Les applications jurisprudentielles prennent alors, dans le système de droit anglais, la place des dispositions que le législateur a édictées."[43]

The crucial point is that the legal comparatists insist on the idea that an enactment can not be perceived apart from its interpretation, because they form a unique phenomenon, being the legal rule itself. A legal rule is, to reproduce the formula we have just seen above, an enactment as interpreted by the courts of law. In other words the interpretation is a constituent part of a legal rule, along with the enactment it has had as an object.

This opinion of legal comparatists, developed in order to be applied only to the Common law system, seems to be gaining ground, being echoed and spreading its influence among modern legal scholars, active in the field of theory. Modern theorists are influenced by Common law, or it might be that they are guided by an attempt at realistic observance and analysis of the process of the operation of the law.

Ronald Dworkin rejects the positivists' idea of the law as "a set of timeless rules stocked in some conceptual warehouse awaiting discovery by judges".[44]

He is of the opinion that a judge actually applies not only rules but also principles and policies, while performing his task.[45] In Dworkin's view the judges' mission is to give a right answer to a problem they are faced with in the course of the proceedings before them. Judges fulfil their task by way of interpretation, which has its gravitational point in the ideas of fairness and treating like cases alike.[46] To explain the importance of interpretation Dworkin takes the example of the game of chess and compares the rules governing that game to statutory rules. There is a referee in that game, whom the author compares to a judge, in order to underline the role played by legal interpretation. In a game of chess a referee makes decisions in cases of a dispute between the gamesters. This of course is very much like issuing judgments by a judge in legal disputes. However the substance of the decisions of a chess referee is basically different if compared to judgments of a court of law. The main feature making such a difference consists of the fact that the decisions of a chess referee are quite simply justified by the established rules of chess that the referee is

43 Ibid.

44 Dworkin (fn. 32), 15.

45 Dworkin (fn. 32), 22-28. Cf. on Dworkin's attitude: P. Legrand & G. Samuel, *Introduction au common law*, Paris 2008, 95; M. Boumghar, *Une approche de la notion de principe dans le système de la Convention européenne des droits de l'homme*, Paris 2010, 72-73.

46 Dworkin (fn. 32), 113.

strongly attached to. On the other hand "legal rules are much more likely than chess rules to require interpretation."[47]

The comparison between two corpuses of rules and their interpretation clearly shows the importance of a phenomenon, which is much larger in the realm of the law, than in the rules of a game. There can hardly be any evolution of the latter, while the former is constantly developing, and it is in fact the interpretation as a crucial phenomenon that is at the origin of such a development.

This goes along with certain ideas expressed in the French legal doctrine, as regards the role of interpretation and interpreters. Thus Michel Troper insists on the role of the interpreter if considered from the standpoint of the process of operation of the law. For Troper the meaning of a legal text is nothing else but the meaning of the rule expressed by the text. Therefore, he says, it is the interpreter who determines the rule.[48]

It should however be noted that, according to Troper, a judge is not completely free to interpret a text of a statute in the way it pleases him or her. He is constrained by various factors. For instance, a judge can not act on his or her own initiative. A judge's interpretation of a text can be reversed by subsequent legislation. A judge's interpretation is usually subject to the control of a higher instance of the judiciary. The latter is not valid for the supreme courts, but those are reluctant to easily reverse their stances.

The essential point in Troper's line of argument is that there is no true meaning of a statutory text. There can be only coherent and rational choices made by judges in the respective situations in which they are to act under the constraints of the existing circumstances.[49] Therefore, the above-mentioned formula remains – a legal rule is what the authoritative interpreters proclaim it is. A legal rule can not come into being before being interpreted, or in other words, interpretation represents a constituent part of a legal rule.

1.4.5 The Notion of Judicial Creativity

1.4.5.1 Addressing the Problem

Resuming what I have exposed above I should say that various stages of operation of the law are not isolated from one another. On the contrary, their sequence represents a unique process in which some of the stages are tightly linked and almost form a specific unity. This is certainly true for the stages of enactment and interpretation. As we have seen above those two phases of the whole process of the operation of the law can not be separated.

One could imagine an enactment that never comes to be interpreted. Could it be justified to call the content of such an enactment a legal rule? It is very likely that the answer to this

47 Dworkin (fn. 32), 111-112.
48 Troper (fn. 32), 109.
49 Troper (fn. 32), 110-112.

question, given by a positivist or someone belonging to the public at large, would be in the affirmative. To this I must disagree. Legal rules serve the purpose of making the law operate. The substance contained in a text of an enactment and never being subject to interpretation can by no means serve that purpose. In other words, if the process of the operation of the law remains at the stage of enactment and does not go any further the whole process will be hindered and there will be no law at all. It is hardly imaginable that an enactment remaining without interpretation might properly speaking bring the law into existence.

If the law is to be fully realised, the process of its operation must be completed. Therefore, an enactment inevitably needs interpretation, to be able to make the entire mechanism work and pass to its subsequent stages, namely adjudication and enforcement. The interpretation fulfils the task of making the enactment immediately effective and thus set the whole of the law to be operative.

It is perfectly clear that an enactment needs interpretation to become effective, but that is only a primary aspect of the problem. A more important aspect than this is that the enactment has not acquired its proper being and existence without interpretation. Interpretation gives the meaning, *i.e.* the real existence to the enactment, which it had as its own object. Only taken as a whole the enactment and interpretation create a legal rule, which makes me repeat, following Troper once more, that the legal rule is a meaning of the enactment.[50]

This enables me to pass on to the second point of this argumentation and to try to give an answer to the question: what is judicial creativity?

Judicial creativity is to be found in the activity by which judges fulfil their main task of administering justice. The administration of justice can be perceived as the process of the operation of the law. Judges make the law operate and they can do so only if they interpret enactments. The authoritative interpretation of enactments, performed by judges, creates legal rules. At this stage, I must put it clearly, I think Cappelletti was right to insist on the fact that interpretation inevitably comprises a certain amount of appreciation in itself and is therefore creative.[51]

It seems to be a mistake to believe, although this might sound awkward to some, that legal rules properly exist in the enactments. They are shaped and completed at the stage of interpretation, for judges interpret enactments and by their authoritative interpretation complete them and make those reach the status of legal rules.

Enactment texts only seem to contain legal rules. The texts are ineffective *per se.* They have to be completed by jurisprudence. To illustrate this we can take an example from comparative law. Belgium and France have the same civil code text, dating from the times

50 Troper (fn. 32), 87; 105.
51 Cappelletti (fn. 1), 30.

of Napoleon. Yet nobody is of the opinion that the private law of France is identical to the one of Belgium. The reason for this is that the legal rules forming the corpus of the private law in France are different from those in Belgium. The intervention of jurisprudence is at the origin of such a situation.[52] The legal rules shaped by the courts of law in the two countries differ, although they rely on the same text.

The texts become transformed into legal rules if and when interpreted by judges. Judicial creativity is therefore nothing else but completing enactments and shaping those as legal rules. Psychologically speaking, such a process is the one of taking decisions, making choices and by that creating, *i.e.* reaching a phenomenon of a different nature than the one that represented the point of departure. What has been a mere enactment will at the end of a creative process, consisting of interpretation, become a legal rule. Judges do not pose legal rules; they only participate in their determination, and without the intervention of judges legal rules, properly understood, can not come into being.

1.4.5.2 Three Questions

Three questions arise at this point. Are judges absolutely free to complete the enactments they interpret as it pleases them? Do they feel any sort of constraint when they interpret enactments? Does the way of reasoning developed here lead to advocating judicial legislation?

Let me respond to the last question at once: the opinion I have exposed here does not advocate judicial legislation. Judges are not allowed to legislate and in reality they can not assume the role of legislators. This is not so only because judges lack democratic capacity and can not be legitimate to introduce enactments, or in other words, to pass legislation. Judges can not act on their own initiative. They must be properly addressed by the parties to set in motion the mechanism of the judiciary. As they merely interpret the law and do not legislate, their creativity is linked to the objects of their interpretation, in essence the enactments.

If we are aware of such a position of judges then the answer to the second question, posed above, must be in the affirmative. Judges proceed under constraints. They can not escape them. Constraints are the elements of any act of creation, not necessarily judicial. It has been observed that a constraint is everything that enables the process of creation to pass from a state of bad definition to the one which is relatively better.[53] The constraints on judges while fulfilling their task should be subject to sociological analysis. They originate in the community in which the judges exercise their activity, as well as in the social needs the judges have to respond to. Constraints are challenges, which provoke judicial creativity.

---

52 J.L. Thireau, *Introduction historique au droit*, Paris 2009, 10.
53 M-L. Rouquette, *La créativité*, Paris 2007, 61.

It should be underlined that the object of interpretation, being for the most part the enactment text, also represents one of the greatest of constraints.

At this point we come to the most difficult question, which was the first of those posed above. Can judges really interpret, *i.e.* complete the enactments they take as objects of interpretation, in the way it pleases them? Are they allowed to attach any meaning to the text interpreted?

Examples spring easily to one's mind. Was the interpretation given towards the end of the 19th century to the Article 1384 of the French Civil Code sufficiently rooted in its text? It served the noble purpose of introducing strict liability for damages into the French legal system, but the interpretation was based on the words representing nothing more than an introduction to the text of the article as a whole. Or, to remain within the French legal system for this purpose, how did the vast corpus of administrative law emerge in jurisprudence, without being rooted in a code, *i.e.* without proper enactments? It has already been remarked by scholars that French administrative law is mostly a product of jurisprudence.[54]

Let me make a preliminary remark, that in spite of the persuasive character of the examples invoked, the answer to the principal question should be in the negative. Judges are not in the position to interpret enactments in the way it pleases them. At the same time it is true that they can attach various meanings to the text interpreted. The two statements seem to be contradictory and paradoxical. They certainly call for explanation.

The problem that arises from the question of the scope of judges' freedom of choice when interpreting enactments is basically methodological. The question posed might be understood in two different ways, namely whether judges *ought to* behave or whether they *do* behave in a certain way. I shall exclude the first possibility, because it is not my intention to be prescriptive; it is the reality that I wish to explore. Therefore the question is what judges actually do, or how they proceed when they interpret enactments.

It may seem at first sight that the scope of freedom, which judges exercise when interpreting the law could be perceived as unlimited. What else could come to our mind if judges find the institute of unjust enrichment in a text of a code which does not provide on that institute at all? The same applies to the situation in which judges develop a whole branch of law without respective enactments to represent their starting points. It also seems to be valid when judges find strict liability for damages in the words introducing a provision of a code. The judges really give the impression that they are free to find any meaning in any text imaginable.

---

54 For civil liability under the French Civil code cf. Ph. Brun, *Responsabilité civile extracontractuelle*, Paris 2005, 210-14. For the developments in French administrative law cf. Gaudemet, (fn. 6), 24-26, M. Fromont, *Droit administratif des états européens*, Paris 2006, 80-81.

The situation is however, more complex than this simple reasoning and needs further reflection. The circumstances in which the judges' task is performed remind me of the declaration, which Humpty Dumpty makes to Alice on her visit to Wonderland. He says:

> "When I use a word, it means what I choose it to mean; neither more nor less".[55]

Judges seem to enjoy an absolute freedom of choice of meanings they attach to the enactments interpreted. However, they do not perform their task in the imaginary land of fairy tales, but face real and serious problems instead. Judges render justice, which means that the community at large approves of their efforts and results of their work and also acts and behaves in compliance with the effects of their judgments. That is why the judges are at least constrained to avoid absurdities; otherwise the community would neither follow their judgments nor by large approve of their activity.

In the most general terms judges are unable to escape two fundamental constraints. The first one is the text itself, concerning a fair amount of possibilities, but however limiting the judges' choice, no matter how large the scope of their freedom in this respect may be. The second constraint is the social problems demanding solutions, as well as the ideas governing approaches to those and the way of life and usual behaviour practised in the community that put limits on judges and their freedom of choice when deciding cases.

Let me give some examples. A judge in the United States of America issuing a judgment based on the United States Constitution interprets a text adopted in the times when slavery was still recognised nationwide. Can anyone imagine a judge sitting at the bench of an American court of law including in his arguments to a judgment rendered today a reference advocating slavery?

Or another example: Can a judge in a former communist country of Eastern Europe depart from the idea of a revival of the one-party system at the beginning of the 21st century?

In both examples the answers to the questions raised must be in the negative. The reasons are the same for both. It is the constraint that prevents the judges from doing what was suggested by the questions. The constraint can be explained in several ways. We can think of the incompatibility of the suggested inacceptable approaches with the ideas of governing contemporary societies, or of a universally adopted social behaviour, as well as of some other explanation. The conclusion will however remain: judges are not in the position to act as it pleases them; they take decisions in an organised situation, which is socially determined. At this point I agree with Cappelletti's opinion, which is followed by Dyevre. He says that the interpretation is not an activity relying on absolute freedom, but

---

55 The words from Lewis Carrol's novel are quoted by legal scholars to describe what I am trying to describe here; cf. Lord Denning, *The Discipline of Law*, London, 1979, 294 or A. Dyevre, *L'activisme juridictionnel en droit constitutionnel compare*: France, États-Unis, Allemagne, thèse de doctorat à l'Université Paris I, 2007, 64.

it nevertheless has creative aspects.[56] The judges' contribution to the operation of the law is thus fundamentally a creation.

Another important aspect of constraint on judges consists in the fact that the object of their interpretation may not exclusively consist in a certain enactment. That was the hypothesis I have followed so far for the purposes of the easy development of reasoning. Judges may however go beyond that and interpret the corpus of enactments, or in other words, they can interpret the law in general, which as a matter of fact they very often do. The constraints seem to be different in the two cases and the judges seem to be less constrained when they interpret the whole of the law than when they take a single enactment as an object of interpretation.

The amount of constraint on judges when interpreting the law as a whole, if compared to the interpretation of enactments, is diminished because there is no text pertinent to the issue at stake, on which judges are to rely, when deciding a case. Legal gaps are the circumstances in which judges often have recourse to such interpretation. When a judge is to fill a gap existing in the legal system he or she has to turn to the law as a whole in order to find grounds for a judgment. The social component of the constraint on judges remains untouched in such circumstances in spite of the absence of a text.

A judge is not absolutely free in the case of a legal gap to choose any solution he or she might wish, because the social situation, subject to the complex game of social forces, provides guidelines for his or her judgment. This is perfectly clear in the famous Article 1 of the Swiss Civil Code, which has somehow canonised those guidelines. The relevant provision of the code prescribes that a judge, acting in the absence of a statutory provision is to decide a case "in accordance with the rule which he would, were he the legislator, adopt". This is already a guideline, because a judge must try to follow the spirit of the legislation, taken as a whole, but the provision I have just quoted also contains some more precise recommendations. A judge, while filling a legal gap, must pay attention to accepted doctrine and tradition, as well.[57] The judges' scope of creativity is however plainly admitted by the code, which recently provoked a legal historian to make a remark that "the old lack of confidence towards judges, stemming from the times of enlightenment does not seem to have penetrated into Swiss valleys and mountains".[58]

Judges are not free to give to the texts arbitrarily such meanings as may please them. On the contrary, they are constrained to find meanings that can fulfil social tasks. Otherwise their judgments would, at least in the long run, prove to be useless and ineffective, or in other words the judges would cease being what they are. Rendering ineffective judgments would have put an end to their authority.

---

56 Cf. Dyevre (fn. 55), 80, with a reference to Cappelletti (fn. 1), 29.

57 Cf. K. Zweigert & H. Kötz, *An Introduction to Comparative Law* (translated by T. Weir), Oxford – New York 1998, 176.

58 P. Grossi, *L'Europa del diritto*, Roma-Bari 2007, 180.

At this point it is necessary to make some distinctions, concerning judicial creativity, in respect of some similar notions. Two of these certainly come to our mind. One is judicial activity and the other is judicial discretion.

Judicial activity is an expression that came into use in order to denote the legislative activity, allegedly performed by judges. The term is therefore to be abandoned, for as I have tried to explain in this passage, judges quite simply do not legislate.

The expression judicial discretion is less extreme in character than the previous one. It gives the impression that the role of judges is one in which they are allowed either to depart from the rules posed by legislators, or even stick to a certain amount of arbitrariness. Neither of the two is a characteristic feature of judges' activity.

Judges neither legislate nor deviate from statutory provisions. Their role on the other hand, if properly understood, is inevitably creative in everything they do. Judicial creativity consists of completing enactments, or, in other words, giving meaning, which results in finalising legal rules. It is a figure of speech whether we say that the enactments contain only imperfect legal rules, which are subsequently completed by judges, or that they do not contain any legal rules at all, because the intervention of judges is indispensable in their proper formulation.

II Judicial Creativity and the Protection of Human Rights in Europe

2.1 The International Character of the European Court of Human Rights

2.1.1 The Mechanism of Protection of Human Rights in Europe

The European Court of Human Rights (hereinafter referred to as the ECHR or the Court) represents a part of the mechanism set up by the Convention for the Protection of Human Rights and Fundamental Freedoms (hereinafter referred to as the Convention), adopted in 1950 in order to protect human rights in Europe. [1]

Originally the mission to protect human rights was conferred to three organs within the Council of Europe – the ECHR, the European Commission of Human Rights and the Committee of Ministers of the Council of Europe. After the reform of the system based on the adoption of the 11th Additional Protocol to the Convention, the Commission ceased to exist.[2] Abolishing the Commission by the 11th Additional Protocol augmented the Court's competence. The Court became competent to decide both on admissibility and merits of a case. The former task had been previously vested with the Commission.

The Court sits in Strasbourg and each of the member states that have ratified the Convention has one judge sitting at the Court.

The Committee of Ministers was not set up by the Convention. The legal basis of its work and composition are laid down by the Statute of the Council of Europe. The Committee of Ministers is a body in which all ministers of foreign affairs of the Council Europe member states have a seat. The ministers are usually represented by the ambassadors of respective states accredited to the Council of Europe with the seat in Strasbourg. That is why the Committee is practically in permanent session.

1 On the Court, its history and background see: P. van Dijk et al. (eds), *Theory and Practice of the European Convention on Human Rights*, Antwerpen – Oxford, 2006, 32-46; Jacobs and White (C. Ovey and R. White), Oxford – New York, 2002, 1-14; F. Sudre, *Droit européen et international des droits de l'homme*, Paris 2005, 531-565; Ch. Grabenwarter, *Europäische Menschenrechtskonvention*, München – Wien 2003, 53-58.

2 On the Commission, its organisation, competence and work see in extenso: J.G. Merrills & A.H. Robertson, *Human Rights in Europe*, Manchester 2001, 271-283.

The Committee of Ministers is competent to survey the execution of the ECHR judgments. Therefore it represents a body, which is necessary in the mechanism of protecting human rights in Europe, in order to make the whole system effective. It is true that the Committee of Ministers is a body of a political nature and character. Its practice has shown so far that such a character does not represent an impediment to its functioning in purely legal matters concerning the execution of the Court's judgments.

2.1.2 *The Composition of the Court*

Each and every member state of the Council of Europe, being at the same time a High Contracting Party to the Convention has one sitting judge at the Court. Judges are elected by the Parliamentary Assembly of the Council of Europe by the majority of votes cast, from a list of three candidates presented by the government of a member state. Judges sit at the Court in their private capacity and do not represent their respective countries.

The Court has five sections and as the current number of member states of the Council of Europe is fourty-seven, each section is composed of at least nine judges. Chambers of seven and committees of three judges are formed within sections to take decisions on the merits as well as on the admissibility of the applications filed with the Court.

In exceptional cases, when either a serious question affecting the interpretation or the implementation of the Convention or a serious issue of general importance is at stake, the Court sits in its Grand Chamber formation. The Grand Chamber of the Court is composed of seventeen judges, whose names are drawn by lots for each particular case.

It should also be noted that a judge elected on the list of a country (the so-called "national judge") must sit on the bench when an application is filed against that country. The national judge's expertise on his or her national legal system of the respective member state is indispensable for the decision to be taken by the Court's formation.

Judges come from their countries and national legal systems in which they are educated, a fact which makes the Court represent a focal point of various attitudes, legal practices, and legal standards, organisations of judiciary, legislation and all other possible sources of diversity in respect of legal provisions and their implementation. The international character of the Court and its diversity are the most outstanding features of its organisation and work. Judges' diverse backgrounds produce a fair amount of impact on the Court's activity.

Several years ago, Drzemczewski made a valuable effort tending to identify what he labelled "legal families" within the Court and its sections. The outcome of his approach was that he found some six different "legal families", each of those being represented within a section. The families thus identified were the following: Latin – Western Mediterranean, Balkans – Eastern Mediterranean, Eastern Europe, Anglo – Scandinavian countries, Central

Europe (embracing the Benelux and German-speaking countries) and the group of states in which the countries of the former Soviet Union and the Baltic states are included.[3]

The problem with the conclusion reached by Drzemczewski concerns above all his method and approach to the issue he researched. His starting point was the composition of the Court's sections and interviews with a number of judges. A lack of a more profound analysis of the "legal families" found is the feeblest point of the method applied. The families seem to be rather geographical. They do not even seem to be sufficiently historically rooted.

The effort to identify similarities and tendencies to give specific answers to certain legal issues by lawyers from some countries is by all means significant. However, whether specialists in comparative law would be ready to follow Drzemczewski's conclusions is doubtful. Maybe the "legal families" are less numerous than he thought, but such families do exist and lawyers educated in one of those are closer to one another than to their colleagues who have been educated in another family.

European countries belong either to the Common law or the Civil law families. Some comparatists are inclined to find smaller families within the Civil law countries; others would add that countries that had been parts of the Soviet Union once upon a time form a family of their own.[4] This is not the right place to discuss problems of this kind, but it is to be noted anyway that various types of legal systems coexist in Europe, being represented within the Court, where the judges inevitably co-operate, irrespectively of their formative background. This brings a strong impulse of creativity to the Court's work. The composition of the Court favours the possibility for a fruitful confrontation of the ideas and legal methods that judges are used to.

Judges sitting at the Court's bench implement the Convention, which, for its part, in a specific way also contributes to the Court's creativity.

2.2 THE CONVENTION'S PROVISIONS AS FOUNDATIONS OF THE COURT'S CREATIVITY

2.2.1 Abstract Concepts

The provisions of the Convention represent for their part one of the challenges of judicial creativity. These provisions are formulated in a rather abstract manner, corresponding to

3 A. Drzemczewski, "The internal organisation of the European Court of Human Rights: the composition of chambers and the Grand Chamber", *European Human Rights Law Review* 3/2000, 237.

4 For legal families within the Civil law group cf. Zweigert & Kötz (fn. 60), 74-180; 276-286. For the post-Soviet legal family cf. M. Fromont, *Grand systèmes de droit étrangers*, Paris 2001, 14-76; 147-169.

the spirit of the continental, romanistic legal system of the Civil law countries.[5] The Convention's provisions often lack precise technical concepts and definitions. The lawyers educated in the Anglo-Saxon system are sometimes inclined to consider such provisions to contain principles rather than legal propositions. As has already been observed in the previous chapter, I am sympathetic to this approach.

To illustrate this let me quote here Article 3 of the Convention:

> "No one shall be subjected to torture or to inhuman or degrading treatment or punishment."

There are several concepts in this text (*e.g.torture, treatment, punishment or subjection to a certain treatment or punishment*). Neither of these is defined, either in this particular text, or elsewhere in the Convention. It is therefore left to the interpretation and interpreters to find out whether a particular type of human behaviour, pertinent to a case before the Court, fulfils the standards of the provision.

We can not discern from the text itself what *torture* is. It is also impossible to learn from the text what are the circumstances in which someone is *subjected* to either *treatment* or *punishment*. An authoritative interpretation must intervene to put an end to dilemmas of the person reading the text, who inevitably remains puzzled because of its abstract character.

It has therefore been observed among scholars that "the Convention provisions are abstract and sparse".

For this reason "the key to resolving individual complaints (under the Convention) ultimately lies in how the text is interpreted".[6]

The fact that principles are contained in the text of the Convention along with real rules has been recently put forward by the current president of the Court, who explicitly said in a public lecture:

> "Many articles of the Convention are drafted to include principles."[7]

---

5 More on the subject to be found in my book published in Serbian; cf. Popović, *Uvod u uporedno pravo/Introduction to Comparitive Law*, Beograd 2007, 105-106.

6 S. Greer, *The European Convention on Human Rights – Achievements, Problems and Prospects*, Cambridge 2006, 193 (with a reference to an article published by C. Gearty in *Cambridge Law Journal* 52/1993).

7 J.P. Costa, "The Evolution and Current Challenges of the European Court of Human Rights", *Regent Journal of Law & Public Policy* 1/2009, 28. President Costa invoked the example of Article 10 of the Convention. He added that it however delineates the way in which a country is authorised to interfere with the freedom of expression. This echoes my additional argumentation, to be found below. On principles and their importance for the Court's jurisprudence see Boumghar, *Une approche de la notion de principe dans le système de la Convention européenne des droits de l'homme,* Paris 2010, 248-303.

One should however admit that some of the provisions of the Convention escape the abstract approach that I have just tried to describe. For instance if we turn to Article 5 of the Convention, granting right to liberty and security and in that context prescribing patterns of lawful detention, we shall easily see the difference in the approach. Article 5.1 enumerates six exceptional cases of lawful detention, thus enabling us to consider the existence of unlawful detention whenever one of the six exceptional cases does not apply.

To conclude this passage, for all the reasons mentioned above one can consider the attitude expressed by Danièle Lochak in order to describe drafting of the text of the United Nations' Universal Declaration on Human Rights of 1948. She says that it tended to reconcile the French tradition of abstract and concise proclamations with the Anglo-Saxon tradition which always takes into account details and descriptions of procedure.[8]

It is true that the text of the Convention tended to incorporate both traditions of the European legal families, but it is also important to underline the fact that the presence of abstract concepts in the text have primarily called for the Court's creativity.

2.2.2 *Interpreting the Convention as a Whole*

On several occasions the Court has showed a tendency to interpret the Convention as a whole. The approach to the text of the Convention as a whole is more abstract than the approach to a particular provision of the Convention. This approach of the Court reminds one of the pattern of approach to the problem of interpretation I discussed above, concerning the interpretation of a legal system as a whole. The Convention, together with the abundant case-law, which is based on its provisions, is indeed a well-developed legal system of its own.

There are scholars who insist on the purposive or teleological interpretation of the Convention, which according to them finds grounds in the Convention's preamble.[9] The aim of the Council of Europe proclaimed in the preamble of the Convention is "the maintenance and further realisation of human rights and fundamental freedoms", because they are "the foundation of justice and peace in the world". When the Court interprets the Convention as far as its preamble is concerned it inevitably takes into account the Convention as a whole. This puts the Court in the position described above, in respect of any interpretation, not necessarily the one of the Convention, and it increases the level of the Court's creativity.

The Court has pronounced itself in favour of the necessity of interpreting the Convention as a whole. In the case of *Otto-Preminger Institut v. Austria* the Court found two

8 D. Lochak, *Les droits de l'homme*, Paris 2002, 52.
9 Thus, Grabenwarter, (fn. 1), 49; cf. also J.F. Renucci, *Droit européen des droits de l'homme*, Paris 2002, 501.

articles of the Convention to be in conflict.[10] The case concerned a blasphemous film, offending religious feelings of the Roman Catholic majority in the Tyrol region of Austria, which was seized by the authorities and forbidden to be presented to the public at large. In the Court's view Article 9 of the Convention, granting freedom of thought, conscience and religion was in this case in conflict with Article 10, granting freedom of expression. The latter was invoked by the applicants.

The Court's finding was that the provocative movie could be regarded as a violation of the spirit of tolerance, which is one of the characteristic features of a democratic society. Therefore, the Court concluded:

> "The Convention is to be read as a whole and therefore the interpretation and application of Article 10 in the present case must be in harmony with the logic of the Convention". (para. 47 of the judgment)

It is evident that an interpretation of the Convention taken as a whole led the Court in this judgment. The logic of the Convention that the Court mentioned is the logic of a system, and it was exactly the guideline which made the Court find a path to rendering justice in this particular case.

The Grand Chamber of the Court has recently confirmed the Court's attachment to the interpretation of the Convention as a whole in the somewhat complex case of *Stec and Others v. The United Kingdom.*[11] The case concerned equal treatment of men and women as regards certain social security benefits of non-contributory nature.

The problem for the Court was to find a proper interpretation of Article 1 First Protocol in respect of the applicability of Article 6.1. of the Convention. The Court used the approach of interpreting the Convention as a whole as an instrument to approach the issue and stated in paragraph 48 of the decision on admissibility:

> "The Convention must also be read as a whole, and interpreted in such a way as to promote internal consistency and harmony between its various provisions."

It has been observed among commentators that the consistency of the interpretation of the Convention as a whole is one of the leading rules of its interpretation.[12] Judges must find solid ground for their rulings and when they depart from the idea of interpreting the Convention as a whole the outcome of their work is by far more complex than when they

10 *Otto-Preminger Institut v. Austria,* A 295 (1994).

11 *Stec and Others v. The United Kingdom,* ECHR 2005-X.

12 D. Harris, M. O'Boyle & C. Warbrick et al., *Law of the Convention on Human Rights,* Oxford – New York 2009, 15.

apply a single provision of the Convention. At the same time the result is situated at a more creative level.

The Court's approach to interpret the Convention as a whole does not necessarily mean that the interpretation includes the entire text of the Convention, indeed the aim is to find and use its spirit as a guideline in a certain case.

The Court interprets the Convention in a way which might be labelled as systematic and it sometimes uses the article of the Convention that was invoked by an application in conjunction with certain other articles for specific reasons of a case. That is exactly what the Court did in *Lautsi v. Italy.*[13] The complaint was under Article 2 First Protocol, Article 9 and Article 14 of the Convention. The Court however stated in paragraph 47 of the judgment that it was related to Articles 8 and 10 of the Convention as well and it also cited a judgment rendered under Article 11. The case was about exposing crucifix in public schools in Italy and the Court found violations of Articles 9 and 14 of the Convention, as well as Article 2 First Protocol. Such an approach of the Court takes place quite frequently and this is just an illustration of the Court's creative manner in handling cases.

The Court's effort to interpret the Convention as a whole and in a systematic way therefore substantially contributes to the Court's creativity in general. It goes along with the Court's handling of abstract concepts of the provisions of the Convention, but also with another phenomenon, gaining grounds today. The phenomenon is the dialogue of jurisdictions, in which the Court takes part. It has spread both in the field of international law and at the horizontal level of national laws and jurisdictions.

2.3 Dialogue of Jurisdictions

2.3.1 *Radiating Influence*

The Court is in a sort of permanent dialogue with the jurisdictions of Council of Europe member states. Many techniques of the Court's approach to the cases, such as, for instance, the evolutive interpretation, influence those jurisdictions. The same applies to the autonomous concepts the Court uses, as well as to the doctrine of the margin of appreciation, accorded to the member states.[14]

National jurisdictions of our time are inclined, while developing arguments for their judgments, to follow a path which brings an impartial observer to conclude that they rely more than ever on the universal idea of justice. One of the examples invoked by scholars

---

13 *Lautsi v. Italy*, app. no. 30814/06, chamber judgment of 3 November 2009.

14 Cf. P. Mahoney, "The Comparative Method of the European Court of Human Rights: Reference Back to National Law", in: Publications of the Swiss Institute of Comparative Law, 43 – *The Role of Comparative Law in the Emergence of European Law*, Lausanne – Zürich, 2000, 143-157.

to illustrate this process is that the judgments concerning human rights at national level are strongly influenced by ECHR standards.[15] In other words, the Court has been radiating its influence on national jurisdictions, and especially on those of the Council of Europe member states.

It has also been observed among scholars that judges at national level generally and usually take account of the jurisprudence of the ECHR. The co-operation between the two levels is based on mutual attention, and it is by no means a dialogue of the deaf.[16]

2.3.2 *The Horizontal Level of Dialogue*

National jurisdictions take account of the arguments put forward in similar cases irrespective of the fact that these are borrowed from abroad and have their roots outside the national law. A specific dialogue of national jurisdictions at the horizontal level has emerged in modern times and it shows the signs of vitality and considerable growth.

Such an interchangeable approach of the courts of law to cases and a specific commerce of ideas has always been a characteristic feature of the Anglo-Saxon legal family.[17] Recently, the English Law Lords have gone beyond, by searching inspiration outside their legal family, namely in Roman law, whereas the Supreme Court of the United States made for the first time reference to an ECHR judgment in 2003.[18]

A national judge no longer searches for arguments and grounds for a judgment exclusively in his or her domestic law. The scope of the foundation that judges pose their judgments on has been made wider and the search for grounds and motivations of these has become much larger than they once used to be. It is the authority of argument that counts nowadays and not the argument of authority of a national source of law.[19]

2.3.3 *Receiving Influences*

The mutual influences and circulation of ideas among national jurisdictions, as well as the impact of the ECHR on the national levels of jurisdiction, go hand in hand with the influences of the national jurisdictions on the jurisprudence of the ECHR. The Court turns to the law of the Council of Europe member states when seeking inspiration, but also to the

15 Cf. J. Allard & A. Garapon, *Les juges dans la mondialisation*, Paris 2005, 85-86.

16 K. Lucas-Alberni, *Le revirement de jurisprudence de la Court européenne des droits de l'homme*, Bruxelles 2008, 239.

17 G. Canivet, "La pratique du droit comparé par les cours suprêmes", *Tulane Law Review* 80, 1/2005, 229.

18 B. Stirn, D. Fairgrave & M. Guyomar, *Droits et libertés en France et au Royaume-Uni*, Paris 2006, 51; Ch. Rozakis, "The European Judge as Comparatist", *Tulane Law Review*, 80, 1/2005, 277.

19 See also my article on the subject: D. Popović, "La raison comparatiste et la liberté", *Mélanges en honneur de Slobodan Milacic*, Bruxelles 2007, 243

laws of extra-European states and international law sources.[20] National and international jurisdictions thus have a considerable impact on the Court's jurisprudence and it is indeed the Court's creativity which largely contributes to its realisation.

A phenomenon given the name of "ascending co-operation" has been observed by the scholars, studying the Court's case-law.[21] A coherent motivation of a judgment or a decision, stemming from the national level is often adopted by the Court and finds place in its proper judgments and decisions. It is to be noted that the Court does not receive such influences exclusively from the jurisdictions of member states of the Council of Europe, although those examples are the most numerous.

In *Tyrer v. The United Kingdom* the Court held that

> "it cannot but be influenced by the developments and commonly accepted standards in the penal policy of the member States of the Council of Europe in this field".[22]

The case was about maintaining corporal punishments for minors at the Isle of Man, belonging to the British Crown and enjoying a fair amount of autonomy, which enabled the local legislation to preserve such punishments until 1978. The Court ruled they were inacceptable under the Convention.

The Court based its ruling in *Tyrer* on the legal developments of the Council of Europe member states taken as a whole. In another case the Court took account of the legal developments that occurred exclusively in the respondent state, being the United Kingdom, once again. In the *Stafford* case the Secretary of State rejected the recommendation of the Parole Board to release the applicant on licence. The judicial review of such a decision proved unsuccessful, because the House of Lords dismissed the applicant's appeal. The Court found a violation of Article 5 of the Convention, but for our purpose here it is important to underline that the Court stated that it "[had] regard to the changing conditions in Contracting States".

The Court further ruled that it was bound by "any emerging consensus discernible within the domestic legal order of the respondent Contracting State".[23]

There was no need for the Court to try to establish the existence of a consensus among all the member states; it was sufficient to follow the line of legal developments in the respondent state in order to reach a decision on the case.

---

20 See my article: D. Popovic, "Le droit comparé dans l'accomplissement des tâches de la Cour européenne des droits de l'homme", in: *Liber Amicorum Luzius Wildhaber – Human Rights* – Strasbourg Views, Kehl – Strasbourg – Arlington, 2007, 380-386.

21 I am borrowing the expression from Katia Lucas-Alberni; cf. Lucas-Alberni (fn. 16), 240.

22 *Tyrer v. The United Kingdom*, Judgments and Decisions A 26 (1978), paragraph 31.

23 *Stafford v. The United Kingdom*, ECHR 2002-IV, paragraphs 68 and 69.

Apart from receiving influences from the Council of Europe member states the Court has proven to be susceptible to finding inspiration in legal developments from extra-European countries, as well as from the international jurisdictions.

There is a wide range of sources of inspiration of the Court's case-law in this field. For instance, in the *Goodwin* case the Court sought inspiration in various foreign legal systems, such as those of Australia, Canada, Israel, New Zealand Singapore, South Africa, and the United States of America.[24] The case concerned gender readjustment and the question was whether its consequences should be fully recognised under national law. This was however exceptional. If the Court makes reference to extra-European laws it usually does so by invoking judgments of only one or two jurisdictions.[25]

The Court also refers to the judgments of international jurisdictions, which sometimes serve as the basis of the Court's arguments. An example of this is to be found in the well known *Oçalan* case, in which the Court made reference to a judgment of the Inter-American Court of Human Rights.[26]

Judgments of international jurisdictions have not only served as a source of inspiration for the Court. The same applies to international law in general. Literature has established various approaches of the Court in using the international law as a point of reference in its judgments. The Court is influenced by the conventions concluded within the framework of the Council of Europe. It also uses its soft-law, as well as the law of the European Union, both at the level of texts and jurisprudence. Finally, as we have just seen, the Court uses the judgments of extra-European jurisdictions as a source of inspiration.[27]

All these various influences largely contribute to the enrichment of the Court's case-law. Being receptive to the ideas coming from different jurisdictions is a feature that could be expected from an international jurisdiction, such as the Court. Its task has thus been efficiently achieved. As a matter of fact it was fulfilled much better than the Court would have performed it, had it stayed isolated.

---

24 *Christine Goodwin v. The United Kingdom*, ECHR 2002-VI.

25 Such as for instance in the following cases: *Pretty v. The United Kingdom*, ECHR 2002-III (a reference to Canadian law), or *Appleby v. The United Kingdom*, ECHR 2003-VI (a reference to the US and Canadian laws), or *Hirst v. The United Kingdom (No. 2)*, ECHR 2005-IX (a reference to Canadian and South African law).

26 *Oçalan v. Turkey*, ECHR 2005-IV.

27 Flauss, "Du droit international comparé des droits de l'homme dans la jurisprudence de la Cour européenne des droit de l'homme", in: *Publications of the Swiss Institute of Comparative Law 43 – The Role of Comparative Law in the Emergence of European Law*, Lausanne – Zurich, 2000, 159-182.

2.3.4 *Enhancing Creativity*

Constant mutual influences between the Court and other jurisdictions, national as well as international, serve the purpose of enhancing the Court's creativity. A fruitful exchange of ideas in which the Court takes part has made its approach to the provisions of the Convention and the interpretation of these richer in arguments, more subtle on certain occasions and well adapted to the demands of justice. The Court's case-law has become a point of convergence of various legal traditions, attitudes and interpretation devices, applied worldwide either at a national or international level of jurisdiction.

As I have tried to show above while judicial creativity consists of completing the legal rules based on provisions of the Convention it should be underlined that the dialogue of jurisdictions has offered many possibilities to enlarge the Court's creativity. Increasing the scope of ideas that the Court has used as guidelines to reach judgments and decisions on particular cases has enabled the Court to achieve a higher degree of creativity.

Conclusion of Part One

Judicial creativity is a specific concept. It can be properly understood only if we take into account the process of the operation of the law as a whole. Judicial creativity plays a decisive role among the various stages of development of the process of operation of the law.

The main function of judicial creativity consists in completing legal rules. It is only when completed by interpretation that enactments reach the stage of legal rules and become effective. Each and every interpretation is creative in itself, but judicial interpretation has a specific feature of its own. It sets the law in motion. This is what makes me conclude that judicial creativity plays the most important role in the work and operation of the complex and rather sensitive mechanism which we commonly label as law.

Judicial creativity also assumes the usual function it fulfils in the field of the protection of human rights in Europe. This is due to the international character of the system of protection of human rights. The fact is not only reflected in the organisation and composition of the ECHR, but also in the specific features of the provisions of the Convention that the work of the ECHR is based on. This has been strongly supported and enhanced by the dialogue of jurisdictions currently existing at a global level, in which the Court takes an active part.

Part 2
The Binding Force of Precedent

INTRODUCTION

The doctrine of precedent in the form we know it today has been a part of Anglo-Saxon legal development and its legacy to modern civilisation. It has emerged over centuries to be shaped in the doctrine of *stare decisis*, which was at its peak at the beginning of the second half of the 20th century. Lord Denning MR, who sat at the British House of Lords between 1957 and 1962, wrote:

> "The House held itself to be absolutely bound by the doctrine of stare decisis."[1]

The doctrine of *stare decisis* laid down the foundation of the principle of the binding force of precedent. Judges were quite simply supposed to follow previous judgments in cases which were identical to the one they had to try. The pure idea of justice stood behind this attitude. Like cases should be treated alike. However, the process of the emergence of the doctrine was slow and the principle of *stare decisis* was elevated into the inflexible dogma only in the early 19th century.[2] The rule of *stare decisis* can be defined by the words an English judge used in a case of 1833. He argued that for the sake of uniformity and consistency of the law, rules derived from precedents were to apply even when they were "not as convenient and reasonable as we ourselves could have devised".[3]

To understand properly the doctrine of precedent one should point out the difference between the two main elements, contained in judgments: *ratio decidendi* and *obiter dicta*. The first element is binding, whereas the second is not. The *ratio decidendi* of a case are "those propositions of law which are necessary for the disposal of the case on the facts".[4]

The *ratio decidendi* must relate both to the facts of a case as well as to the parties' claims. These two connections are indispensable in creating the binding force of a precedent. *Obiter dicta* are all the legal propositions in the judgments which do not have the force of *ratio decidendi*. In other words, they are not binding.[5]

The doctrine of *stare decisis*, as mentioned here in its purest and simplest form has never been completely uncontested. Judges have always been aware of the necessity to adapt the law to the existing social circumstances. It should be noted that even before the doctrine reached its peak there had been judges in England who remarked that the rigidity

1 Lord Denning, *The Discipline of Law*, London 1979, 287.
2 J.H.Baker, *An Introduction to English Legal History*, London 1979, 173.
3 The case was *Mirehouse v. Rennel* (1833); see Baker (fn. 2).
4 S. Whittaker, "Precedent in English Law: A View from the Citadel", in: E.Hondius (ed.), *Precedent and the Law*, Bruxelles 2007, 41 (with a reference to Cross and Harris).
5 Whittaker (fn. 4), 41-42.

should be avoided. In a case which was given judgment towards the end of the 18th century Lord Mansfield CJ stated that "the law must adapt itself to the various situations of mankind."[6]

If pushed to the extreme both attitudes seem to be unacceptable, because they are somewhat exaggerated. On the one hand the principle of *stare decisis* threatens to stiffen and petrify the law and deprive it of the possibility of adapting to changes in society. On the other hand, a constant and rapid adaptation of the law to the existing social circumstances tends to annihilate the whole idea of law. One can deduce that there will be no justice at all if like cases are not treated alike and accordingly decided. The rigidity of the law must be preserved at least to some extent.

It is the idea of justice that can help us overcome this antinomy. Justice itself is the ideal that should represent the goal of each and every lawyer.

"Just as the scientist seeks for truth so the lawyer should seek for justice", says Lord Denning.[7] It is, and should always be above all, justice alone that is guiding judges while performing their task.

I have already tried to convince the reader in Part One of this book that it was judges who participated in fulfilling the task of completing legal rules. This goes hand in hand with another splendid idea of the Anglo-Saxons, or rather common lawyers, who believe their law to be "an unchanging body of common sense and reasoning".[8]

A continental lawyer must make a footnote to this – it occurs to me that the body as a whole remains unchanged in spite of certain adaptations to the parts of its organism, considered as a whole. If some approaches to particular issues may differ over the course of time, the whole body of the law still remains unchanged and preserved in its entirety.

The role of precedent has had a considerable degree of importance in the process of the emergence of European human rights law. The latter has been developed by the ECHR and by way of its abundant jurisprudence. The Court has been completing the rules of the Convention, but at the same time such a task would have turned out to be a mission impossible without fixing the Court's own case-law. It was to that purpose that the Court had to take a stand towards the role of precedent in its proper meaning.

Although the role of precedent in the Court's jurisprudence is subject to disputes and controversy, I should say that the use of precedent in the Court's practice represented the second pillar of the development leading to the emergence of the European human rights law. It is unnecessary to mention, but let me repeat however, that the first pillar of the whole process was the Court's creativity. This I developed in Part One of this book.

6 The case was *Johnson v. Spiller (1784)*; see J.H.Baker (fn. 2), 174.
7 Lord Denning (fn. 1), 292.
8 Baker (fn. 2), 169.

The Court's creativity would have been unbalanced without the role played by the precedent. Therefore to conclude this introduction I would like to invoke the words of an English Law Lord, with which he tried to put limits on the use of precedent. It was Lord Lowry who mentioned "aids to navigation across an uncertainly charted sea of judicial legislation".[9]

Although the Honourable Lord was speaking of requirements for judges when using precedents in English law I dare say his words perfectly apply to the mode of handling the precedents in the jurisprudence of the ECHR. Precedents were the means of introducing consistency in the Court's jurisprudence. That is why I can rephrase Lord Denning's sentence to apply to the ECHR: By standing by their previous decisions the ECHR judges have kept the Court's case-law on a good course.[10]

The three chapters of this part of the book shall firstly expose the Court's general approach to the rule of precedent and its binding force, as far as it can be distilled from the Court's case-law. Secondly, the topic will be how the Court follows its own precedents and thirdly how the Court overrules these from time to time.

---

9 As quoted by Whittaker (fn. 4), 65.

10 Lord Denning (fn. 1), 314 (in respect of the development of common law).

III The Role of Precedent in the Court's Jurisprudence

3.1 Absence of *Stare Decisis* Doctrine

It is indeed commonplace to say that the Court has not developed the doctrine of *stare decisis,* which would be identical to the one existing in Common law. Such a statement might seduce an observer who does not pay enough attention to think that the concept of precedent does not play any role in the Court's jurisprudence. A conclusion of that kind would however be a great mistake. The truth is that, on the contrary, precedents not only play a significant role in the Court's practice, but they are crucial for understanding the European human rights law in general.

Before I turn to the Court's case-law in order to try to discuss the role of precedent, let me mention two things. Firstly, it has been remarked in the scholarship that the Court's practice has developed a method comparable to the one of Common law, as well as that it can be discerned from the Court's case-law that the Court sticks to its own precedents for the sake of legal certainty.[1]

Secondly, the existence of the binding force of precedent can not be confirmed exclusively relying on a written text, or by invoking a certain classical statement or the like. To be able to learn whether precedents have a binding force within a legal system one should analyse the attitude of judges and their feelings in that regard. This is a rather difficult task to achieve, but it is not completely impossible to research the topic.

A former president of the Court, Judge Wildhaber, writing on the role of precedent in the Court's jurisprudence, has left a valuable testimony concerning the subject. Let me hand over to him in order to present reader with the state of affairs within the Court in respect of handling precedents by the sitting judges:

> "Discussions inside the European Court of Human Rights relatively often reveal disagreements as to whether an earlier precedent should be followed. This is

1 K. Lucas-Alberni, *Le revirement de jurisprudence de la Cour européenne des droits de l'homme*, Bruxelles 2008, 34, 44-45 (on page 34 a reference is made to an article of Franz Matscher, published in 1997). For an opinion opposed to this one and denying the binding force of precedent in the Court's practice cf. D.J. Harris, M. O'Boyle & C. Warbrick, *Law of the European Convention on Human Rights*, Oxford – New York 2009, 17.

> not surprising in an international court with so many different legal orders and traditions."[2]

President Wildhaber's words describe fairly well the situation of judges at the ECHR and the legal environment in which they work. We learn from the former president not only that the Court's precedents are generally followed, but also that there is controversy over whether a certain precedent should be followed or not in a particular case. What we learn above all is the fact that there is a whole atmosphere surrounding judges and creating an environment in which following precedents is a part of the Court's day-to-day practice. It really is a rule that judges have adopted over time throughout the Court's history. They can not and probably do not want to escape the environment that has been created by their common efforts, I dare say, already through generations of judges sitting at the Court.

Despite the absence of a coherent doctrine on the binding force of precedents these are usually followed by the Court and at this point we should turn to the question of what the Court's position with respect to the binding force of precedent is precisely.

3.2 Court's Principal Position

3.2.1 Approach to the Problem

It is not easy to find out what the Court's position towards the binding force of precedent really is. So far we have been able to see that there is an absence of a doctrine corresponding to the one of *stare decisis* in Common law. The formulation of a doctrine is, by the way, a task for legal scholars and not for judges themselves to fulfil. The absence of a properly formulated doctrine does not necessarily mean the absence of a corresponding practice of the Court. On the contrary, it is clear that the Court follows its own precedents in subsequent cases identical to previous ones.

The Court's principal position on the binding force of precedent can only be deduced from the Court's case-law, which is quite abundant. The development of case-law proves the existence of a certain readjustment of the Court's attitude to the changing circumstances over the course of time. The Court's attitude towards the subject did not evolve without facing complicated points and issues. Two periods can be identified in the development of the Court's attitude on the subject.

---

2 L.Wildhaber, "Precedent in the European Court of Human Rights", in: L. Wildhaber, *The European Court of Human Rights 1998-2006 – History, Achievements, Reform*, Kehl – Strasbourg – Arlington, Va. 2006, 157.

3.2.2 *Earlier Stages of Evolution*

The earlier stage of evolution of the Court's principal attitude towards the binding force of precedent can be deemed to have lasted until the beginning of the 1990s. The position of the Court in two Belgian cases, in which the same issue was raised, warrants further examination. The first case was *Delcourt v. Belgium.*[3] In this case a company director had been charged with criminal offences and convicted to prison. The proceedings against the director had been instituted by a state official, whose title was *Procureur du Roi*. The director lodged an application with the ECHR and his complaint was under Article 6 of the Convention.

The main grounds for the applicant's complaint consisted of the fact that a member of the department of the state official in charge of prosecution before the Cassation Court (*Procureur général*), after having developed submissions at the oral hearing, also participated in the deliberations from which the parties were excluded. The officer who had initiated the proceedings was in a way subordinated to the one who took part at the oral hearing in the Cassation Court although the Belgian legislation was not quite clear at that point.

The majority of the Commission of Human Rights, the body then competent to decide on the admissibility of the application, expressed the opinion that the fact that a prosecuting officer had taken part in deliberations of the Cassation Court was not incompatible with the Convention. On the contrary the minority of the Commission was of opinion that such a practice in the Cassation Court of Belgium did not comply with the Convention. The Commission however declared the case admissible and the Court had to decide on the merits.

The Court found Article 6 of the Convention applicable to the case, but held unanimously that there was no breach of that provision. The reasons for the decision were mainly based on the Court's findings that the *Procureur général*'s department at the Belgian Cassation Court was completely independent from the Minister of Justice and therefore not attached to the executive power. The Court also found that the state official in question was not an adversary of a party before the Cassation Court, but an adjunct and an adviser of that court. The ECHR therefore held that the whole system existing in Belgian law since 1815, as applied in practice, was not incompatible with Article 6 of the Convention.[4]

The *Delcourt* case would probably have not been of such importance if the same issue had not been raised in another Belgian case twenty years later. It was in *Borgers v. Belgium* that the Court addressed the same issue.[5]

---

3 *Delcourt v. Belgium*, Judgments and Decisions A 11 (1970); for bibliography V. Berger, *Jurisprudence de la Cour européenne des droits de l'Homme*, Paris 2009, 280.

4 See paragraphs 31-37 of the judgment.

5 *Borgers v. Belgium*, Judgments and Decisions A 214 B (1991); for bibliography Berger (fn. 3), 282.

A practising lawyer had been charged with accusations of forgery and using forged documents and he was condemned to a suspended sentence of imprisonment and a fine. He lodged an application with the ECHR, alleging violation of Article 6 of the Convention. The applicant did so on the grounds that he had been unable to reply to the submissions of the *avocat général*, to address the court last. He also complained of the fact that the latter participated in the deliberations, which took place immediately after the hearing.

The Commission of Human Rights ruled that the case was admissible. Furthermore, it expressed by fourteen votes to one the opinion that there had been a violation of Article 6 of the Convention. The Commission's opinion was however not binding for the Court that had to decide on the merits of the case.

It is interesting to note that the Court first took a stand on the binding force of its own previous jurisprudence. The Court stated in paragraph 24 of the judgment:

> "The Court notes in the first place that the findings in the Delcourt judgment on the question of the independence and impartiality of the Court of Cassation and its procureur général's department remain entirely valid... Having regard to the grounds set out in that judgment, the Court does not perceive any breach of the Convention requirements on this issue."

This statement of the Court's is fundamental for our purpose here. The sitting judges expressed their firm conviction and thus declared themselves to have been bound by a Court's previous ruling. However, what the Court stated in paragraph 24 of the judgment was in a certain way contradicted by the Court's final ruling on the case. The Court found a violation of Article 6 of the Convention on the grounds exposed in paragraphs 26-28 of the judgment. In paragraph 26 the Court found that the state official in question could not be regarded as neutral from the point of view of the parties to the cassation proceedings. In paragraph 27 the Court found that the applicant could not reply to the *avocat général*'s submissions and ruled that such restrictions of the rights of the defence were not justified. Finally in paragraph 28 of the judgment it was found that the Cassation Court's deliberations in the presence of the said state official could give the latter the opportunity to promote his submissions, without fear of contradiction by the applicant. The Court's judgment was rendered by eighteen votes to four. It overruled *Delcourt*.[6]

The opinions of the dissenting judges, as well as of those concurring, which are the subject of our discussion, shed more light on the situation.

Judge Thor Vilhjalmsson dissented on several points. The strong traditions of Belgian judiciary were in his opinion sufficient to guarantee its independence effectively. He rejected the question of appearances for the same reasons, being convinced that the traditions

6 Cf. Wildhaber (fn. 2), 158-159.

provided solid grounds for the objective impartiality of the judiciary. It should be underlined that Judge Thor Vilhjalmsson above all dissented on the ground that he held the legal analysis in *Delcourt* still valid. He felt himself bound by a previous precedent.

Judges Pinheiro Farinha and Morenilla took a similar stand in their concurring opinion. They rejected the affirmation of the majority of judges that the findings in *Delcourt* were entirely valid. They stated that they would have preferred instead if the Court had departed from the contents of the paragraphs 32-38 of the *Delcourt* judgment. This leads to a conclusion that the two concurring judges also felt the binding force of a precedent, for which they wanted a clearer expression in a judgment in which previous jurisprudence was overruled.

Judge Cremona dissented on a fact, which he stated quite openly in his dissenting opinion. The fact was that the Court overruled the precedent, posed by the Court's ruling in *Delcourt*. Like the two concurring judges, whose opinions were just mentioned above, he was dissatisfied with paragraph 24 of the judgment in *Borgers*, which he considered a justification for overruling *Delcourt*. He opposed the exhaustive references to the Court's previous judgments, made in paragraph 24, as irrelevant to the case. A remark on this from the author of this book would be that these citations also represented a sign of the binding force of precedent, irrespective of the issue of relevance raised by the dissenting judge.

In a somewhat lengthy dissenting opinion, Judge Martens clearly stated his stance that the *Delcourt* precedent had been overruled and opposed the majority ruling on these grounds. He invoked the rule in *Cossey* that I am going to start the next heading with.[7] That judgment was rendered in September 1990, only a year before the *Borgers* judgment, given in October 1991. That was the end of the earlier stage of development and the beginning of the next period.[8]

Judge Martens argued, based on the rule in *Cossey*, that the Court was allowed to overrule its previous stance only if there were cogent reasons for such a course of action. Those were inexistent in his opinion, but for the purpose of this passage I should point out that Judge Martens indeed confirmed the binding force of precedent in the Court's practice.

If we are to take account of all dissenting and concurring opinions in the light of the judgment rendered on the case, and especially its paragraph 24, it seems inevitable to conclude that the binding force of precedent had emerged in the Court's jurisprudence certainly before 1990. In October 1991 it was difficult to overrule a precedent, as the *Borgers* case clearly shows.

---

7 *Cossey v. The United Kingdom*, Judgments and Decisions A 184 (1990).

8 The Court's deliberations took place in January 1991, when the case was relinquished to the then competent Plenary Court. Further deliberations were held in March and September of the same year.

The fact that overruling a precedent was not easy in the 1980s and 1990s, and consequently that precedents were systematically followed, has been underlined by former President of the Court, Judge Wildhaber, with reference to the Swiss cases of *Schiesser* and *Huber*.[9] In the latter case the majority was in favour of overruling the former, but the minority resistance on the issue clearly shows the state of mind within the Court and among the sitting judges in respect of the force of precedent.

The Court held in *Schiesser* that "other officer authorised by law" within the meaning of Article 5.3. of the Convention was not necessarily identical to a judge, but however had to satisfy certain conditions of independence. A district attorney under Swiss law was susceptible of fulfilling those conditions. There was no violation of Article 5.3.

On the contrary, in *Huber* the Court found a violation on the grounds that the impartiality of the judicial officer, who orders detentions, but also carries out other duties, appears to be "open to doubt".

3.2.3 *A Comparison*

We have seen under the previous heading that Judge Martens invoked the rule in *Cossey* in respect of precedents and their binding force. *Cossey v. The United Kingdom* was a case concerning post-operative male-to-female transsexual who was unable to obtain a birth certificate showing her sex as female and to contract a valid marriage with a man. By ten votes to six, the Court found a violation of Article 12 of the Convention on the case. The issue of binding force of precedent was then raised before the Court.

The question for the Court was whether it was bound by its judgment in a previous case. It was the case of *Rees v. The United Kingdom*, where the Court unanimously found no violation of Article 12 of the Convention.[10] The case was about non recognition for legal purposes of a post-operative transsexual's new identity.

The first issue raised in *Cossey* was whether that case was distinguishable on its facts from the *Rees* case. In paragraph 34 of the judgment the Court stated its finding that the case was not materially distinguishable on the facts from the previous one.

The next question was should the Court depart from its *Rees* judgment. Responding to this question the Court set a rule containing its stance towards the binding force of precedent. The Court stated in paragraph 35 of the judgment:

> "The Court is not bound by its previous judgments. However, it usually follows and applies its own precedents, such a course being in the interests of legal

9 *Schiesser v. Switzerland*, Judgments and Decisions A 34 (1979) and *Huber v. Switzerland*, Judgments and Decisions A 188 (1990); see Wildhaber (fn. 2), 158-159.

10 *Rees v. The United Kingdom* A 106 (1986).

> certainty and the orderly development of the Convention case-law. Nevertheless, this would not prevent the Court from departing from an earlier decision if it was persuaded that there were cogent reasons for doing so."

At this point the Court invoked its judgment in the *Inze* case, in which the Court favoured the principle of equality of treatment of children born in and out of wedlock.[11] What the Court did in *Inze* was not to depart from its own previous ruling, but rather to combat and overrun the margin of appreciation of a member state to the Convention, and its discriminatory legislation.

The Court's attitude in *Cossey* deserves some reflection. First of all it must be pointed out that the binding force of precedent has had a certain development at its source, in England, years before the issue was raised before the Court. The Law Lords gave a statement in 1966:

> "Their Lordships nevertheless recognise that too rigid adherence to precedent may lead to injustice in a particular case and also unduly restrict the proper development of the law. They propose, therefore, to modify their present practice and, while treating former decisions of this House as normally binding, to depart from a previous decision when it appears right to do so."[12]

If we compare the Court's position expressed in paragraph 35 of the *Cossey* judgment to the statement of the Law Lords of 1966, I dare say that similarities are striking. However, the starting points differ. The Court departed from the idea that it was not bound by precedents, while the Law Lords did just the opposite. The conclusions reached in both stances are nevertheless very close. Both the Law Lords and the Court expressed the opinion that it was justified to depart from previous decisions. It is for the sake of the different starting points of the two statements that the Court insisted on legal certainty, whereas the Law Lords invoked the excess of rigidity in order to justify their views.

Both statements considered above invoke reasons for legal developments, and that is a fact I should like to stress. The role of precedent is crucial for the evolution of the law. Precedent seemingly tends to petrify the law. What it actually does is to improve and

11 *Inze v. Austria,* Judgments and Decisions A 126 (1987), paragraph 41.

12 Practice Note (1966) as reproduced in Lord Denning, *The Discipline of Law,* London 1979, 296-297. On the contents see also J.H. Baker, *An Introduction to English Legal History,* London 1979, 175. It should be noted that the Constitutional Reform Act of 2005 modified the composition and altered the name of the highest judiciary instance; instead of the previous House of Lords there is now the Supreme Court of the United Kingdom. See D. Frison, *Introduction au droit anglais et aux institutions britanniques*, Paris 2005, 39.

enhance judicial creativity.[13] That is the way the law keeps evolving and develops fairly in the long run. An effort to overrule previous jurisprudence calls for a considerable amount of judicial creativity.

3.2.4 Further Developments

Paragraph 35 of the *Cossey* judgment declared the Court's principal position towards the binding force of precedent. It could be understood as generally denying the binding force of previous judgments, while at the same time declaring the Court's resolute attitude to follow its own judgments for the sake of legal certainty. Therefore some authors are of the opinion that although the Court does not feel legally bound by its previous judgments, it is the respect of precedent that guides the Court while performing its task.[14] Such a stance was reproduced in the Court's subsequent judgments.

In *Beard v. the United Kingdom*, as well as in *Chapman v. The United Kingdom* the Court revisited the issue of the binding force of precedent.[15] The cases concerned gypsies or Roma people, who were moving between official sites and unofficial stopping places in England. They complained under Article 8 of the Convention of the refusal of permission to station caravans, or their mobile homes on their own land. By ten votes to seven the Court found that there was no violation of Article 8 of the Convention in both cases.

The Court revisited the precedent issue in paragraph 81 of the *Beard* judgment, where it was stated:

> "The Court considers that while it is not formally bound to follow any of its previous judgments, it is in the interests of legal certainty, foreseeability and equality before the law that it should not depart, without good reason, from precedents laid down in previous cases."

This text is exactly the same as the one used in paragraph 70 of the *Chapman* judgment. If compared to the formula used in *Cossey* the *dicta* in *Chapman* and *Beard* show only slight modifications. The starting point remains the same – there is no formal grounds for a binding force of precedent, but the Court nevertheless follows its own previous rulings. The reason for such an attitude was slightly altered in *Beard*, for it was stated that foreseeability and equality before the law were the reasons for the Court's stance, apart from the

13 This has been underlined by the scholarship. Cf. B. Stirn, D. Fairgrave & M. Guyomar, *Droits et libertés en France et au Royaume-Uni*, Paris 2006, 36-38 ; see the authors' further references on those pages. See also D. Frison (fn. 12), 65-66.

14 Lucas-Alberni (fn. 1), 64, 82, 187.

15 *Beard v. The United Kingdom*, app. 24882/94. A judgment of 18 January 2001; *Chapman v. The United Kingdom*, ECHR 2001-I, a judgment rendered on the same day as the previous one.

legal certainty that had already been mentioned in *Cossey*. The development of the case-law, invoked in *Cossey* does not figure in the *Chapman-Beard* formula. That is why one gets the impression that the statement in *Cossey* is a bit closer to the Practice Note of the Law Lords of 1966 than the *dicta* in *Beard* and in *Chapman*.

The second parts of the formulas used by the Court in 1990 and 2001 are very much alike. Although it does not have to, the Court follows its own precedents and can depart from those only if sufficiently good reasons apply and speak in favour of such a step to be taken. The *Cossey* formula speaks of cogent reasons, whereas those in *Beard* and in *Chapman* mention good reason. There is no substantial difference between the two. Both are close to the expression used by the Law Lords in 1966 – "when it appears right".

The literature insists on the difference between the old and the new Court, concerning this issue, which does not seem well-founded to me. Thus Katia Lucas-Alberni in her voluminous thesis on the reversal of the jurisprudence of the Court tends to interpret the ruling in *Chapman*, as a milestone, just because it stems from the new Court, whereas *Cossey* was a judgment of the old Court[16]. This is true, as far as the dates of the judgments are concerned, but in my opinion it is much more important to remark the continuing development of the Court's principal stance on the role of precedent than to draw a line in order to delimit two periods of the Court's organisation.

The Court's principal position on the role of precedent was once more repeated in the *Stafford* case, which concerned continued detention and the lawfulness of its review.[17] The Grand Chamber unanimously found violations of Article 5 of the Convention on the case.

The formula on the binding force of precedent was reproduced in paragraph 81 of the judgment:

> "While the Court is not formally bound to follow any of its previous judgments, it is in the interests of legal certainty, foreseeability and equality before the law that it should not depart, without cogent reason, from precedents laid down in previous cases."

The text was almost the same as those in *Chapman* and in *Beard*, with the exception that the word cogent was used from the earlier text in *Cossey*. Therefore one can find no substantial changes in the Court's attitude: although they are not formally binding, the precedents are followed by the Court.

Literally the same text was reproduced by paragraph 74 of the judgment in *Christine Goodwin v. The United Kingdom*, a case which concerned the absence of legal recognition

---

16 Lucas-Alberni (fn. 1), 58.

17 *Stafford v. The United Kingdom*, ECHR 2002-IV.

of change of sex, where the Grand Chamber unanimously found violations of Articles 8, 12, 13 and 14 of the Convention.[18]

A slight alteration to the Court's usual formula on the binding force of precedent occurred in the *Mamatkulov* case, which primarily concerned Articles 3 and 6 of the Convention, but also Article 34 because of non-compliance of the respondent state with interim measures indicated by the Court.[19] The Court stated in paragraph 121 of the judgment:

> "While the Court is not formally bound to follow its previous judgments, in the interests of legal certainty and foreseeability it should not depart, without good reason, from its own precedents."

It is to be noted that equality before the law was omitted from the grounds for following previous judgments. The "good reason" of the *Chapman-Beard* formula was reintroduced instead of "cogent reason", which we met in *Stafford* and in *Christine Goodwin* cases. One should nevertheless come to the conclusion that the Court's jurisprudence managed to provide a formula on the issue of the binding force of precedent and stick to it in the course of the development of the Court's case-law. Small drafting alterations to the adopted formula on the principal position towards precedents can not lead us to conclude that the Court was hesitating in following its own precedents. On the contrary, following precedents has been and still remains a firm and unchanged attitude of the Court. This attitude seems to be confirmed in some of the most recent academic contributions of the judges sitting in the Court. The Vice-President of the Court, Judge Rozakis, has recently pointed out in an article that the Court, although not being obliged to maintain its own case-law, indeed "[follows] its own precedents and creates case-law to which it adheres".[20]

Let me conclude this passage by returning to the comparison mentioned under the previous heading. What the ECHR does corresponds to the perception that continental lawyers have of the attitude of the English courts of law towards the issue. To illustrate this I shall give the floor to the Fleiners:

> "The common law is a legal system that has developed out of the practice and decisions of the various courts. In England, every court makes decisions based on relevant precedents, thereby contributing to the development of the law with new precedents. The development of the law has been entrusted to the

---

18 *Christine Goodwin v. The United Kingdom*, ECHR 2002-VI.

19 *Mamatkulov and Askarov v. Turkey*, ECHR 2005-I.

20 Ch. Rozakis, "Is the Case-Law of the European Court of Human Rights a Procrustean Bed? Or is it a Contribution to the Creation of a European Public Order? A Modest Reply to Lord Hoffmann's Criticisms", *UCL Human Rights Review* 2/2009, 60-61.

> jurisdiction of the courts, which make decisions based on the principle of stare decisis, applying legal principles developed through the precedents of the respective courts."[21]

The opinion of the two continental lawyers I have just quoted reflects fairly the essence of the Anglo-Saxon system of jurisprudence. It is indeed the most important feature of the system that each and every court of law follows its own precedents. This seems to have grounds in the idea of distributive justice, as perceived in the Aristotelian way.

Legal developments on the European continent have put forward the role of case-law. It has been rightly observed that in German law, for instance, the courts of law interpret the texts of the written law not only *praeter legem*, but also *contra legem*. Such approaches of the courts have been developed in order to meet the "changing ideas of justice".[22]

The ECHR, by remaining faithful to its own previous jurisprudence has made itself a part of that mainstream of developments. This was confirmed by a remark by the Court's Vice-President, whose experience based on the years of sitting on the bench must not be underestimated. Judge Rozakis expressed himself in a clear way, by stating:

> "[The Court] undoubtedly operates rather more as a common-law court than as a continental European (civil law) court."[23]

This feature of the Court has become evident over time and that is what puts the Court at the crossroads of various influences, coming from the States Parties to the Convention. Some of these have turned out to be preponderant and brought the Court in line with the idea of the binding force of precedent, which is no longer to be questioned, as far as the Court's jurisprudence is concerned.

---

21 Th. Fleiner & L.R. Basta-Fleiner, *Constitutional Democracy in a Multicultural and Globalised World*, Springer 2009, 137.

22 H. Simon, G. Funk-Baker, *Einfürung in das deutsche Recht und die deutsche Rechtssprache*, München – Paris – Kopenhagen – Athen – Bern 2006, 23.

23 Rozakis (fn. 20), 53.

IV Following Precedents

4.1 The Court's Technique

The Court has so far usually and constantly followed its own precedents. The pattern applied by the Court while developing such a practice corresponds for the most part to the one known in the Anglo-Saxon legal family.

The precedents can firstly be identified by the Court's technique which consists in making references to its own previous judgments.[1] Secondly, it should be pointed out that the references to the Court's previous judgments take account of the essential element of these. What is considered binding is the *ratio decidendi*, although I must admit that the Court does not use this particular expression. The expression is however used by judges of the Court in their academic contributions.[2]

In the light of what has been shown earlier, it is of the greatest importance to conclude that, when making references to previous jurisprudence of its own, the Court primarily takes account of the legal proposition which is necessary for the disposal of a case. As the Court very often cites its previous rulings, it is to be made clear that only those citations are relevant in respect of the topic of following precedents, that concern reasons for issuing a certain judgment.[3] This must be underlined because the Court's citations of its own jurisprudence are abundant.

The Court invokes its previous rulings when exposing arguments and not exclusively when it follows its own precedents in the essential sense of the term, *i.e.* when following a *ratio decidendi* of a previous judgment. However the reasons for following previous jurisprudence in the strict sense of the expression can be properly identified in the Court's judgments.

Scholars insist on the fact that the judge or judges issuing a certain judgment do not necessarily determine themselves the crucial reasons for the particular decision made. It

1 K. Lucas-Alberni, *Le revirement de la jurisprudence de la Cour européenne des droits de l'homme,* Bruxelles 2008, 56-65.

2 B. Zupančič, *O tumačenju prethodnih odluka (presedana) i presuda Evropskog suda za ljudska prava,* manuscript 2004, p. 7, 14. I am indebted to my colleague, Judge Zupančič, who was so kind as to let me use the Serbian version of his manuscript, written in 2004. The English translation of the title of the text would be: On the Interpretation of Precedents and Judgments of the European Court of Human Rights. It is worth noting that some scholars deny the distinction of *ratio decidendi* and *obiter dicta* in the Court's case-law. Cf. D.J. Harris, M. O'Boyle & C. Warbrick, *Law of the European Convention on Human Rights,* Oxford – New York 2009, 17.

3 Zupančič (fn. 2), 7.

happens more often that the judges who follow a certain ruling are in a position to consider the crucial reasons, thus attributing to those the rank of *ratio decidendi* of the previous judgment, which is followed.[4]

Some characteristic examples can illustrate the Court's technique of following its own precedents. The most suitable among those are the precedents that were followed on a huge number of occasions. They thus stand as leading cases at the beginning of a line of what is sometimes called clone or repetitive cases, although the expressions do not perfectly fit the substance.

4.2 FOLLOWING *GÖÇ*

The case of *Göç v. Turkey* was a Grand Chamber case, which was decided by a nine to eight vote. The applicant complained *inter alia* under Article 6 of the Convention that he had not been given an opportunity to reply to the written opinion which the Principal Public Prosecutor had submitted to the Court of Cassation on the merits of his appeal. The Court's ruling in paragraph 57 of the judgment was that to fulfil the demand of fairness

> "it was incumbent on the registry of the Court of Cassation to inform the applicant that the opinion had been filed and that he could, if he so wished, comment on it in writing".[5]

The Grand Chamber therefore found a violation of Article 6 of the Convention in this case. The violation was found on the grounds of non-communication to the other party of the public prosecutor's remarks before the Court of Cassation. To comply with the Convention it was not sufficient that a party to the proceedings was able to consult the case file. It was for the court of law at the national level to take the initiative to inform the party about the files.[6]

As the practice in the Court of Cassation in Turkey did not change immediately after this judgment of the Court there is a whole line of Court's judgments in which the ruling in *Göç* was followed. Whenever there was a complaint that the public prosecutor's remarks were not communicated to the other party in the proceedings of the Court of Cassation of Turkey the Court found a violation of Article 6 of the Convention.

---

4 Whittaker (fn. 4), 42; R. David & C. Jauffret-Spinosi, *Les grands systèmes de droit contemporains*, Paris 2002, 283 ; P. Legrand & G. Samuel, *Introduction au common law*, Paris 2008, 82-83.

5 *Göç v. Turkey*, ECHR 2002-V.

6 Harris, O'Boyle & Warbrick (fn. 2), 254.

To illustrate the way in which the precedent was followed on this particular issue I would like to refer to two cases taken at random.[7]

In *Sentürk* the Court stated bluntly in paragraph 14 of the judgment:

> "The Court observes that it has examined the present case and finds no particular circumstances which would require it to depart from its established case-law on the matter."

In the paragraph cited, the Court made reference to its ruling in *Göç*. The Court found a violation of Article 6 of the Convention and its main reason for doing so, was quite simply that it had to stick to its own previous precedents, which the Court obviously considered binding.

Basically the Court had the same approach in *Hünkar Demirel*, where it held in paragraph 8 of the judgment:

> "La Cour rappelle avoir examiné un grief identique à celui présenté par la requérante et avoir conclu à la violation de l'article 6.1 de la Convention du fait de la non-communication de l'avis du procureur général, compte tenu de la nature des observations de celui-ci et de l'impossibilité pour un justiciable d'y répondre par écrit."

At this point the Court also made a reference to *Göç*, but at the same time it referred to the fact that information had been received by the Court on the recent alterations and amendments in Turkish legislation.

The purpose of the amendments was to make the Turkish legislation comply with the Court's stance concerning the issue of communication of the public prosecutor's remarks on the merits before the Cassation Court of Turkey. However the Court ruled that it could not take account of the new legislation in this particular case. The reason for such an attitude of the Court was that the violation had been committed while the old legislation was still in force.

The number of cases in which the so-called *Göç* complaint has been raised by applicants is considerable. Let me therefore make a footnote here with some examples only, without going into detail in respect of the way in which the Court handled these cases, because it was substantially the same as in the cases I have made comments on above.[8]

7 *Sentürk v. Turkey*, app. no. 27577/04; *Hünkar Demirel (no. 2) v. Turkey*, app. no. 12166/03.

8 *Parsil v. Turkey*, app. no. 39465/98, judgment of 25 April 2005; *Ozata v. Turkey*, app. no. 19578/02, judgment of 20 October 2005; *Ayçoban and Others v. Turkey*, app. nos. 42208/02, 43491/02 and 43495/02, judgment of 22 December 2005; *Demirci v. Turkey*, app. no. 21843/02, judgment of 3 June 2008; *Turgay v. Turkey*, app. no. 21085/02, judgment of 12 April 2007; *Abdülkerim Arslan v. Turkey*, 67136/01, judgment of

4.3 FOLLOWING *BURDOV*

In the case of *Burdov v. Russia* the applicant raised issues under Article 6. of the Convention, as well as under Article 1. First Protocol.[9] However it is mostly the complaint under Article 6 of the Convention which is of interest.

On a domestic level the case originated in the Chernobyl nuclear plant catastrophe. The applicant had been awarded compensation back in 1991 for having been exposed to radiation during those events. He later brought proceedings against local social security service in order to get the compensation paid and was awarded an outstanding compensation in 1997. The latter was indexed by a domestic court decision in the year 2000, but it was only in March 2001 that the outstanding sum was actually paid to the applicant.

Before the ECHR the applicant complained that the substantial and unjustified delays in the execution of the final judgments violated his rights under Article 6 of the Convention, as well as under Article 1 First Protocol. The Chamber found unanimously for the applicant on both issues. It is on the issue concerning Article 6 of the Convention that the judgment became a leading case.

The Court's finding in respect of Article 6 of the Convention was that it was actually the access to court that was at stake. The Russian state had invoked financial problems as a reason for the delayed payment, which the Court refused to subscribe to. Lack of available funds can not be considered as a good reason for a state's failure to execute a judgment.[10] That is why the Court stated in paragraph 35 of the judgment:

> "In the instant case, the applicant should not have been prevented from benefiting from the success of the litigation, which concerned compensation for damage to his health caused by obligatory participation in an emergency operation, on the ground of alleged financial difficulties experienced by the State."

The Court set the general rule on enforcement of decisions taken on a national level in paragraph 37 of the judgment, which reads as follows:

---

20 September 2007; *Erdal Taç v. Turkey (no 2)*, app. no. 13021/02, judgment of 20 September 2007; *Ozmen and Others v. Turkey*, app. no. 9149/03, judgment of 14 June 2007; *Fuad Caliçkan v. Turkey*, app. no. 25506/03, judgment of 20 October 2009; *Cimen v. Turkey*, app. no. 19582/02, judgment of 3 February 2009; *Hakan Duman v. Turkey*, app. no. 28439/03, judgment of 2 March 2010.

9 *Burdov v. Russia*, ECHR 2002-III. For bibliography see V. Berger, *Jurisprudence de la Cour européenne des droits de l'homme*, Paris 2009, 312-314.

10 Harris, O'Boyle & Warbrick (fn. 2), 234; Ph. Leach, *Taking a Case to the European Court of Human Rights*, Oxford 2005; 171, 252, 359.

> "By failing for years to take the necessary measures to comply with the final judicial decisions… the authorities deprived the provisions of Article 6.1. [of the Convention] of all usual effect."

One could interpret the rule in *Burdov* as providing an obligation for member states, parties to the Convention to comply with the Court's judgments in order to avoid its responsibility for violating Article 6 of the Convention. That rule was followed by the Court's case-law.

One of the cases in which the rule in *Burdov* was followed was *Timofeyev v. Russia.*[11] The case concerned a compensation claim of a Russian citizen who had been persecuted under the Soviet regime and rehabilitated afterwards, as well as the enforcement of compensation based on the claim in question.

The applicant was granted compensation by a judgment on a domestic level in 1998, but the enforcement was stayed in the year 2000 and in the third quarter of 2002 it was still not executed. The Court found unanimously for the applicant both under Article 6 of the Convention and Article 1 First Protocol. In doing so, the Court followed *Burdov* in several aspects. One of those concerns the victim's status, which is not of a particular interest to us here. The other two aspects in which the rule in *Burdov* was followed were the violations of Article 6 of the Convention and Article 1 First Protocol. As to the complaint under Article 6 the Court ruled in paragraph 42 of the judgment that "the applicant should not pay the price of the omissions of the State".

The Court referred to the fact that the non-execution of a final judgment issued on a domestic level in this case was for the most part due to the bailiffs' unlawful actions, for which the applicant was not responsible and therefore should not bear the consequences.

As regards the violation of Article 1 First Protocol, the Court also invoked the *Burdov* judgment to give a ruling in paragraph 45 of the *Timofeyev* judgment that the applicant's claim on a domestic level constituted a possession in terms of the protection of property.

The rule in *Burdov* was also followed in the case of *Jeličić v. Bosnia and Herzegovina.*[12] The case mainly concerned protection of property under Article 1 First Protocol, but it also comprised an issue in regard of Article 6 of the Convention.

The applicant had a foreign currency account with a domestic bank. Such accounts were frozen by virtue of a legislative intervention, which meant that the persons who had saving accounts could not recover their deposits. They were to receive those by annual instalments for a certain period.

The applicant had however obtained a final judgment on a domestic level ordering the bank to pay her the amount deposited before the restrictive legislation came into force. The final judgment rendered on a domestic level remained unexecuted at the moment in

11 *Timofeyev v. Russia*, app. no. 58263/00, judgment of 23 October 2003.
12 *Jeličić v. Bosnia and Herzegovina*, app. no. 41183/02, judgment of 31 October 2006.

which the ECHR gave its ruling. The question therefore was whether a state could be entitled not to execute a final judgment, given by domestic courts of law, invoking internal legislation and citing lack of funds as grounds for non-execution.

The Court referred to the rule in *Burdov* in paragraph 40 of the *Jeličić* judgment:

> "a delay in the execution of a judgment may be justified in particular circumstances, but the delay may not be such as to impair the essence of the right protected under Article 6.1."

The Court thus made a clear reference to the previous judgment, which served as a precedent. It is to be noted however that *Burdov* was also followed in this judgment in respect of the property issue *i.e.* Article 1 First Protocol. This is evident in paragraph 48 of the judgment, where the Court also made an appropriate reference to its previous ruling.

Apart from the above-mentioned cases the rule in *Burdov* was followed in many others. The precedent has become a point of reference in the affairs concerning non execution of judgments on a domestic level.[13]

4.4 FOLLOWING *SCORDINO*

In *Scordino v. Italy (No. 1)* the Grand Chamber of the Court gave its judgment on 29 March 2006.[14] The applicants in *Scordino* inherited several plots of land in Reggio di Calabria. Their land was made subject to an expropriation permit under the general development plan. It was expropriated and the applicants were awarded compensation. Dissatisfied with the amount of the compensation, they brought proceedings on a domestic level in order to contest the amount. They also initiated proceedings under the so-called "Pinto Law" for the excessive length of the main proceedings in which the amount of the compensation was contested.

Before the ECHR the applicants complained of alleged violations of Article 1 First Protocol and Article 6.1 of the Convention.

The Court found a violation of Article 1 First Protocol on account that the compensation awarded to the applicants was inadequate and also of Article 6.1 of the Convention, because the length of the proceedings on a domestic level was excessive and failed to meet the "reasonable time" requirement.[15] It should be noted that the Court found a double violation

---

13 Cf. p.ex. *Bora v. Turkey*, app. no. 14719/03, judgment of 19 January 2010; *Nurten Yavuz v. Turkey*, app. no. 14295/05, judgment of 29 April 2010; *Tchitchinadze v. Georgia*, app. no. 18156/05, judgment of 4 May 2010.

14 *Scordino v. Italy (No. 1)*, ECHR 2006-V; for bibliography see Berger (fn. 9), 323-327.

15 Ibid. paragraphs 103-104; 226-227.

of Article 6.1 of the Convention, because it also ruled that there was a violation of that provision on account of the unfairness of the proceedings.[16]

As for the complaint under Article 1 First Protocol the Court set a rule in paragraph 102 of the judgment. The Court's statement was the following:

> "The present case concerns a distinct expropriation, and one which was neither carried out as part of a process of economic, social or political reform nor linked to any other specific circumstances. Accordingly, in this case, the Court does not discern any legitimate objective 'in the public interest' capable of justifying less than reimbursement of the market value."

The rule in *Scordino* thus only confirmed the well-established rule of the Court's case-law, which provides for a fair balance to be struck between public and private interests in cases of expropriation of property.[17]

The Court has gone a step further in respect of the fair balance test, because it insisted in *Scordino* that reimbursement in cases of expropriation should amount to the market value of the goods expropriated.

Applying Article 46 of the Convention the Court found in this case that:

> "The unjustified hindrance in obtaining compensation for expropriation 'reasonably related to the value of the property' was not caused by an isolated incident; neither is it attributable to the particular turn taken by events in the case of the applicants. It arises from the application of a law to a specific category of citizens, namely, persons affected by the expropriation of land."[18]

The Court thus insisted on a systemic nature of the problem in Italian law and invited the respondent government to take measures under the supervision of the Committee of Ministers to overcome the problem originating in a systemic or structural cause.[19] It should be noted that the Court altered the wording in paragraph 229 of the judgment, compared to the one expressed in paragraph 102, quoted above. In paragraph 102 the Court's formula could be interpreted as if the fair balance could not be struck in the presence of a reimbursement "less than the market value", whereas in paragraph 229 the Court insisted on a compensation "reasonably related to the value of the property".

---

16 Ibid. paragraphs 132-133.

17 Cf. D. Popovic, *Protecting Property in European Human Rights Law*, Utrecht 2009, 58-64.

18 *Scordino v. Italy (No. 1)*, ECHR 2006-V, paragraph 229.

19 Ibid. paragraph 237. On systemic violations and measures to redress these see Part III.

The rule in *Scordino* has been followed in many subsequent judgments in which the Court had to deal with the same issue. Some cases taken at random can be illustrative in this respect.

In *Gennari v. Italy* the issue was the amount of compensation for a plot of land expropriated in Rovigo. The applicant was paid compensation of slightly more than 22.000 EUR, whereas the value of the plot of land was estimated at more than 73.000 EUR.[20] The Court referred to *Scordino* in paragraph 19 of the judgment and stated:

> "La Cour renvoie à l'arrêt *Scordino c. Italie (No 1)* pour la récapitulation des principes pertinents et pour aperçu de sa jurisprudence en la matière."

This extremely simplified way of following a previous judgment, consisting of making a short reference to the jurisprudence followed, was not characteristic for this particular judgment alone. One might even that say such a way of referring to prior judgments became a rule.

In another judgment rendered on the same day the Court reiterated this approach. In *Vacca v. Italy* the issue was the amount for an expropriated plot of land, situated in Bitonto.[21] A remark should be made here that the applicant in *Gennari* did not claim just satisfaction before the ECHR. That is why the Court only found a violation of Article 1 First Protocol. On the contrary, the applicant in *Vacca* made such a claim and he was awarded a considerable sum of 130.000 EUR, which the Court found reasonable.

As to the way in which the *Scordino* precedent was followed by the Court in this judgment there is no difference between *Gennari* and *Vacca*. The text of paragraph 19 of the former case, cited above, was literally reproduced in paragraph 22 of the latter judgment.

4.5 FOLLOWING *SALDUZ*

The case *Salduz v. Turkey* was given a Grand Chamber judgment towards the end of 2008.[22] The applicant had complained under Article 6.1 and 6.3.c of the Convention, about the fairness of the domestic proceedings in a criminal case. For our purposes it is the complaint under Article 6.3.c that is of interest. The decisive point is that the applicant had not been assisted by a lawyer while in police custody. The chamber found no violation on that ground. The case was referred to the Grand Chamber. Before the Grand Chamber the

---

20 *Gennari v. Italy*, app. no. 32550/03, judgment of 17 November 2009 (the judgment is in French).

21 *Vacca v. Italy*, app. no. 8061/05, judgment of 17 November 2009. The rule in *Scordino* was followed in cases concerning various respondent states; cf. p.ex. *Sarica and Dilaver v. Turkey*, app. no. 11765/05, judgment of 4 May 2010 (text in French).

22 *Salduz v. Turkey*, app. no. 36391/02, Grand Chamber judgment of 27 November 2008.

respondent government invoked the legislative amendments of the year 2005. These were however posterior to the events forming the set of relevant facts to the case, which had taken place in 2001.

The Grand Chamber based its ruling on the right to legal assistance consecrated by Article 6 of the Convention. It stated in paragraph 54 of the judgment:

> "This right indeed presupposes that the prosecution in a criminal case seek to prove their case against the accused without resort to evidence obtained through methods of coercion or oppression in defiance of the will of the accused."

The Grand Chamber confirmed the existence of a possibility for an accused person to waive his or her right, either expressly or tacitly, but insisted in paragraph 59 of the judgment on the fact that this must be established in an unequivocal manner and be accompanied by minimum safeguards commensurate to its importance.

The Grand Chamber found at the same time that the restriction imposed on the right of access to a lawyer was systematic in Turkish law and applied to everyone held in custody. The Court's main ruling, to be found in paragraph 62 of the judgment, was that "the absence of a lawyer while [a person is] in police custody irretrievably [affects] defence rights".

The Grand Chamber was unanimous in finding a violation of Article 6.3.c of the Convention, but the judges of the bench expressed subtle differences in their attached concurring opinions. Two of those are significant for our purpose. One is Judge Bratza's concurring opinion and the other the concurring opinion of Judge Zagrebelsky, joined by Judges Casadevall and Türmen.

The two concurring opinions I have just mentioned have a common denominator and follow the same idea. Judge Bratza interpreted the judgment rendered on the case in the sense that

> "a suspect should be granted access to legal advice from the moment he is taken into police custody or pre-trial detention".[23]

Judge Zagrebelsky, followed by two colleagues, as mentioned above, expressed the same standpoint in this way:

23 See judge Bratza's concurring opinion attached to the judgment.

> "It is therefore at the very beginning of police custody or pre-trial detention that a person accused of an offence must have the possibility of being assisted by a lawyer, and not only while being questioned."[24]

The idea was very much the same in both opinions. In order to prevent obtaining statements under pressure and the exercise of any sort of influence on a person in custody, the protection under Article 6.3.c should be considered to exist from the moment of apprehension of a person by the police.

The judgment in *Salduz* has become the leading case in the field and it was followed in many of the Court's other judgments.

In *Amutgan v. Turkey*, the Court referred to the respective paragraphs of the *Salduz* judgment without invoking any details or providing new arguments for the purpose of explanation.[25] The Court put it bluntly in paragraph 17 of the judgment:

> "The Court reiterates the basic principles laid down in the *Salduz* judgment."

The Court did exactly the same in the case of *Sukran Yildiz v. Turkey* in paragraph 34 of the judgment.[26]

In some other cases the Court had to specify its reasoning because the facts were slightly different from those of the leading case, although the Court nevertheless remained faithful to its previous ruling. An example can be found in *Fatma Tunc v. Turkey (No. 2)*. The applicant in that case was allowed to meet with her lawyer for 5 minutes only on the 4th day of her custody.[27] However, the applicant's statement was taken by the police on that same day in the absence of her lawyer.

The Court's main reasoning is to be found in paragraph 14 of the judgment. It says:

> "The Court recalls that in its *Salduz* judgment it underlined the importance of the investigation stage for the preparation of the criminal proceedings, as the evidence obtained during this stage determines the framework in which the offence charged will be considered at the trial. In order for the right to a fair hearing to remain sufficiently 'practical and effective' Article 6.1 requires, as a rule, access to a lawyer as from the first interrogation of a suspect by the police, unless it is demonstrated in the particular circumstances of the particular case that there are compelling reasons to restrict this right."

---

24 See concurring opinion of Judge Zagrebelsky, joined by Judges Casadevall and Türmen.
25 *Amutgan v. Turkey*, app. no. 5138/04, judgment of 3 February 2009.
26 *Sukran Yildiz v. Turkey*, app. no. 4661/02, judgment of 3 February 2009.
27 *Fatma Tunc v. Turkey (No. 2)*, app. no. 18532/05, judgment of 13 October 2009.

It is to be noted that the Court in this case referred to the *Salduz* judgment in line with the concurring opinions of judges I have cited above. It stressed the necessity of a certain and specific interpretation of the ruling given in the leading case, which the Court followed precisely.

The Court had the same approach to the leading precedent in another judgment rendered on the same day as the one in *Fatma Tunc (No. 2)*. It was in *Dayanan v. Turkey* that the Court stated in paragraph 32 of the judgment:

> "un accusé doit, dès qu'il est privé de liberté, pouvoir bénéficier de l'assistance d'un avocat".[28]

The Court's attitude shows a clear tendency to follow the precedent in its particular interpretation, which the Court evidently finds more appropriate and better suited to the issue than other possible interpretations, including the one given in the text of the ruling followed, if understood without reference to the concurring opinions of judges. This seems to be a way of not merely following, but also developing the Court's jurisprudence, which is performed in a rather scrupulous manner and within the limits of the practice of following precedents and remaining faithful to the Court's previous rulings.[29]

4.6 FOLLOWING *TURGUT*

Turgut and Others v. Turkey was a case that concerned what is called public forest domain in Turkey.[30] A plot of land situated in the small village of Kefken in the Black Sea region of Turkey was at issue. In the 1960s the public authorities began proceedings tending to annul the applicants' property titles, on the grounds that the plot of land belonging to

28 *Dayanan v. Turkey*, app. no. 7377/03, judgment of 13 October 2009 (the text in French).

29 Some other cases in which the rule in *Salduz* was followed should be cited here: *Ek and Siktas v. Turkey*, app. nos. 6058/02 and 18074/03, judgment of 17 February 2009; *Mehmet Zeki Dogan v. Turkey*, app. no. 38114/03, judgment of 6 October 2009; *Gürova v. Turkey*, app. no. 22088/03, judgment of 6 October 2009; *Azru v. Turkey*, app. no. 1915/03, judgment of 15 September 2009; *Ditaban v. Turkey*, app. no. 69006/01, judgment of 14 April 2009; *Tagac and Others v. Turkey*, app. no. 71864/01, judgment of 7 July 2009; *Fikret Cetin v. Turkey*, app. no. 24829/03, judgment of 13 October 2009; *Demirkaya v. Turkey*, app. no. 31721/02, judgment of 13 October 2009; *Geçgel and Celik v. Turkey*, app. nos. 8747/02 and 34509/03, judgment of 13 October 2009; *Ogras v. Turkey*, app. no. 13918/03, judgment of 13 October 2009; *Bolukoç and Others v. Turkey*, app. no. 35392/04, judgment of 20 October 2009; *Satir v. Turkey*, app. no. 17879/04, judgment of 10 November 2009; *Yesilkaya v. Turkey*, app. no. 59780/00, judgment of 17 November 2009; *Adalmis and Kilic v. Turkey*, app. no. 25301/04, judgment of 1 December 2009; *Atli v. Turkey*, app. no. 43529/04, judgment of 5 January 2010; *Çoban v. Turkey (No. 2)*, app. no. 4977/04, judgment of 5 January 2010; *Savgin v. Turkey*, app. no. 13304/03, judgment of 12 January 2010; *Boz v. Turkey*, app. no. 2039/04, judgment of 19 January 2010; *Ayhan Isik v. Turkey*, app. no. 33102/04, judgment of 9 March 2010.

30 *Turgut and Others v. Turkey*, app. no. 1411/03, judgment of 8 July 2008 (text of the judgment in French).

them actually represented part of the forest area and therefore could not be used for a private property.

After decades of litigation and based on various expert opinions the domestic courts had found against the applicants. Their property titles were annulled, which made them file a complaint with the ECHR, invoking Article 1 First Protocol.

The Court's finding was that there was a deprivation of property, which had occurred by way of a domestic court's decision. The Court ruled that a fair balance had not been struck in the absence of compensation for the deprivation of property. The Court's crucial stance was expressed in paragraph 92 of the judgment:

> "La Cour estime en conséquence que l'absence de toute indemnisation des requérants rompt, en leur défaveur, le juste équilibre à ménager entre les exigences de l'intérêt général de la communauté et les impératifs de la sauvegarde des droits individuels."

On those grounds the Court found a violation of Article 1 First Protocol in this case. At the same time it is to be noted that in the *Turgut* judgment the Court made no reference to Article 46 of the Convention. The problem which was at the origin of this case did not seem at first to be of a systemic nature. However, it turned out to be the initial case in a line of identical ones, concerning expropriation in Turkey.

One of the examples in which the rule in *Turgut* was followed, was the judgment given in the case *Satir v. Turkey*.[31] The facts of the case were following.

A plot of land near Izmir was registered in 1988 as the applicant's property. However, in 1990 a cadastral revision took place and the authorities found that the plot of land in question belonged to the forest domain *i.e.* it could not be the object of a private property title. That is why the plot of land was registered in the Land Registry as one belonging to the Public Treasury. The applicant brought proceedings to combat the authorities' finding of 1990 and finally lost the case on a domestic level in 2003. It was in the same year that he filed a complaint under Article 1 First Protocol with the ECHR.

The Court's findings were that the applicant was deprived of his property title without any compensation and it found a violation of Article 1 First Protocol. The peculiarity of the Court's approach in *Satir* consisted in the fact that, although basically following the rule in *Turgut*, it did so in the broader context of the pattern of the deprivation of property without compensation. Therefore the Court did not refer exclusively to *Turgut*, but also to other cases in which the reason for finding a violation had been the same. The Court concluded in paragraph 34 of the judgment, *in fine*:

31 *Satir v. Turkey*, app. no. 36192/03, judgment of 10 March 2009 (the text in French).

> "En l'espèce, le requérant n'a reçu aucune indemnité pour le transfert de son bien au Trésor public. La Cour note que le Gouvernement n'a invoqué aucune circonstance exceptionnelle pour justifier l'absence totale d'indemnisation."

The Court's approach in *Satir* was actually broader than following only one precedent, despite the fact that the rule in *Turgut* was as a matter of fact the closest to the issue, because it concerned the forest domain in Turkey.

On the same date on which the judgment in *Satir* was adopted the Court gave three other judgments of the same type in Turkish forest domain cases in which the Court's approach was identical. The Court always referred to the broader context of deprivation of property without compensation.[32] The cases were *Nural Vural, Rimer and Others* and *Temel Conta Sanayi Ve Ticaret A.S.* The respondent state was Turkey in all three and the cases concerned Article 1 First Protocol issues.[33]

Another case in which the *Turgut* precedent was followed was *Kök and Others v. Turkey*.[34] The facts of the case were the following.

In 1957 two plots of land were registered as objects of property of the applicants' parents. The plots of land were qualified in the Land Registry as agricultural land. However, in the course of a cadastral revision carried out in the 1990s, the same plots of land were qualified as forests. The applicants instituted proceedings in order to retain their titles, in the meantime registered with the Land Registry, but their claims were dismissed by the domestic courts of law.

The Court found that there was an interference with the peaceful enjoyment of property in the sense of Article 1 First Protocol. The Court further remarked further, referring to *Turgut*, that it had already examined a complaint identical to the one at issue in this particular case. Therefore, the Court concluded in paragraph 23 of the judgment:

> "En l'espèce, les requérants n'ont reçu aucune indemnisation pour le transfert de propriété de leur bien à la Direction générale des forêts. La Cour constate que le Gouvernement n'a fourni aucun fait ni argument convaincant pouvant mener à une conclusion différente en l'espèce."

At this point the Court referred to both the *Turgut* and *Satir* judgments, which was somehow a way of preserving the broader context of expropriation without compensation being as relevant. However, the cases referred to in the *Satir* judgment, as mentioned above,

32 Cf. on the issue: Popovic (fn. 17), 58-64.

33 See: *Nural Vural v. Turkey*, app. no. 16009/04, paragraph 32; *Rimer and Others v. Turkey*, app. no. 18257/04, paragraph 39 and *Temel Conta Sanayi Ve Ticaret A.S. v. Turkey*, app. no. 45651/04, paragraph 43; judgments of 10 March 2009.

34 *Kök and Others v. Turkey*, app. no. 20868/04, judgment of 3 November 2009 (the text in French).

were in this case only made reference to by the intermediary of that particular judgment. One gets the impression that the Court focused on the most relevant of precedents it was following, although still referring to the broader context of the affair.

The pattern of following previous jurisprudence in *Turgut* type cases can therefore be considered to be basically similar to that already seen in other types of cases. The Court briefly refers to the main case followed, after having decided on the identity of the case at issue by comparing it with a previous one.[35] This has been a widespread technique in the Court's case-law, which has been applied in many cases, concerning various issues, in which the Court followed its own precedent.

35 Some other cases in which the rule in *Turgut* is followed are the following: *Ali Tas v. Turkey*, app. no. 10250/02, judgment of 22 September 2009; *Bozak v. Turkey*, app. no. 32697/02, judgment of 20 October 2009; *Cin and Others v. Turkey*, app. no. 305/03, judgment of 10 November 2009; *Serpil Kaya and Others v. Turkey*, app. no. 21313/05, judgment of 8 December 2009; *Ocak v. Turkey*, app. no. 33675/04, judgment of 15 December 2009; *Nazmi Apaydin v. Turkey*, app. no. 33742/05, judgment of 15 December 2009; *Keçeli and Baspinar v. Turkey*, app. no. 21426/03, judgment of 5 January 2010; *Pak v. Turkey*, app. no. 21516/04, judgment of 5 January 2010; *Erkmen and Others v. Turkey*, app. no. 6950/05, judgment of 23 February 2010; *Arif Erdem v. Turkey*, app. no. 37171/04, judgment of 2 March 2010; *S.S. Göller Bölgesi Konut Yapi Koop v. Turkey*, app. 35802/02, judgment of 2 March 2010; *Caglar v. Turkey*, app. no. 11192/05, judgment of 23 March 2010; *Adem Yilmaz Dogan and Others v. Turkey*, app. no. 25700/05, judgment of 25 May 2010.

V Overruling Precedents

5.1 The Court's Attitude on the Reversal of Jurisprudence

The Court's principal attitude towards its own jurisprudence is marked by the fact that the Court, although not being bound by its previous rulings, is basically not allowed to depart from these, unless there is good reason for doing so.[1] The issue of overruling the Court's precedents was the subject of meticulous research, which resulted in a brilliant doctorate thesis of Katia Lucas-Alberni. The thesis was defended in 2006 at the University of Montpellier I. It was published in Bruxelles two years later.[2]

Katia Lucas-Alberni insists on the existence of a psychological element as a foundation of the Court's reversal of jurisprudence, to which she gives the name of *animus mutandi*.[3] The latter exists when the judges deliberately take a new approach and decide not to follow a previous ruling of their own on a certain issue, but take a new stance instead. This author admits, however, that, as far as the wording of judgments is concerned, the Court is not always willing to state openly its intention to overrule a previous precedent.[4] That is why the author is of the opinion that it was in the *Pellegrin* case when the Court, for the first time, declared its own *animus mutandi* in clear-cut terms, *i.e.* expressed itself in favour of creating what the author calls an explicit reversal of jurisprudence.[5] I can not fully agree, with this particular conclusion of the author and I shall return to this point further on in this chapter.

The insisting on a psychological element while overruling Court's precedents is well founded on the Court's main stance on the rule of precedent as such. Namely, as we have seen above, the Court only avails itself of a possibility to overrule its previous ruling in the presence of circumstances that must be established in order to justify the reversal of jurisprudence. In other words the Court must provide in its reasoning clear, solid and fully convincing arguments for overruling a precedent. Once exposed these arguments testify the existence of the Court's wish to overrule its previous jurisprudence.

The mode in which the Court expresses its intention to overrule a precedent can vary from one case to another. Let me invoke in that respect, for the sake of illustrative purposes,

1 See paragraph 4.1.

2 K. Lucas-Alberni, *Le revirement de la jurisprudence de la Cour européenne des droits de l'homme*, Bruxelles 2008.

3 Ibid. 50, 158.

4 Ibid. 163 (with a reference to F. Matscher).

5 Ibid. 183-184; 229-230. For the *Pellegrin* case see paragraph 5.3.

a striking confrontation of two judgments mentioned by Katia Lucas-Alberni. In the *Pellegrin* judgment the Court gave reasoning on the reversal of jurisprudence in one single paragraph, whereas in *Christine Goodwin* it took the Court none less than nineteen paragraphs to fulfil the same task.[6]

The Court can not overrule a previous ruling without stating justified reasons for such a move, but the way the Court made the reversal should be researched in particular cases before we try to make a conclusion on the reversal of jurisprudence, as well as on the binding force of precedent in the Court's practice in general. Let me therefore expose some outstanding examples of the reversal of the Court's jurisprudence.

5.2 FROM *DELCOURT* TO *BORGERS*

The cases of *Delcourt* and *Borgers* have already been the subject of our attention in this book.[7] It is of interest at this point to comment on the mode of reversal of jurisprudence, which occurred in the latter case in which the issue was the same as in the former. Let me therefore first briefly remind the reader of the facts.

The Court found in *Delcourt* that the fact that a non-judiciary state official attended deliberations of the Cassation court of Belgium in an advisory capacity and without voting did not infringe the Convention. It was 21 years later that this was overruled in the *Borgers* case.[8]

The Court found in paragraph 24 of the *Borgers* judgment that its own findings in *Delcourt* remained valid, as far as the independence and impartiality of the Cassation court of Belgium were concerned. It however stressed the importance of the appearances that have meanwhile grown in the Court's case-law. To support the theory of the existence of an evolution of its case-law on the issue the Court cited rulings in ten judgments. It is indeed the second part of the paragraph 24 that I have just mentioned, which provided the reason for overruling *Delcourt*. The equality of arms was at stake and it had to be reflected in the appearances. Therefore the Court stated:

> "It is however necessary to consider whether the proceedings before the Court of Cassation also respected the rights of the defence and the principle of the equality of arms, which are features of the wider concept of the fair trial."

6 Ibid. 233.

7 See paragraph 4.2.2; *Delcourt v. Belgium*, Judgments and Decisions A 11 (1970); *Borgers v. Belgium*, Judgments and Decisions A 214 B (1991).

8 Wildhaber, 158; see also M.B. Dembour, *Who Believes in Human Rights? Reflections on the European Convention*, Cambridge 2006, 167, who insists on cultural relativism in weighing up the arguments in favour and against the overruling.

This represented the reason for overruling *Delcourt*. It was the concept of the fair trial, as perceived by the Court, which made judges depart from a previous ruling. The fact of overruling a precedent was somewhat timidly expressed in the judgment. It was however clear to the judges sitting on the bench, and that is something one can easily learn from the text of the dissenting opinions. One of the dissenters in this case, Judge Cremona, stated:

> "I am not much impressed by the host of judgments cited in paragraph 24 insofar as they are held out as some sort of justification for overruling *Delcourt*."

Judge Martens was also explicit in this respect. At the beginning of his dissenting opinion he declared quite clearly:

> "In its judgment the Court has overruled the *Delcourt* decision."

Therefore it was beyond doubt that the majority of sitting judges had an intention to overrule a previous precedent. In the light of this conclusion I must say I agree with the former Court's president Wildhaber, who speaks of overruling and reversal of jurisprudence in *Borgers*. At the same time I disagree with Katia Lucas-Alberni that the Court has for the first time shown its *animus mutandi* in the *Pellegrin* case. The intention to overrule previous jurisprudence was already clearly visible in *Borgers*.[9] Even if the opinion expressed by Ms. Lucas-Alberni were to apply to the so-called "new Court", *i.e.* to the ECHR after the adoption of the 11th Additional Protocol to the Convention, I would disagree, because I do not see enough reason to separate the old Court from the new Court. The evolution of the ECHR seems to be a continuous and uninterrupted process, especially in respect of the topic treated in this book.

It is worth noting that the decision to reverse previous jurisprudence was taken by a majority vote of eighteen to four, but more than that it is important to underline the fact that the Court cited in paragraph 24 of the *Borgers* judgment several cases which led the Court to proceed to overruling. These were judgments given in various cases on certain issues that were not the main issue in *Borgers*. The Court considered these rulings to be signs of the evolution which increased the sensitivity of the public at large towards the fair administration of justice, thus representing a cogent reason for overruling a precedent.

9 Cf. Wildhaber (fn. 8), 158; in the same sense Dembour (fn. 8), 167; Lucas-Alberni (fn. 2), 183-184, 229-230.

5.3 From Pellegrin to *Eskelinen*

The story of the *Pellegrin* case begins with the judgments in cases preceding it to which the rule in *Pellegrin* brought a new approach and a fresh response that reversed previous jurisprudence.[10] These previous cases concerned the same main issue as in *Pellegrin*.

The issue in *Pellegrin* was whether disputes relating to the recruitment, careers and termination of service of civil servants were susceptible to the protection of Article 6 of the Convention. The applicant had been recruited by the French Ministry of Co-operation and Development to assume a post of a technical adviser, responsible for budgetary matters, to the governments in some states of West Africa. To become finally eligible the applicant had to fulfil the requirements for such a post. One of those was to obtain a medical certificate stating he was fit for service overseas. A medical specialist declared the applicant permanently unfit for such service and issued a document containing the relevant diagnosis.

The applicant complained under Article 6 of the Convention about the length of proceedings, for his case was pending with the Paris Administrative Court of Appeal more than 8 years after he had brought proceedings on a domestic level. The question before the ECHR was whether Article 6 of the Convention was applicable to this case.

The French Government's position was that the Court should follow its own case-law on civil servants *i.e.* its own rulings in previous similar cases. In the Government's view Article 6 of the Convention could not apply to the case on account of the specific nature of the diplomatic responsibilities entrusted to the applicant. The applicant had taken part in a public service assignment and therefore in the exercise of state sovereignty.

As Article 6 of the Convention applies to either a criminal charge against a person, or to civil rights and obligations, it was the latter notion which was relevant to the case, namely whether the case on a domestic level concerned the applicant's civil rights and obligations. If so, it would fulfil the requirements to be protected by Article 6 of the Convention. To respond to this the Court first turned to its own case-law, revisiting several relevant cases, which made it conclude in paragraph 59 of the judgment:

> "Article 6.1 applies where the claim in issue relates to a 'purely economic' right – such as payment of salary – or an 'essentially economic' one and does not mainly call in question 'the authorities' discretionary powers."

The rule was based on the Court's case-law with reference to several Italian and French cases that the Court cited in the above mentioned paragraph. The Court however concluded in paragraph 63 of the judgment that it was necessary to establish an autonomous interpre-

10 *Pellegrin v. France*, Reports 1999-VIII.

tation of the notion of civil service in order to afford the equal treatment of public servants in the States Parties to the Convention.

Following that line the Court stated in the next paragraph of the judgment that it should adopt a functional criterion, based on the nature of the employee's duties and responsibilities, and accordingly a restrictive interpretation of the exceptions of the safeguards granted by Article 6.1 of the Convention. The Court set the rule in paragraph 66 of the judgment, stating:

> "The Court therefore rules that the only disputes excluded from the scope of Article 6.1 of the Convention are those which are raised by public servants whose duties typify the specific activities of the public service in so far as the latter is acting as the depositary of public authority responsible for protecting the general interests of the State or other public authorities. A manifest example of such activities is provided by the armed forces and the police...The Court will ascertain whether the applicant's post entails – in the light of the nature of the duties and responsibilities appertaining to it – direct or indirect participation in the exercise of powers conferred by public law and duties designed to safeguard the general interests of the State or of other public authorities."

The Court carried out a further examination of the nature of the applicant's duties and responsibilities in the course of his employment and accepted the government's argument in respect of the nature of the applicant's post and work. As it concerned public finances, *i.e.* a sphere in which a state exercises its sovereign power, the Court found that the applicant's duties were designed to safeguard the general interests of the state. The Court therefore ruled by thirteen votes to four that Article 6 of the Convention was not applicable to the case. This departed from previous jurisprudence, made by the Court, and was qualified as spectacular by some commentators.[11]

The rule in *Pellegrin* thus excluded civil servants participating in the exercise of the sovereign power from the protection of Article 6 of the Convention. The Court remained faithful to the ruling in *Pellegrin* for years although there were critics pointing out deficiencies in the Court's new approach. It was mentioned for instance, that the introduction of the functional criterion might give rise to new problems and uncertainties.[12]

After more than six years and having given many judgments in line with the rule in *Pellegrin* and having sustained a certain amount of criticism concerning the rule, expressed

11 Cf. F. Sudre, *Droit européen et international des droits de l'homme*, Paris 2005, 325.

12 P. van Dijk et al., *Theory and Practice of the European Convention on Human Rights*, Antwerpen – Oxford 2006, 533; D.J. Harris, M. O'Boyle & C. Warbrick, *Law of the European Convention on Human Rights*, Oxford – New York 2009, 221.

in legal literature, the Grand Chamber of the Court revisited in a Finish case the issue it had dealt with in *Pellegrin*.

The case was *Vilho Eskelinen and Others v. Finland.*[13] The applicants were policemen who on a domestic level had instituted proceedings claiming certain wage supplements and bonuses, as they alleged they were entitled to remote-area allowances. The litigation had begun in 1993 and ended in the year 2000. The applicants complained before the ECHR about the excessive length of proceedings. The question of applicability of Article 6 of the Convention was raised, because the government put forward that the applicants' duties entailed their direct participation in the exercise of powers conferred by public law and they were designed to safeguard the general interests of the state.

The applicants contested the government's view, claiming that their service and their salaries were not related to the exercise of powers conferred by public law and that it was actually only the right to their salaries that was at stake.

Examining the issue of applicability of Article 6 of the Convention to the case, the Grand Chamber made a summary of the case-law, starting with the jurisprudence preceding the *Pellegrin* case, then following the rule in *Pellegrin* and the functional criterion it introduced, together with the restrictive interpretation of the exceptions.

The Court also made a remark on the consequences of its approach in *Pellegrin*. It is noteworthy that the Court very much seemed to go along with the criticism expressed in the literature.[14] The Grand Chamber stated in paragraph 52 of the judgment:

> "An examination of the cases decided since *Pellegrin* shows that ascertaining the nature and status of the applicant's functions has not been an easy task; nor has the category of public service in which the applicant works always been clearly distinguishable on the basis of his or her actual role. In some cases it has not been apparent the extent to which inclusion in a particular sector of public service was sufficient to remove the applicability of Article 6 without consideration of the nature of the individual's responsibilities."

The Court concluded further that the functional criterion has neither simplified the analysis of the applicability of Article 6 of the Convention, nor brought a greater degree of certainty in its application.

On the basis of its findings the Grand Chamber set a new rule on the issue of the applicability of Article 6 of the Convention to the disputes of civil servants with the state. It was in paragraph 62 of the judgment that the Court stipulated:

13 *Vilho Eskelinen and Others v. Finland*, ECHR 2007.
14 See footnote 11 and 12.

> "In order for the respondent State to be able to rely before the Court on the applicant's status as a civil servant in excluding the protection embodied in Article 6, two conditions must be fulfilled. Firstly, the State in its national law must have expressly excluded access to a court for the post or category of staff in question. Secondly, the exclusion must be justified on objective grounds in the State's interest."

The Court thus declared it was not inclined to acknowledge the existence of what is called "the special bond of trust and loyalty" between a civil servant and the state even if a civil servant participates in the exercise of the state's sovereign power, unless it finds the two above mentioned requirements fulfilled. It is clear enough that the second requirement was subject to the Court's scrutiny. It was for the Court to establish whether objective grounds existed for excluding some types of cases from access to court on a domestic level.

The Grand Chamber ruled Article 6 of the Convention to be applicable to the case and found its violation on account of the length of the proceedings. The judgment was given with a majority vote, by twelve votes to five. The dissenting judges – Judges Costa, Wildhaber, Türmen, Borrego Borrego and Jočiene insisted on following the rule in *Pellegrin*, which they preferred to remain faithful to. One of the arguments they invoked in favour of such an approach deserves our particular attention. The dissenting judges stated in item 7 of their joint dissenting opinion:

> "The Court has overruled its well-established case-law. Admittedly, it is entitled to do so (even if the case-law in question is relatively recent). In general, however, the Court takes this step where there are new developments and where a new need arises. This is not the case here. Abandoning a solid precedent in such conditions creates legal uncertainty and, in our opinion, will make it difficult for the States to identify the extent of their obligations."

This opinion has found a somewhat negative echo in the most recent literature. Although supporting the majority approach in *Eskelinen*, a remark was made that the Court still needs to go further and indeed so far as to consider a dispute concerning employment in public service to be subject to Article 6 of the Convention without exception.[15]

Our special interest concerns above all the fact that the dissenting judges insisted on the recent character of the previous jurisprudence, the one that had been overruled. Only 6,5 years had elapsed between the judgments in *Pellegrin* and in *Eskelinen*. Stressing the importance of that fact, the dissenting judges confirmed the role which a precedent has

15 Harris, O'Boyle & Warbrick (fn. 12), 221.

acquired in the Court's practice. The dissenters felt bound by the precedent, among other reasons, because of its recent character.

Last but not least, the dissenting judges invoked the Court's principal stance towards a precedent, even without mentioning it. They contested the majority approach on the grounds that, as they put it, "no new needs" had arisen, which might justify a reversal of the Court's jurisprudence on the subject. This goes along with the necessity of "cogent reasons" for overruling, which is essential for the Court's principal attitude, as we have seen earlier in this part of the book.

5.4 From *Fretté* to *E.B. v. France*

Fretté v. France was a case in which an unmarried homosexual was refused authorisation to adopt a child on account of his "choice of lifestyle".[16] It is of interest to note that the applicant's complaints are based on Articles 8 and 14 of the Convention.

The applicant complained that he had been refused permission to adopt a child on the grounds of his sexual orientation alone. This ruled out the possibility for a category of persons defined exclusively according to their sexual orientation to adopt in a legal system which authorised adoption by a single person.

The Court found Article 14 of the Convention, taken in conjunction with Article 8, to be applicable to the case.

The Court's crucial finding was stated in paragraph 37 of the judgment:

> "The Court observes that it has found that the decision contested by the applicant was based decisively on the latter's avowed homosexuality. Although the relevant authorities also had regard to other circumstances, these appeared to be secondary grounds."

The Court expressed the view that the right not to be discriminated against in the enjoyment of rights guaranteed under the Convention could be violated if a member state, party to the Convention treated differently persons whose situations were not significantly different. A member state may do so only if it can provide a reasonable and objective justification for such a differentiated treatment. The Court found further on that there was no common ground among the member states, parties to the Convention on this particular subject.

The government of France insisted on the existence of competing interests of the applicant on the one side and the children eligible for adoption on the other. The government expressed doubts, based on scientific works and contributions in the fields of psychi-

16 *Fretté v. France*, ECHR 2002-I.

atry and psychology, in respect of a child's development if adopted by one or more homosexual parents. The government further invoked the margin of appreciation of a member state and submitted to the Court that the decision taken on a domestic level was in the child's best interests. Therefore, in the view of the respondent government, the principle of proportionality was not infringed in this case.

The Court ruled for the government and stated in paragraph 43 of the judgment:

> "The justification given by the Government appears objective and reasonable and the difference in treatment complained of is not discriminatory within the meaning of Article 14 of the Convention."

The judgment in *Fretté* was given by a majority of four to three on the issue of Article 14 in conjunction of Article 8 of the Convention. Judges Bratza, Fuhrmann and Tulkens dissented. [17] They were in favour of finding a violation on the case.

It was in February 2002 that the judgment in *Fretté* was given by one of the Court's chambers. I sat on the bench 5,5 years later in a chamber which decided to relinquish a similar case to the Grand Chamber. The case was *E.B. v. France* and it was given a Grand Chamber judgment towards the end of 2007. The latter was made public at the beginning of 2008.[18]

The applicant in *E.B. v. France* was a woman, a nursery school teacher, who has been in a stable relationship with another woman, who is a psychologist. The applicant was refused authorisation for adoption on a domestic level. The *Conseil d'Etat* ruled as the highest instance on the matter and stated three reasons for the refusal.

Firstly it relied on the absence of a paternal role model and the ambivalence of the commitment of each member of the household to the adoptive child. This was due to the fact that although the applicant's partner did not oppose the adoption, she was not in favour of it.

Secondly, the *Conseil d'Etat* found that there was no breach of the combined requirements of Articles 8 and 14 of the Convention, because the decision to refuse authorisation was not based exclusively on the applicant's sexual orientation.

Thirdly, the highest administrative court of France ruled that the applicant did not provide requisite safeguards for adopting a child. Such a conclusion was reached after having examined the case from a family, child-rearing and psychological perspective.

The applicant complained before the ECHR that she had suffered discriminatory treatment based on her sexual orientation. She invoked Article 14 of the Convention, taken in conjunction with Article 8. The Grand Chamber of the Court ruled in paragraph 51 of

17 Cf. their joint dissenting opinion; see also: Harris, O'Boyle & Warbrick (fn. 12), 597.
18 *E.B. v. France*, ECHR 2008-.

the judgment that Article 14 of the Convention, taken in conjunction with Article 8 was applicable to the case.

The applicant submitted to the Court that the final judgment on a domestic level had been worded in the same terms as the judgment in the case of *Fretté*, which in the applicant's view took a discriminatory approach to the same problem. At first sight this sounds a bit peculiar because the Court ruled in *Fretté* in favour of the respondent government, a fact which would hardly inspire an applicant to argue in this way. The applicant however insisted in her submissions that there had been a steady development in the law in favour of adoption by same-sex couples since *Fretté*. No less than ten member states of the Council of Europe had meanwhile altered their legislation in that respect.[19]

The government on the other hand put forward the argument that the present conditions have not sufficiently changed since *Fretté*. The conclusion reached by the Court in the previous judgment had been based on a division in the scientific community regarding the issue, which still existed, as well as huge differences in the public opinion towards it.[20]

The Grand Chamber distinguished between the *E.B. case* and *Fretté*. It did so, on several important issues. First, the Grand Chamber found that this time the French authorities had not mentioned the "choice of lifestyle", as they had in the previous case. They also mentioned the applicant's qualities in raising children and finally, they took account of the applicant's partner in respect of the adoption planned.

The applicant's partner's view and her attitude towards the adoption was however problematic, because the application for adoption was filed by the applicant as a single person. Her partner's attitude might have led the domestic authorities to an arbitrary refusal to grant adoption on the grounds of her homosexuality.

The Court admitted that the applicant's partner's attitude towards the adoption was of relevance for the decision on a domestic level. It stated that the applicant could not be considered to have been discriminated against on the ground of sexual orientation because the partner's attitude was included in the analysis of the applicant's situation.

However the Court took overall account of the reasons given and the decision reached on a national level of jurisdiction in paragraph 89 of the judgment, saying:

> "The reference to the applicant's homosexuality was, if not explicit, at least implicit. The influence of the applicant's avowed homosexuality on the assessment of her application has been established and having regard to the foregoing, was a decisive factor leading to the decision to refuse her authorisation to adopt."

19 Cf. paragraphs 53 and 61 of the judgment in *E.B. v. France*.
20 Cf. paragraphs 64, 66 and 67 of the judgment.

The Grand Chamber reiterated the approach made in *Fretté*, according to which a lack of objective and reasonable justification for a differentiated treatment was required in order for that treatment to be declared discriminatory. Therefore the Court concluded in paragraph 93 of the judgment:

> "If the reasons advanced for such a difference in treatment were based solely on considerations regarding the applicant's sexual orientation this would amount to discrimination under the Convention."

This was the Court's crucial ruling on the issue. The previous jurisprudence was overruled because the Court found in its final analysis that in substance there was nothing other than the homosexuality, which were the grounds for the decision taken on a national level. The Court consequently found a breach of Article 14 of the Convention, taken in conjunction with Article 8.

The Grand Chamber judgment was given on the case by eleven votes to six. The positions of the dissenting judges, although given in favour of non violation, differed in approaches as well as in arguments.

The national judge, Judge Jean-Paul Costa, expressed a dissenting opinion, which was followed by Judges Türmen, Ugrekhelidze and Jočiene. Judge Costa stated *expressis verbis* that the previous jurisprudence of the Court, *i.e.* the ruling given in *Fretté*, was overruled. His main reason for dissent was not on the issue whether adoption by a single person would be allowed in French law. It was founded on the arguments for refusal given on a national level.

Judge Costa pointed out the fact that the *Conseil d'Etat* based its ruling on two reasons. One was the lack of a male or parental referent within the family if the adoption were to be granted. The other was the lack of interest of the applicant's partner for the adoption. He ruled that the second reason for refusal to grant adoption was neither unreasonable nor disproportionate.[21]

Judge Zupančič dissented on the grounds that the applicant had no rights under Article 8 of the Convention. To be granted a possibility to adopt a child is a privilege and a refusal to grant somebody a privilege could not infringe the Convention.[22]

Judge Loucaides expressed himself quite clearly in favour of the previous jurisprudence stating:

21 See the dissenting opinion of Judge Costa, attached to the judgment.
22 See the dissenting opinion attached to the judgment (Zupančič).

> "I find that the decision of the domestic authorities to refuse the applicant authorisation to adopt a child was legitimate and well within the margin of appreciation."[23]

Judge Mularoni reiterated in her dissent the arguments for the decision not to grant adoption put forward on a domestic level. As to the lack of paternal referent she expressed serious doubts and ruled that the issue should fall within the margin of appreciation of a member state, party to the Convention. Moreover she agreed with the national judge as far as the second argument given on a domestic level was concerned. Judge Mularoni considered that argument to be on its own a sufficient and relevant reason for refusing to grant the adoption.[24]

The judgment in *E.B.* overruled *Fretté* in a way which on the one hand was rooted in a change of opinion of the Court, whereas on the other hand such a change did not seem to be thoroughly explained. The main reason for switching from one theory to the other could be found by looking at the social evolution that had been invoked by the applicant. The Court's jurisprudence thus followed the mainstream of modern legal developments in Europe.

5.5 FROM *ACHOUR* TO *SCOPPOLA*

The case *Achour v. France* was one of those in which the Grand Chamber overruled the stance of the chamber; however this is not our topic.[25] The applicant in *Achour* was a person who had been sentenced in 1984 to three years' imprisonment for drug trafficking. He finished serving his sentence in July 1986. On 1 March 1994 amended provisions of the criminal code on recidivism came into force.

The legislative amendments introduced provided that the maximum sentence and fine that could be imposed were to be doubled in the event of recidivism. At the same time the relevant period for this purpose was increased from five years, as prescribed by the previous legislation, to ten years from the expiry of the previous sentence or of the time allowed for its enforcement.

The applicant was charged with drug trafficking in December 1995 and in April 1997 a court of law of the first instance found him guilty as charged and sentenced him to eight years imprisonment. The public prosecutor appealed and in November 1997 a court of appeal held that the applicant was subject to the rules of recidivism and increased the sentence to twelve years of imprisonment. The Court of Cassation dismissed the applicant's

23 See the dissenting opinion attached to the judgment (Loucaides).
24 See the dissenting opinion attached to the judgment (Mularoni).
25 *Achour v. France*, ECHR 2006-IV.

appeal on points of law. According to the Court of Cassation the new provisions on recidivism could apply immediately and for that it was sufficient that the second offence was committed after their entry into force.

The applicant complained under Article 7 of the Convention that he had been treated as a recidivist despite the fact that the period which should have been taken into consideration had already expired under the old legislation. The main finding of the Chamber was that a heavier penalty was imposed on the applicant than the one prescribed because of a retrospective application of the new legislation on recidivism.

The Chamber therefore ruled for the applicant by a majority of four to three, but at the request of the respondent government the case was referred to the Grand Chamber.

Before the Grand Chamber the applicant put forward that between 13 July 1986, *i.e.* the date on which he had finished serving his sentence and on 1 March 1994, the date of the entry of the new legislation into force, he could not have been legally treated as recidivist. The relevant period for recidivism expired in his view with final effect.

The Grand Chamber noted in paragraph 51 of the judgment that the applicant's initial conviction had not been expunged and remained in his criminal record. That is why in the Court's view the domestic courts were entitled to take it into account. There was no provision in the legislation in force in France granting the applicant what is called the "right to oblivion", *i.e.* there were no grounds whatsoever to disregard the previous sentence in the light of the new legislation throughout the period of ten years, subsequent to the committing of the applicant's second offense.

The Grand Chamber's crucial finding, expressed in paragraph 60 of the judgment was the following:

> "The sentence imposed on the applicant, who was found guilty and deemed to be recidivist in the proceedings in issue, was applicable at the time when the second offence was committed, pursuant to a 'law' which was accessible and foreseeable as to its effect. Mr Achour should therefore have known at the material time precisely what the legal consequences of his criminal acts would be."

On that ground the Grand Chamber ruled that there was no violation of Article 7 of the Convention.

It was the case in which I sat for the first time in the Grand Chamber formation. It so happened that I was the only dissenter in this case. The decisive point of my reasoning is to be found in paragraph 8 of the dissenting opinion, in which I insisted on combating the margin of appreciation that in my opinion was granted to France as an exception to the general rule. I must confess here that the general rule I invoked was a construction of mine. I made it myself on the basis of my own reading of the Court's jurisprudence in order to support the theory of the admissibility of the rule for resolving conflict between successive criminal laws. The rule I gathered from the Court's jurisprudence says that the more lenient law should apply.[26] I must also underline that the majority that sat on the bench would never have agreed to such an interpretation of the Court's jurisprudence.

My major disagreement with the majority was exactly on the issue of whether the more lenient law should apply in a case of successive conflicting criminal statutes. That was the crucial point on which my dissent was founded. I had to give an interpretation of my own of the relevant Court's jurisprudence in order to present the dissent.

The development of the Court's case-law was such that I did not have to wait for a long time to see the issue of successive conflicting criminal statutes reconsidered by the Grand Chamber. It was only 3,5 years after giving the judgment in *Achour* that the question was once again put on the agenda, when an applicant *inter alia* invoked my dissenting opinion, attached to that judgment in order to support his argument. It was in the case of *Scoppola v. Italy*.[27] Once again I was in the formation on the bench.

The facts in *Scoppola* were the following. After a fight with his two sons the applicant killed his wife and injured one of the sons. It was in September 1999. The applicant was sentenced on 24 November 2000 to a life imprisonment. However, as he had opted to stand trial under the summary procedure, envisaged by the Italian law on criminal procedure, he was accorded a benefit and the sitting judge sentenced him to a term of thirty years instead.

The public prosecutor appealed on the grounds that a new legislative decree should have applied. The latter entered into force on the day on which the judgment was rendered on the case. The legislative decree in question introduced a more severe penalty, giving life imprisonment with daytime isolation in cases of cumulative offences, *i.e.* such as those committed by the applicant, who killed a person and injured another. The only benefit for the applicant under the new legislation would have been life imprisonment without isolation.

The public prosecutor's appeal was sustained. The domestic courts applied the new legislative decree and the applicant finally lost his case before the Court of Cassation. He filed an application with the ECHR alleging a breach of Article 7 of the Convention. A chamber of the ECHR declared the case admissible and relinquished jurisdiction in favour of the Grand Chamber.

As regards the main issue the Grand Chamber was divided on the merits, and ruled by eleven votes to six in the applicant's favour, thus finding a violation of Article 7 of the Convention.

---

26 See paragraphs 3-5 of the dissenting opinion, where I invoked the Court's case-law, as well as the French legal doctrine.

27 *Scoppola v. Italy*, ECHR 2009, judgment of 17 September 2009. My dissenting opinion was invoked in paragraph 86.

The Court's main finding was that the application of more lenient legislation in favour of the accused was set aside on a domestic level. Another important stance of the Court's was to dismiss the respondent government's interpretation that the new legislative decree was an act merely interpreting earlier legislation.[28]

The Court took a principal stand towards the issue of successive conflicting criminal statutes in paragraph 108 of the judgment in *Scoppola*. The paragraph reads as follows:

> "The Court notes that the obligation to apply, from among several criminal laws, the one whose provisions are the most favourable to the accused is a clarification of the rules on the succession of criminal laws, which is in accord with another essential element of Article 7, namely the foreseeability of penalties."

The Court's verdict on the case, as I have already remarked, was not unanimous. Judge Nicolaou dissented and was followed by Judges Bratza, Lorenzen, Jočiene, Villiger and Sajo.

Judge Nicolaou's main point was that the so-called *lex mitior* principle, *i.e.* the application of the more lenient statute, was originally not included in Article 7 of the Convention. To support the thesis he invoked the preparatory work on the Convention. He also insisted on the case-law of the previous Commission on Human Rights, which was hostile to the interpretation of Article 7 of the Convention in the sense that it included the *lex mitior* principle. This opinion was supported by Judge Nicolaou's interpretation of the Court's case-law too.[29] It should be noted however, that the dissenting opinion did not rely on the *Achour* judgment, although the issue was susceptible to being treated in light of that particular case.

If one is to consider the situation of overruling *Achour* by the Court's verdict in *Scoppola*, it may sound strange that a certain ruling was contradicted without even mentioning it. The only explanation that comes to my mind is that the sitting judges were not willing to defend the Court's stance in *Achour*, but this can not be accepted without reserve. In fact the dissenting judges tended to remain faithful to the rule of the previous precedent in substance and they actually did so. Why it so happened that the ruling in the previous precedent was not invoked by the dissenters is a question which I must leave without a proper answer.

If overruling *Achour* by the *Scoppola* judgment is to be compared with the overruling of *Pellegrin* by *Eskelinen*, it is worth noting that the dissenters in *Scoppola*, ruling in favour

---

28 *Scoppola v. Italy*, ECHR 2009, paragraphs 117 and 118.

29 Cf. partly dissenting opinion of Judge Nicolaou, joined by Judges Bratza, Lorenzen, Jočiene, Villiger and Sajo.

of a previous jurisprudence did not invoke the insufficient lapse of time between the two judgments, as did the dissenters in *Eskelinen*. Only 3,5 years elapsed between the two judgments. This could be explained by the existence of a widely spread opinion on which the judgment in *Achour* was founded and which corresponds with the dissenting opinion in *Scoppola*. The rule of non application of the more lenient law in a situation of conflicting successive criminal statutes seemed to be firmly anchored in the minds of the sitting judges. The verdict in *Achour* was given by a vote of sixteen to one. However in a short time the judges' opinion evolved considerably, so as to overrule the Court's previous stance. The lapse of time was not invoked by the dissenters probably because they felt that their attitude was older than the *Achour* judgment, which only confirmed the existing jurisprudence. The situation was different in *Pellegrin*, because that judgment had overruled the Court's previous stance.

5.6 FROM *PAPAMICHALOPOULOS* TO *GUISO-GALLISAY*

The case of *Papamichalopoulos and Others v. Greece* concerned a protection of property issue.[30] The whole affaire found its origins in the acts of the authoritarian government of Greece, which had been installed in the country after the military coup d'état of 1967. The case was brought to the ECHR by fourteen Greek nationals, who alleged a violation of their peaceful enjoyment of property.

The applicants were owners or co-owners of land in the area of Agia Marina Loimikou, near Marathon, in Attica. In 1963 they envisaged a construction of a hotel complex on the site, for which an American firm of architects drew up plans.

The dictator government of Greece adopted a statute in August 1967 by virtue of which the land in question was transferred to the Navy, to construct a naval base, as well as a holiday resort for its officers. As they were deprived of their possessions the applicants tried to either recover the land or obtain compensation for it, but the cases remained pending with domestic courts even after the restoration of a legitimate government in Greece in 1974. Throughout the 1980s the cases were still pending.[31]

The Court found that the occupation of the land at stake by the Navy represented a clear interference with the applicants' exercise of their right to the peaceful enjoyment of possessions. It amounted to a *de facto* expropriation, because the applicants were unable to sell, bequeath, mortgage or make a gift of their property.

30 *Papamichalopoulos and Others v. Greece*, Judgments and Decisions A 260-B, 1993 (merits) and A 330-B, 1995 (just satisfaction); for bibliography see V. Berger, *Jurisprudence de la Cour européenne des droits de l'homme*, Paris 2009, 740-745.

31 *Papamichalopoulos v. Greece*, A 260-B 1993 (merits), paragraphs 6-27.

What's more, the only one of the applicants who had managed to obtain a final judgment by the domestic courts in his favour, Mr. Petros Papamichalopoulos, was refused access to the land.[32] The Court therefore found a violation of Article 1 First Protocol in this case, but at the same time reserved the further procedure concerning just satisfaction, leaving the parties a possibility to come to a friendly settlement.

The Court revisited the issue of just satisfaction in 1995.[33] Its main ruling was given in paragraph 34 of the judgment, which reads:

> "The Contracting States that are parties to a case are in principle free to choose the means whereby they will comply with a judgment in which the Court has found a breach... If the nature of the breach allows of *restitutio in integrum*, it is for the respondent State to effect it... If, on the other hand, national law does not allow – or allows only partial – reparation to be made for the consequences of the breach... the Court [is] to afford the injured party such satisfaction as appears to it to be appropriate."

The Court referred to its finding in the principal judgment, the one of 1993 that the taking of the land from private individuals, which had been performed by the state, had lasted for 28 years. The Court also found that the compensation which was to be awarded to the applicants should not be limited to the value of their properties at the date on which the Navy occupied them. Experts were appointed in order to estimate the current value of the land occupied 28 years ago.

The Court's main conclusions regarding the compensation for the property that the applicants had been deprived of were put in paragraph 38 of the judgment on just satisfaction. The Court found that the return of the land at stake would put the applicants in a situation equivalent to the one in which they would have been if there had been no violation of Article 1 First Protocol. In other words the Court proclaimed integral restitution in kind to be the rule. However, should the *restitutio in integrum* not take place the Court gave another ruling in paragraph 39 of the judgment on just satisfaction:

> "If the respondent State does not make such restitution within six months from the delivery of this judgment, the Court holds that it is to pay the applicants, for damage and loss of enjoyment since the authorities took possession of the land in 1967, the current value of the land, increased by the appreciation brought about by the existence of the buildings, and the construction costs of the latter."

---

32 Ibid. Paragraphs 41-43.

33 *Papamichalopoulos v. Greece*, A 330-B, 1995 (just satisfaction).

The Court stated in the same paragraph the exact sums to be paid by the respondent state, which amounted to more than four million Greek drachmas for the land and more than one million for the buildings. To those sums the Court awarded 6% interest from the expiry of the period of six months until the day of effectuating the payment.

The Court also awarded a sum to compensate the pecuniary damages, as well as another one for costs and expenses.

The rule in *Papamichalopoulos* thus stated quite clearly that the basic principle was the integral restitution of the goods an applicant is deprived of by an act of state. A substitute rule was that failing integral restitution in kind, the respondent state was to pay, in case of immovable property, the current value of the land increased by the value of the constructions made on the land. The current value means the one existing at the moment the judgment of the ECHR on a case is rendered.

A certain amount of time elapsed and circumstances changed before the fair but also somewhat rigid rule of the *Papamichalopoulos* judgment was questioned in an Italian case. The case concerned the pattern of indirect expropriation, which often occurs in Italy.[34] The main issue of the case was the mode for calculating compensation, as applied by the chamber, which deviated from the rule fixed by the Court's case-law. The case was *Guiso-Gallisay v. Italy* and it was given a Grand Chamber judgment.[35] The facts were the following.

In the 1970s the local authorities of a city in Italy took possession of land using expedited procedure, but subsequently failed to issue an expropriation order. Throughout the 1980s the case was before the domestic judiciary. The applicants claimed before the ECHR that the amount of compensation awarded to them was unsatisfactory. The Court had to revisit its own case-law, beginning with the judgment in *Papamichalopoulos*, which the Court actually did in paragraphs 98-107 of the judgment in *Guiso-Gallisay*.

The Court first stated that its case-law on the arbitrary deprivation of property had been initiated with the judgment in *Papamichalopoulos*. That stance was followed in the Italian cases of *Belvedere Alberghiera* and *Carbonara and Ventura* and it was further confirmed in *Scordino*.[36]

It was at that point that the Court came up against the crucial problem and the most important issue. The Grand Chamber decided to raise the question of appropriateness of the existing case-law of the Court and reflect on its possible change.

34 On indirect expropriation cf. D. Popovic, *Protecting Property in European Human Rights Law*, Utrecht 2009, 38-41.

35 *Guiso-Gallisay v. Italy*, app. no. 58858/00, judgment of 22 December 2009.

36 See paragraphs 98-101 of the *Guiso-Gallisay* judgment. See also *Belvedere Alberghiera v. Italy*, ECHR 2006-VI (merits) and judgment of 30 October in the same case (just satisfaction); *Carbonara and Ventura v. Italy*, ECHR 2006-VI (merits) and judgment of 11 December 2003 in the same case (just satisfaction); *Scordino v. Italy (No. 1)*, ECHR 2006-V.

The Grand Chamber found two reasons for distinguishing the Italian case in question from *Papamichalopoulos*. The first one was that the applicants in the Italian case had lost ownership of their property in 1983, following the construction of public works and had not sought the return of their property in the course of the domestic proceedings. In *Papamichalopoulos* the applicants were deprived of property, received no compensation for it and claimed the return in kind before the domestic courts of law.

The second point for distinguishing between the two cases was that on the one hand in the Greek case a plot of land had been occupied without any legal basis. On the other hand, in the Italian case the deprivation of property occurred under an expedited procedure of expropriation and on the basis of a public-interest declaration, for the purpose of constructing low-rent housing and leisure centres on the land.

Basing its ruling on what I have just mentioned, the Court concluded in paragraph 103 of the judgment as follows:

> "The Court is of the opinion that the particular features of the *Papamichalopoulos* case make it inappropriate to apply the principles laid down in it to cases of constructive expropriation."

The main distinction between the two principles followed. It concerned the date to be taken into consideration when evaluating compensation for a deprivation of property. The Court stated in the same paragraph:

> "The Court considers that the date to be taken into consideration in assessing pecuniary damage should not be the date on which the Court's judgment is delivered, but the date on which [the applicants] lost the ownership of the land."

This new approach of the Court's was guided by justice and it was founded on practical reasons. Indeed in the Greek case mentioned above, as we could clearly see, the value of the land was much higher than those of the buildings constructed on it. In cases of constructive expropriations, such as in the Italian case at issue, the value of the constructions might massively outweigh the value of the land. The Court saw no reason to award a huge amount of compensation, calculated on the basis of the value of the constructions, to the owners who were deprived of their land. Therefore the Court made it clear that the previous stance on the issue should be overruled.

It is, however, worth our attention and should be noted here that the Court proceeded to the overruling on the grounds of distinguishing. Theoretically speaking the latter could have sufficed. The Court's attitude should in any case be evaluated as more appropriate and I dare say thoroughly sincere. The Grand Chamber did not want to take refuge in distinguishing, but boldly expressed its view and proceeded to the overruling instead.

On the grounds of the application of the newly introduced principle the Court awarded a huge amount of more than two million Euros as compensation of pecuniary damages. It is very likely that the sum would have been considerably higher had the older approach of the Court's applied to the case. Therefore it is easy to conclude that the overruling served the purpose of a practical and realistic approach of the ECHR to the problem of compensation in expropriation cases. The distinguishing served as a specific technique to reach a reasonable decision and its main task was to justify the Court's position while overruling a previous precedent.

Conclusion of Part Two

There is no such thing as a coherent *stare decisis* doctrine in the case-law of the ECHR. The Court has however developed its principal position on the matter in a series of judgments. The Court's stance is that it is not formally bound to follow precedents of its own, but the Court actually does so, unless it finds cogent reasons to depart from these.

The techniques used by the Court when following its own precedents vary, although as far as their outcome is concerned, they remain substantially the same – the Court repeatedly gives identical judgments when it finds the similarity of the case it has to try to a previous case, being the leading consideration.

The binding force of precedent in the Court's case-law is also confirmed by judgments in those cases in which the Court has made reversals of previous jurisprudence. Analysing the Court's reasoning in such cases shows the strength of the Court's previous attitudes on certain issues, which the judges have had to rule out. Their reasoning has always been abundant, it tends to be thoroughly convincing and well founded on solid arguments. It takes the judges a fair amount of effort to overrule a previous stance.

Finally, the Court's principal position on the binding force of precedent should be compared to the situation existing in England. Such a comparison inevitably leads to the conclusion that the Court's attitude on the subject is quite close to the one of the British House of Lords, as contained in the Statement of Practice of 1966. The honourable lords, now entitled Justices of the Supreme Court, are bound by their previous judgments, but they are allowed to depart from those when they find it appropriate. The judges of Strasbourg are not formally bound by the previous judgments of their own. However, they indeed follow them, unless cogent reasons intervene, which make them overrule their previous jurisprudence.

The two approaches, however, differ. The judges of Strasbourg are under influence of Common law, but their approach to precedents could not be fully identified with the one of British judges. The reason for this is to be found in basic attitudes towards legal phenomena, which make the main difference between two great legal systems – Common law and European continental law. For my purpose in this book it suffices to say that the judges of the ECHR are constantly getting closer to Common law precepts and ideas.

Part 3
Interpreting the Convention and Evolving Remedies

Introduction

The ECHR interprets the Convention and awards remedies for violations of human rights. As far as remedies are concerned there are two fundamental notions this part of the book is to deal with. One is *just satisfaction,* and the other is *measures of redress*. Some authors are inclined to name the former ordinary remedies, but the term hasn't received much of a support in the academia so far, despite the fact that the denomination of the substance it applies to is justified to a considerable degree.[1]

A measure of redress is a term posterior to the other notion I have just mentioned. It is peculiar that on the one hand, it does not belong to the wealth of concepts we find in the text of the Convention, whereas on the other hand, it is often used by the Committee of Ministers of the Council of Europe.[2]

It has been rightly observed among commentators that the Court "has gradually become more adventurous" in applying Art 46 of the Convention in the sense that its practice has introduced indications of the measures of redress, along with just satisfaction.[3] In other words, the Court has evolved remedies by way of interpreting the Convention rules and such developments are rooted in the implementation of Article 46 of the Convention.

The Court's powers are in general terms laid down by Article 32 of the Convention, which provides on the Court's jurisdiction stating:

> "The jurisdiction of the Court shall extend to all matters concerning the interpretation and application of the Convention and the protocols thereto."

One might therefore conclude at first glance that the Court's powers are to interpret and to apply the Convention. I have already tried to convince the reader in Part One of this book that each and every interpretation comprises creativity on the side of the interpreter and constitutes, in itself, a part of formulating a legal rule. The implementation of the law is thus closely linked to the interpretation, the latter being a part of the former.

The application of the Convention as such basically consists of declaring the existence of violations of human rights and providing remedies to these. The latter means granting reparations that are to be made for violations of human rights committed, which are

1 Cf. M.W. Janis, R.S. Kay, A.W. Bradley, *European Human Rights Law – texts and materials*, Oxford – New York 2008, 98.

2 Cf. p.ex. 'Interim Resolution (2008) 1, concerning Ukraine, or Resolution (2008) 37, concerning Belgium', in: *Council of Europe, Yearbook of the European Convention on Human Rights*, Leiden – Boston 51/2008, 112-119 and 147-150.

3 D.J. Harris, M. O'Boyle & C. Warbrick, *Law of the European Convention on Human Rights*, Oxford – New York 2009, 862

attributable to the member states of the Council of Europe, being contracting parties of the Convention.

The member states undertook an obligation envisaged in Article 46 of the Convention to abide by the final judgment of the Court in any case to which they are parties. The supervision of the execution of the Court's judgments is, by virtue of the same provision, vested with the Committee of Ministers of the Council of Europe.

The powers of the Court thus consist in interpreting the Convention and applying it in the sense of affording reparations or remedies for violations of human rights. The Court is empowered by Article 41 of the Convention to afford just satisfaction to the injured party, if the internal law of the member state concerned allows only partial reparation to be made for a violation of human rights.

Initially, it was the provision of Article 41 of the Convention that was designed to meet the need for reparations in case of violations of human rights, but the Court's jurisprudence made use of Article 46 of the Convention in order to evolve the remedies. The Court based its approach to the remedies and their development by finding support in the supervisory powers of the Committee of Ministers of the Council of Europe. Although these powers apply to both just satisfaction and measures of redress, special attention should be given to the latter, because it was exactly in that field that the development of the Court's remedies took place.

However, I need to mention the Court's power to interpret the Convention first, because that power represented the fundamental point in evolving remedies under European human rights law. In interpreting the Convention, the Court applied techniques that enhanced legal developments, along with some others that were less favourable to the development of law.

VI Interpreting the Convention

6.1 Legal Grounds

The Convention's provisions provide themselves legal grounds for the Court's power to interpret the Convention. Namely, the Court's power to interpret the Convention is provided for by Articles 30 and 32, which pose rules on the Court's jurisdiction as such, as well as on the jurisdiction of one of its formations, namely the Grand Chamber. The power to interpret the Convention can also be seen in its Article 19, providing for the establishment of the Court. The provision says that the main task of the ECHR is to ensure the observance of the engagements undertaken by the member states to the Convention in respect of human rights. Ensuring observance is to be achieved by way of implementing the Convention's provisions and the latter need interpretation to be set in motion.

While interpreting the Convention the Court uses various techniques. Some of these enhance the Court's role in the development of the European human rights law, whereas others escape from fulfilling such a task.

6.2 Techniques of Interpretation Enhancing Legal Developments

The most important among the techniques of interpretation susceptible to enhance legal developments, which have been used by the Court, are the use of autonomous concepts, evolutive interpretation, innovative interpretation and interpretation contrary to the drafters' intentions.

6.2.1 *Autonomous Concepts*

Autonomous concepts are a product of a judge-made law and they emerged in the Court's case-law as a result of the implementation of the Convention's provisions.[1] Autonomous concepts are terms applied by the Court that exist in national legal systems of the member states to the Convention, but which are given a special meaning in the Court's case-law.

1 More on the subject is to be found in a recently published article of mine; cf. D. Popovic, "Autonomous Concepts of the European Human Rights Law", in: M. Jovanovic & I. Krstic (eds.), *Human Rights Today – 60 years of the Universal Declaration*, Utrecht 2010, 107-120. For more specifically relevant references see that text.

The most important features of autonomous concepts are to be found in the fact that they usually escape precise definitions, they quite often contradict the mainstream legal theory, they also lack the support of comparative law and last but not least they are susceptible to evolution. Let me go briefly through all these features.

Escaping Definition

To illustrate how autonomous concepts escape definition one can take the notion of *possessions* in terms of Article 1 First Protocol as an example. The title of the provision I have just mentioned uses the word *property*, whereas its text speaks of *possessions* in the first subsection and then again of *property* in the second. To render the situation with the text more complex the French version of the text of the Convention uses the word *propriété* in the title of the article, but it varies the expression in the first subsection, first using the term *bien*, before returning in that same subsection to the term used in the title. In the second subsection the word *bien* is used again. The question of finding out the appropriate meanings of the terms used in the two official versions of the text of the Convention inevitably arises.

To amuse the reader and make the example more illustrative one can refer to the problem of translations which clearly, show that in some languages due to complicated legal and historic reasons the translation could only follow one of the official texts. Therefore, it was for instance easy for the Italian translation to follow the French version and the expressions used are corresponding (*proprietà* stays for property and *beni* for *biens*). The approach is different in the German translation, where the translator introduced some uniformity, so that there is only one expression in German (*Eigentum*) instead of the two above-mentioned used in the two official languages.[2]

The basic question for a continental lawyer is whether Article 1 First Protocol speaks of *ownership* in the usual sense of the expression. This could be answered in the affirmative but with a considerable amount of reserve. Namely the fact is that what is meant by *possessions* in terms of Article 1 First Protocol can hardly be identified with the notion of *ownership* as we know it in continental Europe either in academic papers, or in legislative texts inspired by the Roman law tradition.

In order to learn what the notion of *possessions* in terms of Article 1 First Protocol really means, one has to research the case-law of the Court, because the concept is an autonomous one. It means that it does not match any of the similar notions existing in the national laws of the member states to the Convention, not even those that legislate in

2 For the sake of similar historical reasons the translator into Serbian, my mother tongue, also had to stick to a uniform expression, like the German one, but he did not use the same term. Instead of *Eigentum*, his choice of wording was *imovina*, which would correspond to the German word *Vermögen*, or to the French word *patrimoine*, which is not at all used in the French official version of the text of the Convention. It could however largely suit the English expression from the title of the provision – *property*.

English. For instance, it includes such notions which are known in French as *propriété industrielle*, like patents and the like. It also includes a specific concept that could hardly be considered to be an asset. It is the concept of *legitimate expectation*, protected under Article 1 First Protocol, which by no means falls into the scope of *ownership* in our romanistic legal minds. The lawyers educated in the Common law tradition would also have a problem to consider it an asset.

Contradicting Mainstream Legal Theory

In the same way that it escapes a definition, except the one done by way of enumeration based on the analysis of the Court's case-law, an autonomous concept of European human rights law may contradict the mainstream legal theory. To illustrate this one can take the example of the notion of *law*. The English word corresponds to two French words, being *loi* and *droit*. The first of the two French expressions stands for a statute or an act of Parliament, whereas the second is to denominate the whole body of law, considered in its entirety.

Now what does the expression *prescribed by law*, or in French, *prévus par la loi*, as used for instance in Articles 9 and 10 of the Convention really mean? Are we to conclude that something must be prescribed by a statute to fall within the ambit of the two articles mentioned above? Could legal rules of jurisprudential origin also apply? The Court looked into the question for the first time towards the end of the 1970s. The case was *The Sunday Times v. The United Kingdom.*[3] In that case an injunction on a domestic level was not issued according to the provisions of a statute. Was it then *prescribed by law / prévue par la loi* in terms of Article 10 of the Convention? That was the question for the Court. The Court gave its reply in paragraph 47 of the judgment, stating:

> "The Court observes that the word 'law' in the expression 'prescribed by law' covers not only statute but also unwritten law."

It is worth noting at this stage that the Court invoked the intention of the drafters of the Convention in favour of its stance. The Court made its own position clear in paragraph 49 of the judgment, where it was underlined that two features were required for a legal norm in order to fulfil conditions of fitting the expression *prescribed by law*. Those features were its accessibility and foreseeability.

On the grounds of what has been shown above one might conclude that the Court recognises the quality of *law* to a legal provision, which is accessible and foreseeable, disregarding the fact of its origin. The latter could be either legislative or jurisprudential.

3 *The Sunday Times v. The United Kingdom*, Judgments and Decisions A 30 (1979) for bibliography see: V. Berger, *Jurisprudence de la Cour européenne des droits de l'homme*, Paris 2009, 564.

Now, if we return to the French text of the Convention it would mean that the expression *prévue par la loi* is understood in such a way that the word *loi* would have been replaced by the word *droit*. Otherwise, the text runs counter to the whole of the continental legal theory in which the French word *loi* can only mean a statute, *i.e.* a legislative act.

Lacking Support of Comparative Law

How an autonomous concept, developed by the Court, may lack the support of comparative law can be shown by the example already invoked for another purpose. The concept of *possessions*, as we have realised above does not correspond with any definition of *ownership*, given either by legislation or academia in continental Europe. At the same time it can hardly fit the complex network of estates, tenancies and leases in England and Wales. The term developed by the ECHR has as a matter of fact no proper parallel in comparative law.

Another example of this kind can be found in the notion of *civil rights and obligations*, as mentioned by Article 6 of the Convention. Those are usually opposed to public duties and rights, but it is impossible to learn the exact meaning of the autonomous concept without consulting the Court's case-law. The concept does not necessarily correspond with the ideas, which continental lawyers have when confronted with the expression. One of the reasons for that lies in the fact that the concept evolved with the development of the Court's case-law.

Susceptibility of Evolution

Let me continue with the same example, in order to show another feature of the autonomous concepts, namely their susceptibility to evolution. At first, the Court was confronted with the question of whether the notion of "civil" could apply to those cases in which the proceedings on a domestic level had taken place before administrative bodies. The ruling on the issue was given in the *Ringeisen v. Austria*.[4] In paragraph 94 of that judgment the Court stated:

> "The French expression '*contestation sur (des) droits et obligations de caractère civil*' covers all proceedings the result of which is decisive for private rights and obligations."

In others words the term civil was interpreted in this judgment as the equivalent of private. It was the nature of the issue that was decisive and not the character of the body competent to hear the case at the national level of jurisdiction.

4 *Ringeisen v. Austria*, Judgments and Decisions A 13 (1971); for bibliography Berger (fn. 3), 331-332.

The approach to the meaning of "civil" was changed many years after the judgment in *Ringeisen* had been given. It happened in the case of *Pellegrin v. France*.[5] The French Ministry of Co-operation and Development recruited the applicant as a technical advisor to governments of West African states. A medical report stated he was permanently unfit to serve overseas, a fact which made him ineligible for the post.

As it has been mentioned earlier in this book, the Court introduced a criterion based on an employee's duties and responsibilities. If these were such as to include what the Court labelled as "participation in the exercise of powers conferred by public law", which according to the Court represented the origin of "a special bond of trust and loyalty" between an employee and the employer, the protection of Article 6 of the Convention would cease. Persons participating in the exercise of sovereign power had special responsibility and a duty of loyalty to that power, which prevented them to claim the "civil" character of their relations to the employer. The rule in *Pellegrin* excluded a whole class of cases from those susceptible to fall under Article 6 of the Convention.

The rule set by the *Pellegrin* judgment was abandoned in a Finish case. It was the case of *Vilho Eskelinen and Others*.[6] In that affair a group of Finish policemen had brought a case before the domestic courts. The case related to the amount and payment of the applicants' salaries. The autonomous concept of "civil" was altered in this case, compared to the previous jurisprudence. Namely, the Court ruled in favour of a presumption of applicability of Article 6 of the Convention to labour disputes. Irrespective of the fact that a civil servant might have participated in the exercise of the sovereign power he or she could claim protection under Article 6 of the Convention if two requirements were fulfilled. These were firstly, that access to court on a domestic level was not excluded in national law and secondly, if such exclusion existed, it must be justified on objective grounds in the state's interest. The justification remains subject to the scrutiny of the ECHR.

To conclude this heading, we see that the autonomous concept of "civil" character of the rights and obligations provided for by Article 6 of the Convention have evolved and developed in the Court's case-law. At first, it was understood according to the nature of the issue at stake and not in respect of a competent body on a national level. Later it was shaped in such a way as to exclude those relations that might have been "civil" by their very nature but they implied special bonds of loyalty to the sovereign power. At a subsequent stage it was no longer important whether such bonds of loyalty existed or not, because it was supposed to embrace all lawsuits being brought to the national level of jurisdiction, except those that were excluded by the national legislation on a justified basis.

5 *Pellegrin v. France*, Reports 1999-VIII.
6 *Vilho Eskelinen and Others v. Finland*, ECHR 2007-IV; for bibliography V. Berger (fn. 3), 319.

6.2.2 *Evolutive Interpretation*

The susceptibility to evolution of the autonomous concepts stands close to a technique of interpretation, which on many occasions has enabled the Court to develop the law of the Convention. The technique is called evolutive interpretation, but it is also known as the Court's living instrument approach. It clearly appeared in the case of *Tyrer v. United Kingdom.*[7]

The *Tyrer* case came to the Court from the Isle of Man, an island located in the Irish Sea belonging to the British Crown. The applicant was a minor, who was punished for having assaulted and occasioned a bodily harm to a senior pupil at the school he attended, because the victim had reported him for having brought beer into the school. The punishment was pronounced by a domestic court of law and it consisted of the birching of the boy in a police station by a police officer and in the presence of his father and a medical practitioner. The question before the Court was whether the corporal punishment of a juvenile amounted to a degrading punishment under Article 3 of the Convention.

The Attorney general of the Isle of Man submitted to the Court that corporal punishment was prescribed by law. He also stated in the defence that such punishments "did not outrage public opinion" on the island. The Court held in paragraph 31 of the judgment:

> "[t]he Convention is a living instrument, which must be interpreted in the light of present-day conditions. In the case now before it the Court cannot but be influenced by the developments and commonly accepted standards in the penal policy of the member States of the Council of Europe in this field."

What the Court stated as the ground for its holding on the merits of the case was the legal developments, which had taken place in member states to the Convention. It has been observed among scholars that the Court actually failed to make it clear how those developments influenced the Court's holding as well as what they really were. The Court did not refer either to a comparative study on corporal punishment or to anything similar that might have supported its approach on the merits of the case.[8]

The Court held in paragraph 33 of the judgment that a corporal punishment, permitted by the law and ordered by judicial authorities, was nothing else but "institutionalised violence". The Court concluded further on, in paragraph 35 of the judgment, that "[t]he applicant was subjected to a punishment in which the element of humiliation attained the level inherent in the notion of 'degrading punishment'".

---

7 *Tyrer v. United Kingdom*, Judgments and Decisions A 26 (1978); for bibliography Berger (fn. 3), 86.

8 Cf. G. Letsas, *A Theory of Interpretation of the European Convention on Human Rights*, Oxford – New York 2007, 76.

The idea behind this approach of the Court's was that the degrading character of a certain punishment was found to be such in 1978, irrespective of the attitudes that the founding fathers of the Convention might have had at the time of its drafting. However, such an attitude was only implied when the Court decided to introduce the living instrument approach for the first time.[9]

Issuing the judgment in *Tyrer*, the Court sided with the opinion that corporal punishment has become unacceptable in European countries. It has somehow been understood or rather promoted by the Court's attitude to be universal, although the Court itself was not unanimous on the issue.[10] The judgment was rendered by six votes to one; Judge Sir Gerald Fitzmaurice dissenting.

Another example of the living instrument approach can be found in the *Dudgeon* case.[11] It concerned Article 8 of the Convention. The question was whether the legislation of Northern Ireland, which prohibited male homosexual practices between consenting adults was in accordance with that provision. The legislation in force in Northern Ireland dated back to the 19th century and in the second half of the 20th motions of reform were brought to the agenda. The Court took account of these as well as of the existing legislation in the member states of the Council of Europe. It held in paragraph 60 of the judgment:

> "As compared with the era when that legislation was enacted, there is now a better understanding, and in consequence an increased tolerance, of homosexual behaviour to the extent that in the great majority of the member States of the Council of Europe it is no longer considered to be necessary or appropriate to treat homosexual practices of the kind now in question as in themselves a matter to which the sanctions of the criminal law should be applied; the Court cannot overlook the marked changes which have occurred in this regard in the domestic law of the member States."

The judgment in this case was rendered by a clear majority of fifteen votes to four, by which the Court invalidated an outdated piece of legislation.

The concept of private life, envisaged by Article 8 of the Convention had evolved and it was no longer appropriate to give it the meaning it once had had.[12] In the academic comments it was remarked that "the core of the Court's reasoning was that Europe's mores

9 Cf. P. Mahoney, "Judicial Activism and Self-Restraint in the European Court of Human Rights: Two Sides of the Same Coin", *Human Rights Law Journal*, 11 (1990) 61.

10 M.B. Dembour, *Who Believes in Human Rights? Reflections on the European Convention*, Cambridge 2006, 175.

11 *Dudgeon v. United Kingdom*, Judgments and Decisions A 45 (1981); for bibliography Berger (fn. 3), 486.

12 Mahoney (fn. 9), 61-62.

had evolved".[13] Some were of opinion that the Court's evolutive approach to the interpretation of the Convention's provisions was "primarily interested in evolution towards the moral truth of the [Convention] rights" and not in the evolution towards a commonly accepted standard. One of the reasons for this was to be found in the Court's attitude that the evolution led to a better understanding of the Convention's rights.[14]

A question may be raised at this point whether the evolutive interpretation of the Convention's provisions, as performed by the Court, may result in judicial lawmaking and a sort of illegitimate judicial activism of the Court's. In response to this it seems to me to be sufficient to quote a rather prudent opinion by Mahoney formulated decades ago, which hasn't lost its value in the course of years. He stated that the special nature of the Convention "compels a flexible and evolutive interpretation of its open-textured terms if the Convention is not to become progressively ineffective with time".[15]

Another topic is also of interest, and I have already discussed it with Mahoney, finding reasons of disagreement.[16] It concerns the scope of evolutive interpretation. Mahoney is of opinion that such an approach of the Court's is by no means likely to permit the Court to create new rights and freedoms, apart from those already protected by the text of the Convention.[17] It has recently been observed, in order to address a reproach to Mahoney, that "as in national law, the line between judicial interpretation and legislation can be a difficult one to draw, particularly in the case of generally worded provisions".[18]

I find Mahoney's viewpoint to be primarily semantic. If we take account of the two cases that have been mentioned here as examples it is easy to conclude that both the concepts of degrading punishment in *Tyrer* and private life in *Dudgeon* were only interpreted in a certain way, but that the concepts as such were basically not altered. However their respective substance has considerably changed in both cases. It is therefore a game of words whether we shall say that from *Tyrer* degrading punishments embrace corporal punishment of juveniles, or that the homosexual practices between male consenting adults after *Dudgeon* fall within the scope of private life of individuals. Indeed changes were significant and one is tempted to admit that the Court has introduced substantial novelties into the body of the still emerging European human rights law. Finally, let me underline the fact that there are cases in which the novelties adopted by the Court can not be confused with or reduced

13 M.D.Goldhaber, *A People's History of the European Court of Human Rights*, New Brunswick - New Jersey - London 2007, 38.
14 Letsas (fn. 8), 79.
15 Mahoney (fn. 9), 65.
16 D. Popovic, "Prevailing of Judicial Activism over Self-Restraint in the Jurisprudence of the European Court of Human Rights", *Creighton Law Review*, Vol. 42, no. 3 (2009) 379-380.
17 Mahoney (fn. 12), 66.
18 D.J. Harris, M. O'Boyle & C. Warbrick, *Law of the European Convention on Human Rights*, Oxford - New York 2009, 7.

to new interpretations. Or, to put it in another way, on certain occasions the Court boldly applied the approach which is called innovative interpretation.

6.2.3 *Innovative Interpretation*

It is clear that the Court's power to interpret the Convention does not include lawmaking. The Court is not allowed to create law, but as we have seen the Court can develop and evolve its interpretation of certain provisions and concepts so as to make these apply to a wider or a different range of phenomena than has previously been the case. This leads to a question of a possible existence of novelties in the Court's practice. These are mostly the results of the mode of interpretation, which the Court applies in certain cases. The Court can sometimes find itself even in the stark contrast with the idea of strict interpretation. By making its interpretation of the Convention less strict the Court may from time to time come close to creating new rights.

One of the most important cases in which the Court did so and as a matter of fact introduced a new path in its own jurisprudence, labelled as innovative interpretation, was the *Golder* case.[19]

In that case a prisoner sought to bring an action of libel against a prison officer, but the Home Secretary, being competent for prisons, refused to allow the prisoner to contact his counsel. The question before the Court was whether Article 6 of the Convention applied to the case. The main problem was the wording of Article 6. It provides for the rights of a person who is already before a court of justice. The applicant in *Golder* actually only sought access to justice on a domestic level, which he was denied by the authorities. That is why it was doubtful whether the above mentioned provision could apply to the case.

The Court's principal finding was expressed in paragraph 28 of the judgment in following words:

> "Article 6 paragraph 1 does not state a right of access to the courts or tribunals in express terms. It enunciates rights which are distinct but stem from the same basic idea and which, taken together, make up a single right not specifically defined in the narrower sense of the term. It is the duty of the Court to ascertain, by means of interpretation, whether access to the courts constitutes one factor or aspect of that right."

The Court's approach was prudent and subtle at the same time. It departed from the idea of a purposive interpretation. As we have just realised from the quotation, the Court

19 *Golder v. United Kingdom*, Judgments and Decisions A 18 (1975); for bibliography Berger (fn. 3), 195-196.

admitted at first that there was no specific right as the one claimed by the applicant. However, the Court went on and concluded in paragraph 32 of the judgment:

> "While the right to a fair, public and expeditious judicial procedure can assuredly apply only to proceedings in being, it does not, however, necessarily follow that a right to the very institution of such proceedings is thereby excluded."

This was the first step in the Court's interpretation tending towards the introduction of an innovation, by way of purposive interpretation. The Court found that a certain phenomenon could not be excluded from the meaning of the provision, of which the interpretation was at stake. The Court also found support for its approach to the case in the Preamble of the Convention, as well as in the provision of the Vienna Convention on international treaties. The Preamble of the Convention lays its foundation among other values, on the rule of law. The Vienna Convention on international treaties provides that, when interpreting international treaties, an account must be taken of the "general principles of law recognized by civilized nations". Both led the Court to a conclusive stage in the interpretation. The Court's crucial ruling found place in Article 35 of the judgment, in which the Court stated:

> "The principle whereby a civil claim must be capable of being submitted to a judge ranks as one of the universally 'recognised' fundamental principles of law; the same is true of the international law which forbids the denial of justice. Article 6 paragraph 1 must be read in the light of these principles."

The main problem for the Court, the one of finding grounds for a certain interpretation was thus solved, by invoking both the fundamental principles of law and those of international law. The outcome was however an innovation – the right of access to court, as discovered and recognised by the jurisprudence of the Court.

The judgment on this case was given by nine votes to three. In his exhaustive dissent, consisting of 48 paragraphs on fifteen pages, Judge Fitzmaurice raised the decisive question,

> "[of] the alleged right of access to the courts – the point here being, not whether the Convention ought to provide for such a right, but whether it actually does".[20]

20 See separate opinion of Judge Sir Gerald Fitzmaurice, attached to the judgment, paragraph 2.

To support his stance against the majority ruling on the case Judge Fitzmaurice took a broader stand and viewed the majority stance from theoretical and historical aspects. These made him find certain passages of the judgment to be:

> "[a] typical cry for the judicial legislator all down the ages – a cry which, whatever justification it may have on the internal or national plane, has little or non in the domain of inter-State treaty or convention based on agreement and governed by that essential fact."[21]

However, Judge Fitzmaurice put a footnote in his text, when referring to the national level and in the footnote he admitted that in England, though "to a diminishing extent", as he put it "[a] certain element of judicial legislation has always been part of the legal system".[22]

Judge Fitzmaurice was not inclined to recognise the existence of the right of access to court as the one guaranteed by the Convention. His reasoning was abundant and his argument quite clear, but the majority of his colleagues went the other way. One might claim today that the dispute between the majority and the minority in this case, the latter being well represented by Sir Gerald Fitzmaurice, has been resolved by further developments of the Court's case-law.[23]

It is also worth noting that the general attitude towards the Convention and its role as an international instrument have meanwhile significantly evolved. Its role is now viewed as the one fulfilling the task of protection of individual human rights from violation by contracting states in the context of the Council of Europe. The set of ideals that the Council of Europe is based on are viewed as fundamental values, which must be followed.[24] The Convention has therefore overcome its primary character of an international treaty. It shows a tendency of becoming a charter, if we are not inclined to go so far as to say a constitutional document, relevant for all of the Council of Europe member states.

The Court has persistently followed its own ruling in *Golder* and the fact is reflected among academics and their opinions, which accept the right of access to court as one of those granted by the European human rights law. That particular right has been commented on by the academia as any other provided for by the text of the Convention.[25]

---

21 Ibid., paragraph 37.

22 Ibid., paragraph 37, footnote 21.

23 On the dissent and conflicting opinions cf. Jacobs & White (C. Ovey & R.C.A. White) *European Convention on Human Rights*, Oxford – New York 2002, 39-40.

24 S. Greer, *The European Convention on Human Rights – Achievements, Problems and Prospects*, Cambridge 2006, 195-196.

25 P. van Dijk e.a. (eds.), *Theory and Practice of the European Convention on Human Rights*, Antwerpen – Oxford 2006, 557-559; Jacobs and White (fn. 23), 151-152; D.J.Harris, M.O'Boyle & C.Warbrick, *Law of the European Convention on Human Rights*, Oxford – New York 2009, 235-236; J.F. Renucci, *Droit européen des droits de l'homme*, Paris 2002, 217-218; J.G. Merrills & A.H. Robertson, *Human Rights in Europe*,

Although the Court's holding in *Golder* accepted the existence of a right which was not mentioned *expressis verbis* in the text of the Convention it did not transgress from the Convention's drafters' intentions. The text of Article 6 of the Convention was neutral as regards whether the concept of the right to a fair trial should be read as broadly as to include access to justice, and the Court was willing to apply such an innovative interpretation and include it. On other occasions the Court had to face the question whether to run counter to the drafters' intentions or not.

6.2.4 Interpretation Contrary to the Drafters' Intentions

The Court interpreted the Convention contrary to the drafters' intentions in an affair which was commonly given the name of the *British Closed Shop* case.[26] The case concerned freedom of assembly and association, being protected by Article 11 of the Convention.

The main issue before the Court in this case was whether an employer was entitled to demand that all his employees of a certain class should be members of the same trade union. This became a matter of controversy and dispute when employees of British Rail brought an action on the grounds that they had no intention of joining a certain trade union because of their disagreement with the trade union's political attitudes and aims.

At the beginning of the 1970s, British Rail had concluded what is called a closed shop agreement with several trade unions, which meant that the employees were required to join these if they wished to preserve their posts. The three applicants refused to comply with such a requirement and were dismissed from work. Having lost their cases on a domestic level they turned to Strasbourg and filed applications with the ECHR.

In order to interpret Article 11 of the Convention, which the applicants' complaints were based on, the Court had to examine the drafting history of that provision. Its crucial finding was formulated in paragraph 51 of the judgment in following words:

> "The Government [...] submitted that Article 11 did not confer or guarantee any right not to be compelled to join an association. They contended that this right had been deliberately excluded from the Convention and that this was demonstrated by [...] the *travaux préparatoires*."

Manchester 2001, 89-91; Ch. Grabenwarter, *Europäische Menschenrechtskonvention*, München – Wien 2003, 354-357; D. Gomien, *Short guide to the European Convention on Human Rights*, Strasbourg 2005, 53-54. It is worth mentioning, just for the sake of illustration of the state of mind among scholars, that Donna Gomien exposes on the right of access to court without even mentioning the *Golder* case, *i.e.* as if such a right were provided for by the text of the Convention itself.

26 *Young, James and Webster v. United Kingdom*, Judgments and Decisions A 44 (1981); for bibliography Berger (fn. 3), 665.

The passage to which the government referred was also reproduced in the same paragraph of the judgment. Its text says as follows:

> "On account of the difficulties raised by the 'closed shop system' in certain countries, the Conference in this connection considered that it was undesirable to introduce into the Convention a rule under which 'no one may be compelled to belong to an association' which features in [Article 20 paragraph 2 of] the United Nations Universal Declaration."

The founding fathers of the Convention have thus made it clear that the closed shop system was not forbidden. It complied with the protection of human rights envisaged by the Convention's provisions. The Court's reasoning, while interpreting Article 11 of the Convention was complex and included a subtle approach to the research on the meaning of its provision.

The Court departed from the finding that if a rule was deliberately omitted from the text of the Convention it could not be regarded as enshrined in the Convention. However, this was not sufficient for the Court to conclude that a negative aspect of the rule inevitably fell outside the ambit of a certain provision. The Court took account of the negative aspect of a person's freedom of association and in paragraph 52 of the judgment formulated the way in which it viewed Article 11 of the Convention:

> "[it] does not follow that the negative aspect of a person's freedom of association falls completely outside the ambit of Article 11 and that each and every compulsion to join a particular trade union is compatible with the intention of that provision. To construe Article 11 as permitting every kind of compulsion in the field of trade union membership would strike at the very substance of the freedom it is designed to guarantee."

The Court emphasised further on in the judgment that its task was not to review the closed shop system as such. The Court was merely called to examine the effects of that system in the applicants' cases.[27] In this regard the Court's finding was expressed in paragraph 55 of the judgment:

> "The situation facing the applicants clearly runs counter to the concept of freedom of association in its negative sense."

27 Van Dijk et al. (fn. 25), 831.

To reach its ruling on the merits the Court used two tools. The first was the negative aspect of a right guaranteed by the Convention and the second was the substance of the right, or rather freedom, guaranteed. The interpretation of Article 11 of the Convention, which the Court gave in this particular case was laid on these two pillars. The negative aspect of a freedom could not be excluded and had that been the case, it would have deprived the freedom guaranteed of its very substance. To achieve this, the Court had to run counter to the drafters' intentions, because they were clearly favourable to the maintenance of the closed shop system in industrial relations. The jurisprudence of the ECHR made a development which could have hardly been envisaged by the founding fathers of the Convention. It was with the support of the rule posed in *Young, James and Webster* that the "individual, as opposed to the collective, dimension of freedom of association prevailed in the context of labour relations".[28]

The judgment on the case was given by the majority of eighteen votes to three. The dissenting Judge, Judge Sorensen, joined by Judges Thor Vilhjalmsson and Lagergren, contested both of the pillars the majority of judges relied on:

> "Reference to the 'substance' of freedom of association is not relevant in the present context. [...] In the present case [...] the problem is whether the negative aspect of the freedom of association is part of the substance of the right guaranteed by Article 11. [...] The States Parties to the Convention must be considered to have agreed not to include the negative aspect, and no canon of interpretation can be adduced in support of extending the scope of the Article to a matter which deliberately has been left out and reserved for regulation according to national law and traditions of each State Party to the Convention."[29]

I must admit I find the dissenting opinion quite convincing from a purely logical standpoint. It relies on the idea of the margin of appreciation accorded to the member states. The fact is however that the development of the Court's case-law sometimes goes beyond the sound arguments, used for the purpose of the interpretation of law. This is due to the circumstance that the Court's guideline has always been primarily justice, which prevails over the canons of interpretation. That is why the Court was compelled to conclude in this case that it was indeed justified to contradict the drafters and their intentions, which the Court did in a sophisticated manner. It applied the usual canons of interpretation, but at the same time these were used to serve the purpose of rendering justice in a particular case. The purpose thus prevailed over the words and the Court's approach to the case favoured the protection

28 Harris, O'Boyle & Warbrick (fn. 25), 548.

29 Cf. dissenting opinion of Judge Sorensen, joined by Judges Thor Vilhjalmsson and Lagergren, attached to the judgment, paragraph 5.

of human rights to the detriment of a strict interpretation of rules relying on the drafters' intentions.

6.3 Techniques of Interpretation Restraining the Court's Creativity

Techniques of interpretation, which the Court used to interpret the Convention that restrained the Court's creativity, have been, because of their prudent approach to cases, less fruitful in respect of legal developments than those analysed so far, which were enhancing the jurisprudential evolution of law. The techniques and approaches of the Court's to cases that are restraining creativity are often in use and they are numerous. The most important among them are the doctrine of the margin of appreciation, the doctrine of fourth instance, the approach consisting of finding no significant disadvantage, as well as inadmissibility issues in general.

6.3.1 *The Doctrine of the Margin of Appreciation*

The notion of the margin of appreciation of member states to the Convention finds its origin in the principle of a subsidiary role of the Convention in the field of the protection of human rights in Europe.[30]

The margin of appreciation is the amount of discretionary power conferred to the member states in respect of their capacity to introduce a framework, which represents a scope of effective application of the rights granted by the Convention.[31] The concept of the margin of appreciation has been subject to criticism among scholars, and recently a question was raised whether in future it should be at all preserved in the Court's jurisprudence.[32]

It was indeed at the very beginning of the functioning of the European system of human rights protection that the idea of the margin of appreciation emerged in the practice of the then existing filtering body – the European Commission of Human Rights. The Commission introduced the doctrine into the practice of the European system, as early as in the late 1950s.[33] The Court followed the Commission and it was in the first judgment issued by

30 Renucci (fn. 25), 522-523; F. Sudre, *Droit européenne et international des droits de l'homme,* Paris 2005, 216-217 ; E. Kastanas, *Unité et diversité: notions autonomes et marge d'appréciation des Etats dans la jurisprudence de la Cour européenne des droits de l'homme,* Bruxelles 1996, 98-99.

31 Basically I am following Sudre, as far as the definition of the notion of the margin of appreciation is concerned; cf. F. Sudre, *Droit européen et international des droits de l'homme,* Paris 2005, 216.

32 Renucci (fn. 25), 524.

33 Kastanas (fn. 30), 113.

the Court that the concept of margin of appreciation played a significant role, although it was not mentioned *expressis verbis.*[34]

In the *Lawless* case the applicant complained to have been detained without trial during a period of almost five months in a military detention camp situated in the territory of the Republic of Ireland, pursuant to an order of the Minister of Justice. The authorities of the Republic of Ireland had been vested in 1957 with special powers of ordering the arrest and detention of persons in view of combating IRA terrorism, growing at that time. The measure was allowed, as stated in paragraph 17 of the judgment on the merits, in order

> "to prevent the commission of offences against peace and order and to prevent the maintaining of military or armed forces other than those authorised by the Constitution".

The applicant had been detained without trial for several months. During the detention he had filed a *habeas corpus* claim, but the latter was dismissed by the Supreme Court of Ireland. The question before the Court was whether the applicant's detention, ordered by the Irish authorities, complied with the Convention.

The Court's finding in paragraph 29 of the judgment was that there had been

> "the imminent danger to the nation caused by the continuance of unlawful activities in Northern Ireland by the IRA and various associated groups, operating from the territory of the Republic of Ireland".

The Court also found that the situation in Ireland in 1957 was such as to justify a derogation from the obligations under the Convention, as well as that the general measures taken by the government were strictly required by the exigencies of the situation. Especially, it was stressed by the Court that administrative detention, "despite its gravity" was a measure required by the circumstances.

This made the Court conclude in paragraph 37 *in fine*:

> "[It] follows from the foregoing that the detention without trial [...] appears to be a measure strictly required by the exigencies of the situation within the meaning of Article 15 of the Convention."

The Court ruled unanimously in the *Lawless* case that

34 *"Lawless"* case, Judgments and Decisions, A 1-3 (1960-61); for bibliography Berger (fn. 3), 140-141.

> "the facts found do not disclose a breach by the Irish Government of their obligations under the European Convention for the Protection of Human Rights and Fundamental Freedoms".

It is clear that the Court departed from an analysis of the state's actions in view of what its internal legal system might find appropriate to combat terrorism, comparing the measures taken according to the exigencies of the Convention. Even if not fully in accordance with the Convention's provisions the State measures were considered acceptable, because of reasons arising from a particular situation. The idea of margin of appreciation stood behind such an attitude by the Court, although it was not labelled as such and put in the judgment in clear cut and unequivocal terms.

It was a decade later that the Court expressed the same idea in a manner which could not raise any doubts as to its meaning and substance. This was done in the so-called *"Vagrancy"* cases in which the Court gave judgment in 1972.[35] The cases concerned three applicants, De Wilde, Ooms and Versyp and the respondent state was Belgium. The applicants were kept in detention ordered by the magistrates in the cities of Charleroi, Namur and Bruxelles in the years 1965 and 1966. De Wilde remained in detention for a little less than seven months, Ooms was detained for one year and Versyp one year, nine months and six days. The applicants were detained on the grounds of the provisions of the Belgian internal legislation, suppressing vagrancy and begging, which had meanwhile been altered to meet the requirements of the Convention.

The Court considered the cases together and found that some of the articles invoked by the applicants were not applicable to the cases, and that others were not breached. Finally, the Court ruled that there had been a violation of Article 5 (4) of the Convention. This was on the grounds that the applicants had no remedy against the decisions ordering their detention.

Paragraph 93 of the judgment on the merits of 18 June 1971 is of particular interest for our topic here. The Court's finding in that paragraph was that the Belgian authorities had sufficient reason to believe that it was necessary to impose certain restrictions for the purpose of the prevention of disorder or crime, the protection of health or morals, and the protection of the rights and freedoms of others. Those restrictions concerned the applicants' private life, for they complained *inter alia* that their correspondence was subject to control, while they were detained.

The Court found, however, that the restrictions of individuals' rights neither applied for a long period, nor were they deemed to have provoked any discrimination or the abuse

---

35 *De Wilde, Ooms and Versyp Cases*, Judgments and Decisions A 12 (1970-1971) and 14 (1972); for bibliography Berger (fn. 3), 161-162.

of power to the prejudice of the applicants. That is why the Court stated in the same paragraph:

> "[The] competent Belgian authorities did not transgress in the present cases the limits of the power of appreciation which Article 8 (2) of the Convention leaves to the Contracting States."

The notion I am discussing here was thus for the first time mentioned in a Court judgment and it was done in a way which was to be abandoned afterwards. The expression used by the Court was "power of appreciation", whereas the one of "margin of appreciation" was to prevail later. However, the concept was the one and the same and it was clearly put forward by the Court. The member states have the power to appreciate within rational limits set by the Court, whether a certain measure should apply or not. Their power to appreciate has created a margin of appreciation. In the original vocabulary the stress had been put on a certain power attributed to the member state, whereas in the subsequent expression it was the result of the use of that power which prevailed.

The judgments in which the margin of appreciation has played a decisive role for the Court's verdict are literally countless. They are for the most part to be analysed on a case to case basis, although it should be put forward that some valuable efforts have been made in the scholarship to introduce elements of a systematic analysis. Let me mention two of those.

Sudre underlines the fact that the ECHR exercises effective control over the scope of the margin of appreciation left to the member states – parties to the Convention. The control is mostly based on the fair balance test and according to this author it concerns three main parameters that the Court usually combines.[36] The first parameter says that in cases primarily concerning the private sphere of an individual the Court tends to apply a stricter approach than in other cases.

The second important issue refers to the aim of the restriction to the protection of human rights that a member state invokes before the Court, the latter being under constraint to take the aim of restriction into account when rendering judgments.

The third point of importance concerns the question whether there exists or not a consensus among the member states on a certain issue. The Court makes use of the three criteria, or parameters as Sudre calls them, in order to achieve a sensitive balance between a standard implementation of the Convention guarantees of rights on the one hand and preserving specific features of each and every member state, which is a contracting party to the Convention, on the other.[37]

---

36 Sudre (fn. 30), 219-221.
37 Ibid. 222.

Kastanas for his part insists on the "normal" character of the standards applying to restrictions of human rights, which fall under the margin of appreciation of a member state.[38] According to this author the Court applies what he labels as a "normality" criterion to legitimate certain interferences with human rights, performed by the member states. For instance, whatever could be considered "normal" in the course of execution of a criminal sanction of imprisonment is acceptable for the Court.

It is of course difficult to learn what the standard of normality really is in a particular case. That is why Kastanas admits that the standard is rather descriptive and not sufficiently dogmatic. It expresses what most frequently happens and does not provide on what should be the rule.[39] The author finally admits the impossibility of defining the standard properly, stating the fact that the margin of appreciation concerns legal and political, as well as practical aspects. He also points out that the margin of appreciation depends on the existence of legal and factual guarantees in the domestic law of a member state that can prevent the abuse of its discretionary power.[40]

6.3.2 *The Doctrine of the Fourth Instance*

The so-called doctrine of fourth instance is one of the techniques of approach to cases, which enables the Court to refrain from excessive interference with the decisions taken by the courts of law in the national justice systems of the member states, which are contracting parties to the Convention. As a matter of fact the Court has neither a complete nor a fully coherent approach in this respect. The main idea is that the Court can by no means be perceived as a fourth instance in rendering justice in a particular case. The ECHR is not superior to the justice system of a member state and a decision issued by a national court of law is not susceptible to the control of the Court. Such facts make it clear that the doctrine of fourth instance is rooted in the principle of the subsidiary role of the Convention. The protection of human rights falls primarily within the competence of the member states, which are contracting parties to the Convention.

The doctrine of fourth instance was clearly expressed in a Spanish case, although it can not be said that it emerged in the judgment on that particular case. The case was *Garcia Ruiz v. Spain*, in which the Grand Chamber of the Court gave judgment on 21 January 1999.[41]

The case was brought to the Court by an applicant who, although a registered member of the Bar, had not been a practising lawyer. As he had carried out some non-contentious

38 Kastanas (fn. 30), 140-145.

39 Ibid. 143.

40 Ibid. 145.

41 *Garcia Ruiz v. Spain*, Reports 1999-I.

work, providing advice and assistance for which he had not been paid, he instituted proceedings on a national level seeking remuneration.

The applicant lost his case in the first instance on a national level, because his case was dismissed on the grounds that he had not proved to have performed the services his claim was based on. The court of appeal on a domestic level repeated the summary of the facts set out in the first-instance judgment endorsing the grounds for dismissal of the case. The Constitutional Court of Spain dismissed the applicant's recourse on the grounds that the case had no constitutional relevance. The applicant then turned to the ECHR filing an application with a complaint based on Article 6 of the Convention. He alleged that the appellate court judgment was not reasoned, which according to him rendered the whole procedure in his case unfair.

The Grand Chamber of the Court unanimously found no violation of the Convention in this case. The Grand Chamber tackled both the issue of the particular case, being the obligation of a court of law to provide a reasoned judgment, and the relation of the Court to the judgments rendered on a domestic level in general. The Court's position on both subjects was given in paragraph 28 of the judgment, which reads as follows:

> "In particular it is not [the Court's] function to deal with errors of fact or law allegedly committed by a national court unless and in so far as they may have infringed rights and freedoms protected by the Convention. Moreover, while Article 6 of the Convention guarantees the right to a fair hearing, it does not lay down any rules on the admissibility of evidence or the way it should be assessed, which are therefore primarily matters for regulation by national law and the national courts."

Although the reasoning in the court of appeal's judgment on a domestic level could have been more exhaustive, it was not for the ECHR to evaluate the mode in which domestic courts of law proceed, because it is not another instance superior to the national courts. The task of the ECHR is specific and its only concern is the protection of human rights. Even if there had been an error committed by a national court of law, the ECHR would not have been competent to redress it, unless the matter raises an issue under the Convention.

It should be remarked that the fourth instance doctrine is frequently used by the Court, serving the purpose of judicial self-restraint. At the same time the doctrine has not reached a status with scholars, which could be seen as corresponding to its frequent use in practice. The major manuals on the European Human Rights Law only occasionally treat the doctrine of fourth instance as a separate issue. Examples of this kind are to be found in Jacobs &

White, as well as in Harris, O'Boyle and Warbrick.[42] The authors usually omit to mention this tool of interpretation, so often exploited by the Court.

6.3.3 *Absence of Significant Disadvantage*

The absence of significant disadvantage as an approach to a decision on a particular case has had a somewhat peculiar evolution in the Court's case-law. The idea to adopt it as a tool had pushed through in the jurisprudence, before it was finally accepted by the 14th Additional Protocol to the Convention. The latter only legitimised an emerging practice of the Court's.

One of the occasions when the concept of the absence of significant disadvantage was apparent was the Grand Chamber case of *Micallef v. Malta.*[43] The somewhat strange case originated in 1985 with an injunction being issued to restrain a lady from hanging her washing to dry over the neighbour's yard. Subsequently many complications intervened, but they are hardly of any interest in this book. At the chamber level within the ECHR the case had been given a judgment by a majority of four to three, before it reached the Grand Chamber.

The Grand Chamber held by eleven votes to six that there had been a violation of Article 6 of the Convention in this case. The joint dissenting opinion of Judges Costa, Jungwiert, Kovler and Fura, attached to the judgment on the case is worth our attention. The dissenters began their reasoning by invoking the concept which is being discussed here. Let me give them the floor:

> "First of all, Mrs. M, the applicant's sister (now deceased), does not appear to us to have incurred a significant disadvantage in this case, which concerned a trivial dispute between neighbours, and respect for human rights did not, in our view, require our Court to examine this case on the merits. [...] It is surprising that the Court – overburdened as it is with applications – did not consider this application to be inadmissible, particularly as an 'abuse of the right of application' within the meaning of Article 35 paragraph 3 *in fine*."[44]

The approach of the dissenting judges could not have been clearer. They were of opinion that the criterion of "no significant disadvantage" should apply to the case, for which they

42 Jacobs & White (fn. 23), 140; Harris, O'Boyle & Warbrick (fn. 25), 202. Even in these two books the doctrine is treated as an introduction to the chapter consecrated to the guarantees of a fair trial.

43 *Micallef v. Malta*, ECHR 2009.

44 See: *Micallef v. Malta*, ECHR 2009, joint dissenting opinion of Judges Costa, Jungwiert, Kovler and Fura, paragraph 1.

found grounds in an article of the Convention, namely the one on the abuse of the right of application. This seems to be well founded and questions may be asked about how it was possible that the Court had never decided to follow such a straightforward approach and a clear path leading to practical gains in terms of lessening the Court's considerable backlog. Whether the Court should be labelled as conservative or scrupulous in this respect is not the most important issue. I dare say the Court is by no means to blame to have given priority to the implementation of principles and a thorough protection of human rights instead of practical considerations.

The dissenting opinion in *Micallef* was formulated at a time when the Court, as well as the public at large, was waiting for the ratification of the 14th Additional Protocol to the Convention, and its coming into force, and the dissenters referred to that fact in their joint dissenting opinion.[45]

To some extent it was probably the same set of circumstances that provided the grounds for another decision, taken by a chamber of the Court, in which the same line of reasoning applied, based on the concept that is being discussed here. It should be however pointed out that the Court made no reference to the forthcoming 14th Additional Protocol and considered the matter exclusively from the standpoint of Article 35 of the Convention.

The case was *Bock v. Germany*, in which a chamber of the Fifth Section of the Court gave decision at the beginning of 2010.[46] The case was peculiar. A civil servant in Germany brought proceedings on a domestic level for the reimbursement of 7,99 EUR that he had spent purchasing magnesium tablets prescribed by his physician. His monthly salary amounted to more than 4.500 EUR and the tablets had nothing to do with his work, being prescribed exclusively for dietetic purposes.

The applicant complained before the ECHR, under Article 6 of the Convention of the length of proceedings on a domestic level, as well as of the absence of effective remedy, under Article 13.

The chamber found the application inadmissible, because of the abuse of the right of application under Article 35 paragraphs 3 and 4 of the Convention. To reach such a decision the chamber took account of the applicant's comfortable financial situation, but it also stated that no question of principle was involved in the case.

The main argument for the decision taken by the chamber was to be found in the following words:

> "In particular [the Court] had regard to the disproportion between the triviality of the facts, namely the pettiness of the amount involved and the fact that the proceedings concerned a dietary supplement, not a pharmaceutical product."

45 Ibid.
46 *Bock v. Germany*, app. no. 22051/07, decision on admissibility of 19 January 2010.

It is therefore clear that the Court's reasoning was based on the trivial character of the matter, although the Court did not mention either the absence of significant disadvantage or the expectance of a new criterion of admissibility of applications to be introduced in the near future by the Protocol 14. What the Court did in *Bock* was quite simply to stick to and confirm the old Roman principle, contained in the adage *de minimis non curat praetor*.

Protocol 14 finally solves the dilemma on the interpretation of Article 35 of the Convention in the light of the abuse of right to application. It provides in Article 12, amending Article 35 paragraph 3 of the Convention:

> "The Court shall declare inadmissible any individual application submitted under Article 34 if it considers that:
> a) the application is incompatible with the provisions of the Convention or the Protocols thereto, manifestly ill-founded, or an abuse of the right of individual application; or
> b) the applicant has not suffered a significant disadvantage, unless respect for human rights as defined in the Convention and the Protocols thereto requires an examination of the application on the merits and provided that no case may be rejected on this ground which has not been duly considered by a domestic tribunal."

The question of no significant disadvantage has thus been entrenched at the level of the text of the Convention. It has been remarked by scholars that the introducing of this provision into the 14th Protocol was inspired by the idea of lessening the Court's burden, consisting of a heavy backlog.[47] That is why it should be repeated that the Court was rather timid in using the concept, which was somehow accessible under Article 35 of the Convention even before amending the text of the Convention by the 14th Protocol. The Court restrained itself from the use of an important tool for combating the backlog by way of judicial self-restraint.

The situation changed with the coming into force of the 14th Additional Protocol to the Convention. In the case of *Adrian Mihai Ioanescu v. Romania* the Court applied the new criterion for the first time on the same day on which the 14th Protocol entered into force.[48] The applicant had claimed before domestic courts the sum of 90 Euros in damages from an international road transport company. His claim had been rejected by the domestic courts and he complained before the Court, invoking Articles 6 and 13 of the Convention. The Court declared the application inadmissible on the grounds that no sig-

---

47 Cf. R. Ergec, *Protection européenne et internationale des droits de l'homme*, Bruxelles 2006, 158.
48 *Adrian Mihai Ioanescu v. Romania*, app. no. 36659/04, judgment of 1 June 2010.

nificant disadvantage occurred. In doing so the Court cited, *inter alia* its previous rulings in *Micallef* and in *Bock*. This approach of the Court's probably heralds a new era on this particular point, as regards the interpretation of the Convention. The Court is probably adopting the old Roman rule – *de minimis non curat praetor*, which is to enhance the Court's efficiency and improve the quality of the Court's work in general, by removing from the agenda applications of minor interest for the protection of human rights.

6.3.4 *Overview of the Court's Power to Interpret the Convention*

An overview of the Court's power to interpret the Convention proves the main stance of the Court's towards the development of the case-law, which tended to adopt an active attitude rather than the one of judicial self-restraint.[49] The Court is always in a position to fulfil its main task, this being the protection of human rights. That is why it has to balance the interests of the individual and those of the community.[50] The way it interprets the Convention serves the Court's main task, which is being the guideline of the interpretation process. The protection of human rights, as performed by the Court, consists in issuing judgments in which the Court either recommends a measure of redress or indeed prescribes one.

49 This goes along with my main theory on the Court's attitude towards interpreting the Convention; cf. Popovic (fn. 16), 396.
50 Dembour (fn. 10), 102.

VII The Court's Remedies

7.1 The Notion of Remedies

A remedy is a relief afforded to the successful claimant in a legal suit.[1] As I have already mentioned in the introduction to this part of the book, various expressions are in current use in European human rights law to denote the same phenomenon.

The ECHR has jurisdiction to afford remedies, or to put it more precisely, in terms of Article 41 of the Convention, the Court is allowed to "afford just satisfaction to the injured party" in case of a violation of human rights. There are scholars and learned commentators of the Convention who insist on the thesis that such wording of the text primarily shows the Court's lack of competence to annul or nullify acts of member states, which are in conflict with the Convention.[2]

There are no separate proceedings for just satisfaction before the ECHR; the question is "dealt with as an element of a larger whole of which the examination of merits forms the first part".[3] It is to be noted that the development of the Court's jurisprudence has clarified the situation in this respect, because in early cases the respondent governments had argued that the applicants were to undertake a "second domestic proceeding to seek remedies, before the Court could apply Article 41 [of the Convention]". The Court rejected this argument as formalistic, alien to international law and contrary to the proper administration of justice.[4] That is how the Court adopted the idea of unity of procedure concerning merits of a case and just satisfaction, being the remedy for a violation of human rights.

The Court can first of all declare that the respondent state had violated the applicant's rights. This is also a remedy, although it gives only a moral satisfaction to the applicant.[5] A declaration of this kind is considered to be a primary remedy. Only after having found a violation, the Court is allowed to proceed to the award of a just satisfaction.[6] That is a part of the Court's technique, which has developed throughout the evolution of the Court's

---

1 I am following Dinah Shelton, who quotes Black's Law Dictionary to support the definition; cf. D. Shelton, *Remedies in International Human Rights Law*, Oxford – New York 2006, 7.

2 Shelton (fn. 53), 189 with reference to S.Thomsen's article in Bernhardt's *Encyclopaedia of Public International Law*.

3 P. van Dijk et al. (eds), *Theory and Practice of the European Convention on Human Right,* Antwerpen – Oxford 2006, 247.

4 Shelton (fn. 53), 195-196.

5 Shelton (fn. 53), 195.

6 Ph. Leach, *Taking a Case to the European Court of Human Rights*, Oxford – New York 2005, 397.

case-law. However, the Court does not apply remedies exclusively under Article 41 of the Convention, but also under Article 46, in a somewhat sophisticated form.

The notion of remedy for a breach of human rights is therefore an overall concept, which applies both to *just satisfaction* and *measures of redress*. They should be distinguished in spite of having legal grounds in common, consisting of the two provisions of the Convention that I have just mentioned.

7.2 Legal Grounds

Legal grounds of remedies, which the ECHR awards, are provided by Articles 41 and 46 of the Convention. Article 41 reads as follows:

> "If the Court finds that there has been a violation of the Convention or the protocols thereto, and if the internal law of the High Contracting Party concerned allows only partial reparation to be made, the Court shall, if necessary, afford just satisfaction to the injured party."

Just satisfaction is thus the most general remedy, which the Court applies. Its substance will be discussed later in this chapter.

Whereas it is clear from the wording of Article 41 of the Convention that it provides a remedy to repair a violation of human rights, it is much less the case of Article 46 of the Convention. This provision has nonetheless served the purpose of developing remedies in the field of the European human rights law. Article 46 of the Convention reads:

> "The High Contracting Parties undertake to abide by the final judgment of the Court in any case to which they are parties.
> The final judgment of the Court shall be transmitted to the Committee of Ministers which shall supervise its execution."

High Contracting Parties to the Convention are sovereign states. They are under an obligation, arising from the international law, to abide by the Court's judgments. The provision I have just cited does not provide details of the conduct of the Committee of Ministers, or the way in which that body will deal with the execution of judgments. Within the framework of the Council of Europe a member state which refuses to enforce a Court's judgment may be suspended, or even excluded. The latter has never occurred so far.

The Committee of Ministers of the Council of Europe is a body which is primarily political in character. The Committee is composed of ministers of foreign affairs of the member states, who are usually represented by the ambassadors accredited to the Council of Europe, residing in Strasbourg. The Committee is therefore in a sort of permanent session and it has supervisory powers as regards the execution of the Court's judgments. These powers consist above all in exercising political pressure on the respondent state, in order to make it comply with a particular judgment, rendered by the Court. Although rooted in political considerations this system has turned out to be effective throughout the history of the protection of human rights in Europe.[7]

It is to be noted that neither Article 41 of the Convention, nor its Article 46 make it clear what just satisfaction nor measures of redress are to consist of. One can think of any possible remedy, but the problems of enforcing these will inevitably arise on the international scale, because of the fact that a certain conduct is to be imposed to a sovereign state.

The legal grounds for the Court's remedies; either just satisfaction or measures of redress for violations of human rights, as laid down by the two articles of the Convention I have cited under this heading inevitably introduce constraint. A member state, which is a Contracting Party to the Convention, must enforce the remedy, contained in a Court's judgment. Although sovereign, the states have undertaken an international obligation to comply with the Court's judgments.

7.3 Just Satisfaction

When applying Article 41 of the Convention the Court first declares its finding of a breach of the Convention. As a consequence of such a declaration the Court usually makes an award of a just satisfaction under three headings. Those are: pecuniary and non-pecuniary damages, as well as costs and expenses.[8]

It should be outlined that the awards the Court makes as just satisfaction are equitable remedies, and as such they fall within the Court's discretion.[9]

As the Court is not empowered to annul an act by domestic authorities it tends to achieve compensation for damages, originating from a violation of human rights, by awarding a sum of money to the applicant, who suffered such a violation.[10] As a sum of money may be awarded in order to cover pecuniary as well as non-pecuniary damages and the Court is not in a position to calculate properly the damages it is to compensate, in the greatest number of the cases it applies the remedy on an equitable basis. Mostly technical considerations guide the Court in this respect.

7 Van Dijk (fn. 3), 44-45; J-F. Renucci, *Droit européen des droits de l'homme,* Paris 2002, 590.

8 D.J. Harris, M. O'Boyle & C. Warbrick, *Law of the European Convention on Human Right,* Oxford – New York 2009, 857-861.

9 Leach (fn. 6), 397.

10 Van Dijk et al. (fn. 3), 261-262.

Awards for pecuniary damages may include different items, such as, for instance, loss of earnings or medical expenses or loss of value of land.[11]

As for the non-pecuniary damages, the Court makes awards for pain and suffering, or frustration, or loss of reputation as well as for other similar reasons.[12]

It is to be noted that the Court does not always specify for what it is awarding a certain amount of money as just satisfaction. Moreover, the Court is also inclined to make an award without specifying whether it is to cover pecuniary or non-pecuniary damages. Quite frequently the Court makes an overall award for both sorts of damages on an equitable basis. The reason for an approach of this kind is to be found in the specific character of the ECHR. It is an international jurisdiction which can not easily establish the facts of a case, and usually does not do so. In most of the cases it deals with the Court relies on the facts established by the domestic courts-of-law.

Many factors influence the Court's decision on the amount, which is to be awarded, and they vary from one case to another. As examples of this kind one can take the duration of detention of a person, or the duration of proceedings on a national level of jurisdiction, or readiness of the respondent government to pay a certain amount to the applicant in terms of compensation and the like.[13] With the support of the Court's case-law some commentators insist on the idea that only those damages that have actually and necessarily been incurred and are also reasonable are susceptible of redress.

The three criteria I have just mentioned also apply to the Court's awards for costs and expenses.[14] The main rule in this respect is that only those legal costs that relate to the violation found by the Court are recoverable. The Court usually awards a certain amount of money to a successful applicant in order to cover these costs and expenses that have occurred during the proceedings before the Court. However, the costs and expenses, which an applicant incurred while litigating on a domestic level are not excluded from recovery. It depends on the circumstances of a case whether the Court will find it necessary to award a sum of money for reparation of these costs as well.

7.4 Measures of Redress

When the Court finds a violation of human rights protected by the Convention and its additional protocols, the respondent state is not only under obligation to pay an amount of money awarded by the Court in just satisfaction to the successful applicant. The

11 See Leach (fn. 6), 402, where no less than ten items are enumerated in this regard, as a result of an analysis of the Court's case-law.
12 Ibid. 404, where eleven items are enumerated.
13 Van Dijk et al. (fn. 3), 262-265.
14 Leach (fn. 6), 407; Van Dijk et al. (fn. 3), 265.

respondent state, provided the Court has so pronounced in its judgment, is also to choose under the supervision of the Committee of Ministers of the Council of Europe general and/or individual measures of redress and apply these in the domestic legal order on a national level.[15]

As I have already pointed out, the Court has slowly developed its practice concerning measures of redress over the course of time to the extent that they nowadays stand parallel to just satisfaction and indeed on many occasions are of primordial importance.[16] It is indeed in the field of measures of redress that the evolution of Court's remedies under Article 46 of the Convention occurred for the most part, making a significant contribution to European human rights law.

The substance of measures of redress may vary and it is not an easy task to define the concept of such measures in terms of a global formula. As a matter of fact a measure of redress to repair a breach of human rights can be any measure pronounced by the Court and supervised by the Committee of Ministers. The Court can demand either passing pieces of legislation or sub-legislation on a national level or merely introducing alterations in administrative practice. I shall examine more exhaustively the modes of introducing such measures in the chapters to come. Let me only note here that measures of redress are regularly followed by respondent states, no matter whether they call for altering of legislation or administrative practice. Learned commentators who have made efforts to illustrate this, could quote cases of compliance with measures of redress exclusively *exempli causa*, because these are different in character and substance.[17]

7.5 Overall Obligation of Restitution

While developing remedies the Court has also clarified its principal position towards repairing human rights violations. The Court held in *Papamichalopoulos v. Greece* in paragraph 34 as follows:

> "[A] judgment in which the Court finds a breach [of the Convention] imposes on the respondent State a legal obligation to put an end to the breach and make reparation for its consequences in such a way as to restore as far as possible the situation existing before the breach."[18]

15 Van Dijk et al. (fn. 3), 257.
16 Harris, O'Boyle & Warbrick (fn. 8), 862; Shelton (fn. 1), 201.
17 Shelton (fn. 1), 202.
18 *Papamichalopoulos v. Greece*, Judgments and Decisions A 330 B (1995).

It was only a bit further in the same paragraph of the *Papamichalopoulos* judgment that the Court expressed the same general rule on restitution in another way, stating:

> "If the nature of the breach allows of *restitutio in integrum*, it is for the respondent State to effect it."[19]

The Court has thus made it clear that an overall obligation of restitution represents the fundamental principle of the European human rights law, which has emerged as an outcome of the Court's jurisprudence. It is true that the respondent state is free to choose the means by which it complies with a judgment by the Court, but at the same time the state may do so only if it is not in a position to perform integral restitution. The latter remains the rule.

It was rightly observed by my learned colleague, Judge Birsan of the ECHR, that the obligation to restore property was not mentioned for the first time in *Papamichalopoulos.*[20] The Court had indeed previously stated in *Hentrich v. France*, in a judgment rendered one year before the one in *Papamichalopoulos* that:

> "the best form of redress would in principle be for the State to return the land [to the applicant]".[21]

However, mentioning the state obligation to restore property in *Hentrich* found its place outside the operative part of the judgment and that is exactly what makes the difference between this judgment and the one in *Papamichalopoulos*. In the latter judgment the Court ruled on the obligation to restore property and put it in the operative part of the judgment, which reads:

> "[The Court unanimously] *Holds* that the respondent State is to return to the applicants, within six months, the land in issue of an area of 104,018sq.m, including the buildings on it."[22]

Judge Birsan also admits that the judgment in *Papamichalopoulos* stands as the leading case. He underlines the fact that it was in that judgment that the Court recognised for the first time a connection between the obligation of a member state, contracting party to the

---

19 Ibid.

20 Cf. C. Birsan, "Les aspects nouveaux de l'application des articles 41 et 46 de la Convention dans la jurisprudence de la Cour européenne des droits de l'homme", in : H. Hartig (ed.), *Trente ans de droit européen des droits de l'homme – études à la mémoire de Wolfgang Strasser*, Bruxelles 2007, 23.

21 *Hentrich v. France*, Judgments and Decisions A 296 (1994), paragraph 71.

22 *Papamichalopoulos v. Greece*, Judgments and Decisions A 330 B (1995).

Convention, to abide by a judgment by the Court under the supervision of the Committee of Ministers and the *restitutio in integrum.*[23]

There is no unanimity among commentators as to the actual significance of the Court's rulings in respect of the obligation to restitution. There are authors who tend to limit this approach to the restitution of property.[24] I am more inclined to follow those who interpret the rule of *restitutio in integrum* as one of a general nature.[25] Finally, there are authors who carry out detailed analyses of the Court's case-law and are still without a clear conclusion as to the meaning of the rule on restitution. It occurs to me that those authors are however closer to its general meaning, because they do not limit its field of application to the restitution of property.[26] I insist on the general meaning of the rule because it seems to me that setting such a rule goes hand in hand with the Court's overall efforts and achievements in respect of the evolving measures of redress. As we have learned so far the measures of redress can be either individual or general, and as far as the mode of their introduction is concerned they can either be recommended or prescribed.

23 Birsan (fn. 20), ibid.
24 Leach (fn. 6), 405-406.
25 Shelton (fn. 1), 199-200.
26 Van Dijk et al. (fn. 3), 252-257.

VIII Recommending Measures of Redress

8.1 The Court's Power to Recommend

The ECHR is an international tribunal, which in principle can not order sovereign states, being contracting parties to the Convention, to take measures under constraint. Although lacking powers to order and urge a member state to apply a certain measure, the Court may however recommend one. Its power to recommend was not envisaged by the text of the Convention, but it has emerged in the Court's case-law, finding its foundation in the general principles of law. The Court's power to recommend has proved to be sufficiently effective because of the Court's undisputed authority. While its power to recommend was evolving, the Court introduced two types of measures of redress for violations of human rights representing the outcome of the use of such a power. Those are individual and general measures of redress.

8.2 Recommending Individual Measures of Redress

The Committee of Ministers of the Council of Europe sought to address problems arising in cases in which there was a lack of appropriate legislation at the level of member states, contracting parties to the Convention. One of the problems was the reopening of proceedings on a domestic level. Despite the fact that there is no such obligation under the Convention on the part of a member state to reopen proceedings, the Committee of Ministers took a stand that the reopening of domestic proceedings which had seriously breached the Convention was of fundamental importance.[1] To address the problem the Committee of Ministers adopted one of its recommendations, anchoring it in the powers the Committee is vested with under Article 46 of the Convention.[2]

The Committee of Ministers insisted in the preamble of the recommendation on the obligation of the member states, contracting parties to the Convention, to achieve the *restitutio in integrum* in case of a breach of human rights protected by the Convention.

1 M.Hunt, "State Obligations Following from a Judgment of the European Court of Human Rights", in: Th. Christou and J.P. Raymond (eds.), *European Court of Human Rights – Remedies and Execution of Judgments*, London 2005, 39.

2 Recommendation No. R (2000) 2 adopted on 19 January 2000.

This means that the respondent state has to put the victim of a violation "in the same situation as he or she enjoyed prior to the violation of the Convention". The text of the recommendation in its substantial part read:

> "[T]he Contracting Parties [are] to ensure that there exist at national level adequate possibilities to achieve, as far as possible, *restitutio in integrum*;
> [The] Contracting Parties [are encouraged] to examine their national legal systems with a view to ensuring that there exist adequate possibilities of re-examination of the case, including reopening of the proceedings, in instances where the Court has found a violation of the Convention, especially where:
> i. the injured party continues to suffer very serious negative consequences because of the outcome of the domestic decision at issue, which are not adequately remedied by the just satisfaction and cannot be rectified except by re-examination or reopening, and
> ii. the judgment of the Court leads to the conclusion that
>   a. the impugned domestic decision is on the merits contrary to the Convention, or
>   b. the violation found is based on procedural errors or shortcomings of such gravity that a serious doubt is cast on the outcome of the domestic proceedings complained of."

It is to be noted that the Committee of Ministers invoked in the explanatory memorandum, attached to this Recommendation, the Court's judgment rendered in *Papamichalopoulos* in support of its own standpoint. The Committee of Ministers also added in the explanation that "an increasing number of States have adopted special legislation providing for the possibility of such re-examination or reopening". At the same time in other member states, contracting parties to the Convention, "this possibility has been developed by the courts and national authorities under existing law".[3]

The leading case in the Court's jurisprudence concerning the recommendation of individual measures of redress in regard to reopening of proceedings is *Gençel v. Turkey*.[4] The issue in that case was that the applicant had been sentenced on a national level for an offense against state security. The competent domestic tribunal had been the State Security Court, which included military judges on its bench. Military judges, being army officers, were submitted to regular military discipline and a chain of command structure. The applicant complained that Article 6 of the Convention had been violated by the presence

3 Ibid. Explanatory Memorandum; for more on the Recommendation (2000) 2 and its Explanatory Memorandum see M. Hunt (fn. 1), 39-42.

4 *Gençel v. Turkey*, app. no. 53431/99, judgment of 23 October 2003 (text in French).

of military judges on the bench. Military officers, submitted to a chain of command in the army could by no means fulfil the requirements of independence and impartiality inherent in Article 6 of the Convention.

The Court ruled in the applicant's favour on the grounds that the composition of the bench including military judges could not meet the requirements of Article 6 of the Convention, granting the right to a fair trial. A tribunal so composed can be considered neither independent nor impartial. Therefore the Court stated in paragraph 27 of the judgment:

> "Lorsque la Cour conclut que la condamnation d'un requérant a été prononcée par un tribunal qui n'était pas indépendant et impartial au sens de l'article 6.1, elle estime qu'un principe le redressement le plus approprié serait de faire rejuger le requérant en temps utile par un tribunal indépendant et impartial."

That was the so-called *Gençel* formula, which was adopted and to a certain extent developed in another Turkish case. It was the Grand Chamber case of *Oçalan v. Turkey.*[5] One of the issues raised in this case was identical to the issue in *Gençel*, for it again concerned the presence of military judges on the bench.

The applicant in *Oçalan* was a prominent leader of the Kurdish opposition, which is not legal in Turkey, because of being accused by the authorities of having a tendency to use violent methods. The applicant had been arrested abroad and extradited to Turkey, where he was tried and sentenced for terrorism by a State Security Court.

The Grand Chamber of the Court reiterated the approach made by the Chamber in *Gençel* and referred to the judgment in that case. While referring to the Court's previous jurisprudence, the Grand Chamber developed the formula on reopening of the proceedings, as recommended to the respondent state. It did so in paragraph 210 of the *Oçalan* judgment, which read *inter alia*:

> "The Grand Chamber endorses the general approach adopted in the above-mentioned case-law. It considers that where an individual, as in the instant case, has been convicted by a court that did not meet the Convention requirements of independence and impartiality, a retrial or reopening of the case, if requested, represents in principle an appropriate way of redressing the violation."

The Grand Chamber developed the formula by introducing an element, which put the measure of redress, *i.e.* the reopening of proceedings on a domestic level, at the disposal of the victim of a violation of human rights. Domestic proceedings should be reopened

5 *Oçalan v. Turkey*, 2005-IV.

only at the demand of the victim of a violation of human rights, who won the case at the ECHR.

It is also to be underlined that both in *Gençel* and in *Oçalan* the recommendations of measures of redress, made by the Court, found their places outside the operative parts of the respective judgments. The Court's approach was prudent. It was primarily rooted in the general principles of law, rather than in the text of the Convention itself. That is what led to the adoption of the idea to recommend a measure of redress in a situation in which the Court could not properly prescribe a certain measure to the respondent state.

Recommendations for reopening domestic proceedings, identical to those stemming from the two judgments that I have just commented on and somehow shaped in what one may call a *Gençel-Oçalan* clause, were repeated in many similar cases, in which Turkey was the respondent state. This led the Turkish government to introduce a bill before the Parliament aiming at the reform of the State Security Court system. The reform bill was adopted and military judges no longer sit on the bench. The measure of redress recommended by the Court thus achieved a broader effect than the one at which the Court aimed. It overcame its individual character and turned out to be effective on a larger scale, for it gave the input for the reform of national legislation.

8.3 RECOMMENDING GENERAL MEASURES OF REDRESS

As we have already seen at the end of the previous heading the fact that the Court recommended an individual measure of redress for a violation of human rights could produce a broader effect which indeed led to the introduction of general measure of redress for violations of human rights on a national level. The Court itself has also proceeded to recommend general measures of redress for violations of human rights. This was the case when the Court recommended to a respondent state to either amend its legislation, being incongruent with the Convention, or to pass a piece of legislation on a situation when it was lacking. The Court's practice in this respect dates back to the 1990s.

In one of its judgments the Court referred to a specific problem, existing in Italy, although by no means limited to that country. The issue was the excessive length of proceedings, to which the Court made reference in *Bottazzi v. Italy*.[6] In paragraph 22 of the judgment the Court first invoked a resolution of the Committee of Ministers dating to 1997, in which the Committee took the stand that

6 *Bottazzi v. Italy*, ECHR 1999-V.

> "[excessive] delays in the administration of justice constitute an important danger, in particular for the respect of the rule of law".[7]

Furthermore the Court stated in the same paragraph of the judgment that it had already delivered sixty-five judgments in cases against Italy in which a violation of human rights was found on the grounds that the civil proceedings before Italian courts of law had exceeded a reasonable time. Therefore, the Court concluded the paragraph in the following way:

> "The frequency with which violations are found shows that there is an accumulation of identical breaches which are sufficiently numerous to amount not merely to isolated incidents. Such breaches reflect a continuing situation that has not yet been remedied and in respect of which litigants have no domestic remedy.
> This accumulation of breaches accordingly constitutes a practice that is incompatible with the Convention."

The only dissenter in the Grand Chamber in this case, although dissenting only partly found that there was

> "[an] ongoing dialogue between the Committee of Ministers of the Council of Europe and the Italian government, in the course of which the government [had] provided detailed information on the measures that [were] being taken, and [would] be taken in the future, in order to solve the problem of the excessive length of proceedings".[8]

It was indeed during a process of adapting the national law of Italy, which had been launched by Resolution 336 (1997) mentioned above, that the judgment in *Bottazzi* was rendered. This explains the brevity of the judgment in general, as well as the formula used to recommend a general measure of redress. The wording was clear, but the recommendation itself was by no means explicit. The Court took account of a problem, found a violation in the case and underlined in general terms the duty of respondent states to organise their judicial systems in such a way as to be able to meet the reasonable time requirement of Article 6 (1) of the Convention.

---

7 Resolution 336 (1997) as cited in the text of the judgment; on the activity of the Committee of Ministers concerning the issue cf. E. Bates, "Supervising the Execution of Judgments Delivered by the European Court of Human Rights: The Challenges Facing the Committee of Ministers", in: Th. Christou and J.P. Raymond (eds.), *European Court of Human Rights – Remedies and Execution of Judgments*, London 2005, 81-32.

8 Cf. partly dissenting opinion of Judge Türmen, attached to the judgment.

It was nonetheless clear that the recommendation addressed to Italy in *Bottazzi* aimed at a general measure of redress. The recommendation served the purpose well, for less than two years after rendering the judgment I have just mentioned the Italian Parliament adopted a special piece of legislation designed to address the problem indicated by the Court in its judgment. In April 2001 the parliament passed the well-known *Pinto-Law (Legge Pinto)*, providing a remedy on a national level in case of excessive length of proceedings.[9] I have no intention to go beyond my task which consists of writing on the development of the Court's practice of recommending measures of redress for violations of human rights, within the scope of the emergence of what we call today European human rights law. I am however tempted to inform the reader about the appreciation of the general measure that is at issue here. Let me therefore hand you over to an Italian author, Marco Fabri, who is a director of a research institute in Bologna. He wrote:

> "The Pinto Law was introduced in 2001 to stop the flooding of cases for the excessive length of judicial proceedings to the European Court of Human Rights. [T]his new law has not solved any problem, but it has just increased both the caseload of the already suffering Courts of Appeal and the state budget deficit (about 118 million Euros). The Pinto Law is an expensive and useless *placebo*, which just tried to sweep problems under the carpet."[10]

The path leading to inferno is sometimes paved by the best of our intentions. One can not deny the fact that the Italian government was ready to follow the Court's recommendation, placed under the supervision of the Committee of Ministers and that is exactly what is of concern to me. Whether the way chosen by the respondent government to address the problem, which provided grounds to issue a certain recommendation, gave a successful result or not, is something outside the realm of this book and should be discussed elsewhere.

Although the Court, because of the facts I have explained, was not fully explicit in formulating the recommendation in *Bottazzi*, it took a different stand in respect of the formula of recommendation in another Italian case. The case was *Scozzari and Giunta v. Italy.*[11] Temporary placement of children in a home by social services and prolonged absence of contact with their mother were at issue in the case.

The Court found that the circumstances of conferring children to social care institutions, given the duty to look after children lacking parental care, did not meet the requirements

9 Cf. D. Popovic, *Evropski sud za ljudska prava* (/European Court of Human Rights), Belgrade 2008, 96. On Pinto Law see also in Serbian: S. Caric, *Pravo na sudjenje u razumnom roku* (Right to a Trial Within Reasonable Time), Belgrade 2008, 38-40.

10 M. M. Fabri, "The Italian Maze Towards Trials Within Reasonable Time", in: *Council of Europe, The Right to Trial Within Reasonable Time*, Round table, Bled 2009, 15-16.

11 *Scozzari and Giunta v. Italy*, ECHR 2000-VIII.

of Article 8 of the Convention. The Court expressed its view in paragraph 216 of the judgment, which read:

> "[T]he authorities have failed to show the degree of prudence and vigilance required in such a delicate and sensitive situation, and have done so to the detriment not just of the first applicant's rights but also of the superior interests of the children."

The wording of the passage cited clearly shows that the Court aimed at a problem existing on a broader scale, affecting a whole class of persons and not only the applicants. The Court's holding in paragraph 249 of the judgment was in parallel to this and extended the idea of reparation for breaches of human rights. It referred to a general measure of redress.

The Court held in paragraph 249:

> "[A] judgment in which the Court finds a breach [of human rights guaranteed by the Convention] imposes on the respondent State a legal obligation not just to pay those concerned the sums awarded by way of just satisfaction, but also to choose, subject to supervision by the Committee of Ministers, the general and/or, if appropriate, individual measures to be adopted in their domestic legal order to put an end to the violation found by the Court and to redress so far as possible the effects."

At this point the Court referred to paragraph 34 of *Papamichalopoulos* judgment, which, as we have seen above, provided for an overall obligation of the respondent state to achieve integral restitution.[12]

If compared to the Court's approach in *Bottazzi*, the one the Court made in its judgment in *Scozzari and Giunta* calls for two remarks. Firstly, it set a rule on adopting measures of redress, and secondly it put these measures on the same footing as just satisfaction. The latter occurred despite the fact that only just satisfaction is mentioned in the text of the Convention as a remedy for violations of human rights. The Court was justified to do so, because it found another remedy in the powers conferred to the Committee of Ministers by Article 46 of the Convention.[13] There are commentators who claim that *Scozzari and Giunta* was the first case in which the Court for the first time applied "the language of Article 41 of the Convention in conjunction with Article 46".[14]

---

12 See 7.5.

13 Cf. Hunt (fn. 1), 33.

14 N. Frangakis, "Systemic Human Rights Violations in the Jurisprudence of the European Court of Human Rights", in: *Nomiko Vima – European Court of Human Rights 50 Years*, Athens 2010, 131.

What is a common feature for judgments' texts in *Bottazzi* and *Scozzari and Giunta* is the fact that the recommendations were contained in the judgments but they found their place among Court's reasoning, *i.e.* outside the operative parts of the judgments. This is easy to understand, for if they had been put in the operative part of a judgment, the Court's recommendations would have lost their character, or rather they would have been transformed into prescriptive clauses.

The original timidity of Court's recommendations can be illustrated by invoking another judgment from 2000, namely the one rendered in the case of *Kudla v. Poland.*[15] In that case violations of Articles 3 and 5 of the Convention were found, but the Grand Chamber went beyond and also found a violation of Article 13 of the Convention. The Court stated in paragraph 156 of the judgment that

> "[t]he correct interpretation of Article 13 is that that provision guarantees an effective remedy before a national authority for an alleged breach of the requirement under Article 6 (1) to hear a case within a reasonable time".

Such an interpretation led the Court to examine the national law of Poland in respect of the remedy in question. The Court's findings in this regard were expressed in paragraphs 158 and 159 of the judgment. Effective remedies were missing on a national level. Therefore, the Court concluded in paragraph 160:

> "In the present case there has been a violation of Article 13 of the Convention in that the applicant had no domestic remedy whereby he could enforce his right to a 'hearing within a reasonable time' as guaranteed by Article 6 (1) of the Convention."

Contrary to the text of the *Bottazzi* judgment, where the Court recommended a measure by way of reference to the number of judgments rendered in identical cases, the text in *Kudla* only implied a recommendation. Properly interpreted however, that judgment must be considered as containing a recommendation.[16]

The Court's wording was hesitant at the beginning. Although in the same year the judgment in *Kudla* was given after the one in *Scozzari and Giunta.* There was however a slight contrast between the judgment in *Scozzari and Giunta* if compared to those given in *Bottazzi* and in *Kudla*. The trend of evolution seems to have been to render the Court's

---

15 *Kudla v. Poland*, ECHR 2000-XI.

16 For bibliography on *Kudla* see V. Berger, *Jurisprudence de la Cour européenne des droits de l'homme*, Paris 2009, 403-404; cf. also F. Tulkens, "The Right to a Trial Within a Reasonable Time: Problems and Solutions", in: Venice Commission (ed.), *Can excessive length of proceedings be remedied?*, Strasbourg 2007, 342-343.

recommendation of a measure of redress for a violation of human rights more and more explicit.

The Court pursued this path, and the outcome has become visible in more recent judgments. Thus, for instance in a Georgian case, the Court made its recommendation much more specific than it was in the Italian and Polish precedents I have mentioned above.

In *Klaus and Iouri Kiladze v. Georgia* the applicants complained of a legislative gap, which prevented them from enjoying benefits of the legislation adopted in order to remedy the victims of persecutions that had taken place in Soviet times.[17] The Court invoked the powers of the Committee of Ministers before making a clear statement on the measures of redress recommended to the respondent state in paragraph 85 of the judgment, which read:

> "Dans ces conditions, la Cour estime que des mesures générales au niveau national s'imposent sans aucun doute dans le cadre de l'exécution du présent arrêt. Des mesures législatives, administratives et budgétaires nécessaires doivent ainsi être prises rapidement afin que les personnes visées par l'article 9 de la loi du 11 décembre 1997 puissent bénéficier effectivement de leur droit garanti par cette disposition."

It is obvious that the formula used in the Georgian case is rather developed and more complex and specific if confronted to the ones we saw in the cases cited above. The Court's recommendations have over the course of time become more detailed or to put it in another way, more indicative, but they have not overstepped the limit set by their nature and character. That is why the Court repeated in paragraph 82 of the judgment of *Klaus and Iouri Kiladze v. Georgia* the main rule in this field, *i.e.* that the respondent state is free to choose a measure of redress for a violation of human rights under the supervision of the Committee of Ministers. However, the Court indicated at the same time that a set of measures to be taken concerned adopting pieces of legislation, altering administrative practice and also providing budgetary resources to make the whole system of compensation for unjustified persecutions workable.

It is the work of the Committee of Ministers that has represented the framework for the Court's jurisprudence in respect of recommending measures of redress for violations of human rights. The proceedings of the Committee of Ministers were based on Article 46 of the Convention.

The pattern we have met in the judgment rendered in the Georgian case I have just mentioned had come into practice before that particular judgment was given. It consisted

---

17 *Klaus and Iouri Kiladze v. Géorgia*, app. no. 7957/06, judgment of 15 December 2009 (text in French).

of introducing a special heading, devoted to Article 46 of the Convention, in the text of the judgments.

One of the examples of this kind of drafting is to be found in a Romanian case, which represents a landmark in the so-called pilot-judgments, a topic to which I shall return later in this book. In *Viasu v. Romania* the issue was the protection of property.[18] The applicant could not recover in kind the property his father had been deprived of by the communist regime. The Court invoked the powers of the Committee of Ministers in a special heading of the judgment, consecrated to the recommendation of general measures of redress for a violation of Article 1 First Protocol to the Convention. The Court found shortcomings in the functioning of the Romanian system of the restitution of property, which had been expropriated once upon a time by the communist regime. Besides awarding just satisfaction to the applicant in *Viasu* the Court also proceeded to recommend general measures of redress. It did it quite explicitly, stating in paragraph 83 of the judgment as follows:

> "Pour aider l'État défendeur à remplir ses obligations au titre de l'article 46, la Cour a cherché à indiquer, à titre purement indicatif, le type de mesures que l'État roumain pourrait prendre pour mettre un terme à la situation structurelle constatée en l'espèce. Elle considère que l'État défendeur doit, avant tout, soit supprimer tout obstacle s'opposant à l'exercice effectif du droit des nombreuses personnes touchées par la situation jugée par elle contraire à la Convention, comme c'est le cas du requérant, ou à défaut, offrir un redressement approprié. L'État défendeur doit donc garantir par des mesures légales et administratives appropriées la réalisation effective et rapide du droit à restitution, qu'il s'agisse d'une restitution en nature ou de l'octroi d'une indemnité, conformément aux principes de la prééminence du droit et de la légalité de la protection des droits patrimoniaux énoncés à l'article 1 du Protocole n° 1, en tenant compte des principes énoncés par la jurisprudence de la Cour en matière d'indemnisation (arrêt *Broniowski* précité, §§ 147-151, 176 et 186). Ces objectifs pourraient être atteints, par exemple, par l'amendement du mécanisme de restitution actuel, dont la Cour a relevé certaines faiblesses, et la mise en place d'urgence de procédures simplifiées et efficaces, fondées sur des mesures législatives et règlementaires cohérentes, qui puissent ménager un juste équilibre entre les différents intérêts en jeu."

The Court has thus developed its own approach to general measures of redress for violations of human rights and the technique of their recommendation. The evolution of the Court's

18 *Viasu v. Romania*, app. no. 75951/01, judgment of 9 December 2008 (text in French). For more details on the case see: D. Popovic, *Protecting Property in European Human Rights Law*, Utrecht 2009, 104-106.

attitude towards the issue has been constant and uninterrupted. The Court has always been trying to introduce more and more details and, as it stated in the judgment I have just cited, to suggest certain types of measures of redress recommended to the respondent states. In this particular case the Court suggested the introduction of a simplified procedure of the restitution of property, which would be provided with grounds in amended legislation, accompanied by appropriate sub-legislation. This was by far more specific and detailed than the general approach the Court had made in *Papamichalopoulos*, the judgment in which the whole evolution of recommending measures of redress begins.

The Court has neither overstepped the limits laid down by Article 46 of the Convention, providing for the framework of the powers of the Committee of Ministers, nor has it destroyed the nature, spirit and character of a recommendation as such. With a recommendation a member state, contracting party to the Convention is only invited to act in a certain way. There is no specific obligation in this respect, although the problem is much more complex than it appears to be at first glance. The consideration of the complex character of the problem is based on two main facts. Firstly, despite the fact that the Court only invites a member state to act and does not give an order, there is an overall obligation of a member state to comply with the Court's judgments. This is what makes it indeed obligatory for the member state to repair a violation of human rights. Secondly, the Court has also introduced its own scrutiny of the measures recommended, aiming to repair violations of human rights.

8.4 The Court's Scrutiny of Measures of Redress

The Court has made it clear that the recommendations of general measures of redress remain under its own scrutiny. The same applies to the individual measures, as well, but it was in a case concerning a general measure of redress that the ECHR made its position on scrutinising measures of redress precise and fully comprehensive. Such a statement of the Court's occurred in the case of *Sejdovic v. Italy*.[19]

The applicant in that case was suspected of having committed a murder in Italy. As he was untraceable to the Italian authorities he was assigned a lawyer and convicted *in absentia*. He was subsequently arrested in Germany under an arrest warrant that had been issued by the Italian authorities, but the German authorities refused his extradition. The reason for refusal was that the Italian law did not provide sufficient guarantees that the proceedings already conducted in the applicant's absence would be reopened. In November 2004 a chamber of the Court held that Italy had violated Article 6 of the Convention in this case.

19 *Sejdovic v. Italy*, ECHR 2006-II.

The case was then referred to the Grand Chamber at the request of the Italian government. The Grand Chamber confirmed the chamber stance that the violation found on the case had originated in a systemic problem. The latter consisted of the lack of an effective mechanism to secure persons convicted *in absentia* with a fresh determination of the merits of the charge against them.

The Italian government's submissions were referred to in paragraphs 110-118 of the Grand Chamber judgment. The paragraph 115 read:

> "The Government stated that they were not opposed in principle to the Court's giving fairly detailed indications of the general measures to be taken. However, the new practice pursued by the Court ran the risk of nullifying the principle that States were free to choose the means of executing judgments. It also ran counter to the spirit of the Convention and lacked a clear legal basis."

The respondent government had made a remark, to which the Court made reference in paragraph 117 of the judgment, on the distribution of powers between the bodies belonging to the mechanism of protection of human rights at the level of the Council of Europe. This concerned especially the relations between the Committee of Ministers and the Court. The government of Italy had suggested, as referred to in paragraph 118 of the judgment, the following:

> "[I]f the practice of indicating general measures were to be continued, it should at least become institutionalised in the Rules of Court or in the questions, which the Court put to the parties, so that the parties could submit observations on whether a violation was 'systemic'."

As a matter of fact the Italian government claimed to have complied with the recommendation of the Court's chamber. In April 2005 *i.e.* only six months after the chamber judgment, a special piece of legislation (Law no. 60/2005) amended the former Article 175 of the Criminal Procedure Code, providing for the possibility of reopening proceedings conducted against a person, who was convicted *in absentia*.

The Grand Chamber of the Court gave its judgment in March 2006, holding that it was too early to estimate the scope and efficiency of the statutory amendment, because the Cassation Court of Italy had not yet developed any jurisprudence concerning the amendment adopted the previous year. The Court's reasoning found its place in paragraph 123 of the judgment, where it was stated:

> "The Court considers that it would be premature at this stage, in the absence of any domestic case-law concerning the application of the provisions of Law

> no. 60/2005, to examine whether the reforms outlined above have achieved the result required by the Convention."

The Grand Chamber invoked as authorities the *Gençel* and *Oçalan* precedents in paragraphs 125 and 126 of the judgment. Furthermore, although without referring to the rule in *Papamichalopoulos*, the Grand Chamber substantially affirmed it in paragraph 127 of the judgment, holding that the respondent state

> "[w]as free, subject to monitoring of the Committee of Ministers, to choose the means by which it will discharge its obligation to put the applicant, as far as possible, in the position he would have been in had the requirements of the Convention not been disregarded".

If we are to interpret the rule in *Sejdovic* it is indispensible to note that the Court rendered obligatory its own appreciation of a general measure of redress for a violation of human rights, taken on a national level. The fact that the Court required domestic case-law as a piece of evidence in this particular case indicates a means by which the Court was to be assured that a general measure, taken on a national level, had been fully effective. The decisive element of the Court's approach is that it was not satisfied to learn that a certain measure of redress for a violation of human rights, recommended by the Court, was introduced in the national legal order. The ECHR submitted the measure to its own scrutiny, demanding evidence of its effective character and proper implementation.

IX Prescribing Measures of Redress

9.1 The Court's Power to Prescribe

The Court's power to recommend a measure of redress for a violation of human rights is relatively easy to understand in terms of the general principles of law. However, the Court's scrutiny of the measures recommended has led to overcoming the classical notion and scope of a recommendation. If a measure is merely recommended to a respondent state then, basically, it may or may not be followed. A recommendation may be accepted by a sovereign state and the ECHR in principle could not go further than that. By introducing its own scrutiny of measures recommended, aiming to redress violations of human rights, the Court has rendered such measures almost obligatory. On certain occasions the Court has gone even beyond that stage.

There were cases in which the Court was tempted to reinterpret its own powers to a certain extent, and it did so in such a way as to indicate a measure of redress for a violation of human rights, and indeed prescribe it, instead of only recommending it. The Court was driven to do so by the force of circumstances in cases which as a matter of fact gave rise to aspect of the Court's powers, namely the one to prescribe a measure of redress for a violation of human rights.

Indicating measures of redress, while at the same time making these prescriptive, leads to two distinct situations corresponding to two types of measures of redress. Like the measures recommended, those prescribed can be either individual or general.

9.2 Prescribing Individual Measures of Redress

The Court's judgments were designed to be binding, but at the same time they are essentially declaratory in character. The introduction of constraint when indicating a measure of redress was indeed an innovation. By doing so, the ECHR limited the choice of a member state, contracting party to the Convention, in its mode and course of complying with a judgment.

As I have already mentioned, the circumstances of certain cases provided the instigation and were indeed the masters of progress in this regard. It so happened that a peculiar political and social situation in a country guided the Court to decide to make a bold move and indeed a step forward in the evolution of the Court's remedies.

The respondent state in the leading case was Georgia, a country burdened with problems and with a complex and troublesome political situation, which did not lack armed conflicts between the central government and some of the component parts of the country. The Ajarian Autonomous Republic, in which the case originated, is an integral part of Georgia and should not be confused with the breakaway province of Abkhazia, which meanwhile declared independence.

The applicant, Mr Assanidze, used to be the mayor of the capitol city of Ajaria and a member of the provincial parliament. He was convicted of a criminal offence in 1994 and consequently imprisoned. In 1995 he was granted pardon by the President of the Republic of Georgia, but due to the existing tensions between the central and the provincial governments the latter refused to release him from prison.[1] The Court found that the province of Ajaria had no standing in international law and ruled that the respondent State was Georgia. The applicant asked for release from prison and as the Court noted in paragraph 166 of the judgment

> "[i]t was his belief that he was being held because it suited the local Ajarian authorities, who wanted him out of the way, the motive being political revenge".

The ECHR ruled in applicant's favour. Affording an amount of money in just satisfaction to the applicant in a situation in which he had actually found himself, being unlawfully detained, would not have provided effective relief, because the applicant's arbitrary detention would have continued. That is why the ECHR faced the dilemma of whether to issue a rather formal judgment devoid of effect or pursue another and quite different path, dealing with the case at hand. The latter led the Court to introduce a novelty, to which the Court placed in the operative part of the judgment, which read in its item 14:

> "[The Court] holds unanimously that the respondent State must secure the applicant's release at the earliest possible date."

The Court gave its reasoning for such a decisive statement in the operative part of the judgment, containing a clear cut prescription to the respondent state in paragraph 202 of the text of the judgment. The Court reiterated its previous stances, *i.e.* a line of authority beginning with *Papamichalopoulos*, which concerned the choice of means to comply with a Court's judgment that the respondent state has always been entitled to. Although confirming its own jurisprudence in general, the Court made a distinction in this particular case, stating:

1 *Assanidze v. Georgia*, ECHR 2004-II paragraphs 20-99.

> "However, by its very nature, the violation found in the instant case does not leave any real choice as to the measures required to remedy it."

The factual situation of the applicant detained, thus provided reasons for the Court's introduction of an innovation in the operative part of the judgment. This was a precedent, which the Court followed in some other similar cases. They also concerned unlawful detention.

In the case of *Ilascu and others* the application was lodged against Moldova and Russia.[2] An integral part of the Republic of Moldova proclaimed secession under the name of Moldavian Republic of Transdnistria. The region of Transdnistria escapes to this date the control of the Moldovan central government. Russian troops remain in the region, which made the Court accept the application against Russia in a case in which several persons alleged to have been unlawfully detained in the region of Transdnistria.

The applicants were four Moldovan nationals, who were arrested in June 1992 by Transdnistria authorities. They were tried by the Supreme Court of the Moldovan Republic of Transdnistria, which sat on a three-judge bench and gave judgment on 9 December 1993. They were found guilty of a number of offences defined in the Criminal Code of the Moldovan Soviet Socialist Republic and severely sentenced to long terms of imprisonment.

Only a few months later, in February 1994, the Supreme Court of the Republic of Moldova examined of its own motion the judgment of 9 December 1993, rendered by the Supreme Court of the secessionist region. The Supreme Court of Moldova quashed the judgment of 9 December on the grounds that the court which had rendered it was unconstitutional. The authorities of Transdnistria did not take account of the judgment of the Supreme Court of Moldova and did not respond to it at all. The applicants remained detained. However, two of the applicants were released in 2001 and 2003 respectively. The two others remained in detention.

The Court found violations of various articles of the Convention in this case, for which the respondent states were held liable. The Court followed its own approach from the *Assanidze* case in item 22 of the operative part of the judgment, which read:

> "[The Court] holds unanimously that the respondent States are to take all necessary measures to put an end to the arbitrary detention of the applicants still imprisoned and secure their immediate release."

---

2 *Ilascu and others v. Moldova and Russia*, ECHR 2004-VII; for bibliography see V. Berger, *Jurisprudence de la Cour européenne des droits de l'homme*, Paris 2009, 68.

The execution of the two judgments, *Assanidze* on the one hand and *Ilascu* on the other, however differed. In the former case the applicant was released, whereas in the latter the Committee of Ministers had to pass a whole series of interim resolutions in an effort to make Russia comply with the judgment. The applicants, being still detained, even filed a new application with the ECHR.[3]

Both of the cases that have just been mentioned, *Assanidze*, as well as *Ilascu*, addressed political issues in new European democracies, which were destabilised by separatist tendencies. It is however noteworthy that the Court's prescriptions of individual measures of redress under Article 46 of the Convention did not take place exclusively in cases of that kind.

As a matter of fact the Court had previously indicated individual measures of redress in certain cases, which can be considered forerunners in this respect. These cases concerned non execution of final judgments rendered on a national level. In such cases the Court simply ordered execution of those judgments. That situation is however different from the one in *Assanidze* or *Ilascu*. In the latter cases the issue was the release of persons unlawfully detained, which made the Court act in a way that included indicating a measure as an *ultima ratio*.

There were also cases in which the Court prescribed a measure in a rather specific way, expressing itself in a conditional mode. These were the cases concerning extraditions. The Court puts an obligation upon a member state, respondent in a case, not to extradite a person. The Court does so by putting in the operative part of its judgment that extraditing the applicant to a country in which he or she might face inhuman or degrading treatment would in itself constitute a violation of the Convention. Thus the Court stated in *Tehrani and Others v. Turkey* in item 4 of the operative part of the judgment:

> "[t]he applicants' deportation to Iran or Iraq would be in violation of Article 3 of the Convention".[4]

In another judgment rendered on the same day the Court used the same technique. It was in the case of *Charahili v. Turkey*, where item 3 of the operative part read as follows:

---

3 More on the subject in: D.J. Harris, M. O'Boyle & C. Warbrick, *Law of the European Convention on Human Rights*, Oxford – New York 2009, 882; on developing the practice of adopting interim resolutions within the Committee of Ministers cf. E. Bates, "Supervising the Execution of Judgments Delivered by the European Court of Human Rights: The Challenges Facing the Committee of Ministers", in: Th. Christou and J.P. Raymond (eds.), *European Court of Human Rights – Remedies and Execution of Judgments*, London 2005, 60-61.

4 *Tehrani and Others v. Turkey*, app. nos. 32940/08; 41626/08; 43616/08, judgment of 23 March 2010.

> "[t]he applicant's deportation to Tunisia would be in violation of Article 3 of the Convention".[5]

Despite the subjunctive in the text the Court's attitude is quite clear and the substance of its pronunciation is quite prescriptive. The Court forbids extraditions in certain cases.

Several judgments can illustrate the Court's approach to indicating the measure consisting of an order to the respondent state to execute a final judgment, given at domestic level.

In *Terem Limited Chechetkin and Olius v. Ukraine* the issue was an irregular seizure of the applicant's property in tax proceedings on a national level.[6] The domestic courts found for the applicants and awarded them a certain amount. The judgment remained unexecuted, which was the reason why the applicants turned to the ECHR, filing an application. The Court quite simply ordered the government of Ukraine to pay the applicants the sum awarded by the domestic courts.

In another case the Court ordered another sort of measure, but the latter had also already been adjudicated on a domestic level of jurisdiction. In *Ilic v. Serbia* the issue was the eviction of a tenant from the applicant's apartment.[7] The Court ordered the respondent government to comply with the final judgment, which had remained unexecuted. It consisted of the eviction of a tenant from the applicant's apartment.

It was convenient for the Court to prescribe a measure of redress that consisted of executing a judgment delivered by the domestic courts of law, because the substance of such a measure had already been determined in a final judgment at the national level of jurisdiction. On the contrary, it seemed to be a more intensive interference with the sovereign state's capacity when the Court ordered a measure of redress, which had not been previously defined on a national level.

9.3 Prescribing General Measures of Redress

The Court proceeded to prescribe general measures of redress for violations of human rights in a number of judgments, usually known as pilot judgments, but which could be labelled as old style pilot judgments. In the beginning prescribing a general measure of redress actually meant putting specific wording in the operative part of a judgment. This element was viewed among commentators as being one of the main features of pilot

5 *Charahili v. Turkey*, app. no. 46605/07, judgment of 23 March 2010. There are other examples of this kind. Cf. p.ex. *Alipour and Hosseinzadagan v. Turkey*, app. nos. 6909/08; 12792/08; 28960/08, judgment of 23 March 2010 (forbidding applicant's extradition to Iran).

6 *Terem Limited Chechetkin and Olius v. Ukraine*, app. no. 70297/01, judgment of 27 September 2005.

7 *Ilic v. Serbia*, app. no. 30312/04, judgment of 10 September 2007; cf. D. Popovic, *Evropski sud za ljudska pravo/European Court of Human Rights*, Beograd 2008, 93.

judgments.[8] An approach of this kind was followed in certain cases, but it was also abandoned in others.

The Court's old style approach was abandoned on certain occasions by moving the measure of redress from of the operative part of a judgment. In doing so, the Court actually transformed the substance of a measure from prescription to recommendation. This fact created a type of new style pilot judgments, which find their origin in *Viasu v. Romania*.[9]

A general measure of redress for a violation of human rights contains a prescription or an order to a member state, contracting party to the Convention, to introduce a measure aimed at meeting demands of a specific situation existing on a national level. The specific situation is characterised by the existence of a systemic violation of human rights, which results in a considerable number of cases pending either before the Court, or on a national level.

To put an end to the systemic violation of human rights, the Court gives a judgment of principle, which is named a pilot judgment. By implementing a pilot-judgment the member state in question is supposed to find a way of redress for all the cases pending with the domestic courts, as well as to those having already reached the Court, for the latter can be referred back to the national level. The idea seemed to be very useful, although its implementation turned out to be more complicated than expected.[10] This avenue of redress saw the light of day in two Polish cases before the Court. Those were the cases of *Broniowski* and *Hutten Czapska*.[11]

At issue in *Broniowski* was the indemnification of individuals repatriated to Poland immediately after World War II. Namely, when Poland's present-day frontiers were drawn, a large number of Poles found themselves east of the Bug River, constituting the country's eastern border. Due to relocation in Poland the repatriated persons had to leave behind the immovable property they owned in the regions they left. The Polish state assumed the obligation to compensate them *i.e.* to allow them to acquire a title to property of adequate value within the Polish borders. The problem remained unsolved for decades and it survived the communist regime in Poland.

---

8 Cf. D. Popovic, "Pilot Judgments of the European Court of Human Rights", in: Council of Europe, *The role of the Supreme Courts in the domestic implementation of the European Convention on Human Rights* (Proceedings of the Regional Conference Belgrade 20-21 September 2007) Strasbourg 2008, 112-114; Ph. Leach, H. Hardman, S. Stephenson & B.K. Blitz, *Responding to Systemic Human Rights Violations*, Antwerp – Oxford – Portland 2010, 22.

9 *Viasu v. Romania*, app. no. 75951/01, judgment of 9 December 2008; see paragraph 9.4. Some authors use the name of "quasi pilot judgments" for this type; cf. Leach et al. (fn. 8), 24-26.

10 R. Deneger and P. Mahoney, "The Prospects for a Test Case Procedure in the European Court of Human Rights", in: H. Hartig (ed.), *Trente ans de droit européen des droits de l'homme – études à la mémoire de Wolfgang Strasser*, Bruxelles 2007, 173-207; Popović (fn. 8), 107-122; Leach et al. (fn. 8), 32-187.

11 *Broniowski v. Poland*, ECHR 2004-V; *Broniowski v. Poland* (friendly settlement), ECHR 2005-IX; *Hutten-Czapska v. Poland*, ECHR 2006-VIII; *Hutten-Czapska v. Poland* (striking out), ECHR 2008. For bibliography see Berger (fn. 2), 735-736 (Broniowski) and 759 (Hutten-Czapska).

The number of indemnification demands pending on a national level was huge. It amounted to 80.000, while some 160 cases of the same kind were pending with the Court when the judgment in *Broniowski* was rendered.[12] The technique of pilot-judgments was for the first time used in the *Broniowski* case, thus representing a new way forward. It was based on the respective recommendations of the Committee of Ministers, which invited the Court to examine the effectiveness of legal remedies in the domestic legislation of a member state, contracting party to the Convention, in order to prevent the emergence of repetitive cases before the Court.[13]

In the operative part of the *Broniowski* judgment the Court first held in items 2 and 3 that there was a violation of Article 1. First Protocol, as well as that it had originated in a systemic problem, connected with the malfunctioning of domestic legislation and practice. The latter consisted of the failure of the respondent government to set up an effective mechanism of indemnification of the so-called Bug River claimants. The Court's prescription of a general measure of redress found its place in item 4 of the operative part of the judgment, which read:

> "[t]he respondent State must, through appropriate legal measures and administrative practices, secure the implementation of the property right in question in respect of the remaining Bug River claimants or provide them with equivalent redress in lieu, in accordance with the principles of protection of property rights under Article 1 of Protocol No. 1."[14]

Although this was in line with one of the recommendations of the Committee of Ministers of 12 May 2004 I have mentioned above, it is to be noted that the wording of the Court's prescription was styled in a rather general manner.[15] As a matter of fact its wording was very much similar to that of a recommendation. It is indeed the place of this text which is decisive, for it was put in the operative part of the judgment and that fact represents the basic distinction between recommendations and prescriptions. Only the latter find themselves in operative parts of judgments. However, if we are to consider the substance of this particular prescription of a measure of redress of the Court's we cannot find any specific orders to a member state. The Parties to the Convention are sovereign states and the Court could not go too far in prescribing general measures of redress. It should also be underlined

12 L. Garlicki, "Broniowski and After: On the Dual Nature of Pilot Judgments", in: L. Caflisch et al. (eds.), *Liber Amicorum Luzius Wildhaber, Human Rights – Strasbourg Views*, Kehl – Strasbourg – Arlington 2007, 180-181.

13 Committee of Ministers' Resolution of 12 May 2004. Res. (2004) 3 and 6. See also V. Zagrebelsky, "Questions autour de Broniowski", in: L. Caflisch et al. (eds.), *Liber Amicorum Luzius Wildhaber, Human Rights – Strasbourg Views*, Kehl – Strasbourg – Arlington 2007, 526-527.

14 *Broniowski v. Poland*, ECHR 2004-V.

15 Cf. D. Popovic, *Protecting Property in European Human Rights Law*, Utrecht 2009, 97.

that in giving its judgment in the *Broniowski* case the ECHR concurred with the stance of the Polish Constitutional Court on the issue. Besides, the Polish government had already introduced a bill in parliament in order to move towards a solution of the problem.[16]

Despite the Court's timid language and a rather diplomatic approach to prescribing general remedies for violations of human rights, a real novelty has been introduced. It was for the first time that the Court put such a prescription in the operative part of a judgment.

In another Polish case the Court used the same approach and the technique of a pilot judgment. The case also concerned Article 1 First Protocol; it was the case of *Hutten-Czapska*.[17] The applicant complained of having been prevented from the peaceful enjoyment of her possessions because of the restrictive legal provisions on a domestic level relating to rent. The restrictive system of rent control was introduced in Poland under the communist regime. It was amended after the restoration of democracy, but it was deemed to be unfavourable or at least unsatisfactory to the owners of apartments. Some provisions of the amended legislation were declared unconstitutional by the Polish Constitutional Court. The problem posed by the rent control regulations was estimated to have affected approximately 100,000 flat owners.

The Court found a violation of Article 1 First Protocol in this case, stating that it arose from a systemic problem. In item 3 of the operative part of the judgment the Court went so far as to specify the origins of the problem, these being connected with the malfunctioning of domestic legislation. The latter consisted of two main features:

> "(a) it imposed, and continues to impose, restrictions on landlords' rights, including defective provisions on the determination of rent;
> (b) it did not and still does not provide for any procedure or mechanism enabling landlords to recover losses incurred in connection with property maintenance."

Despite using such a particularly precise formula to demonstrate the origin of the systemic problem on a domestic level, resulting in violations of human rights, the Court was still prudent in prescribing general measures of redress. Basically, the same formula was used in that respect as the one the Court applied in *Broniowski*. The wording in the two judgments was similar, for the Court stated in item 4 of the operative part of the judgment in *Hutten-Czapska* as follows:

> "[t]he respondent State must, through appropriate legal and/or other measures, secure in its domestic legal order a mechanism maintaining a fair balance

---

16 Cf. Popovic (fn. 15), 115.
17 *Hutten-Czapska v. Poland*, ECHR 2006-VIII.

> between the interests of landlords and the general interests of the community, in accordance with the standards of protection of property rights under the Convention (see paragraph 239 above)".

What was said earlier in this chapter in respect of the *Broniowski* judgment applies to the judgment in *Hutten-Czapska*, as well. The Court refrained from specifying the substance of the general measures of redress. However a small difference between the judgments is to be noted insofar as the formula, concerning measures of redress, used in *Hutten-Czapska* in the operative part of the judgment contains a reference to a paragraph of its text, being paragraph 239. In that paragraph the Court proceeded to reflect upon the substance of measures which were to be introduced on a national level, noting the freedom of choice of the respondent state in respect of such measures. However the Court made a step further by indicating the substance of those. The Court did so in the last passage of the paragraph 239 of the judgment, which read:

> "The Court would, however, observe in passing that the many options open to the [respondent] State certainly include the measures indicated by the Constitutional Court in its June 2005 Recommendations, setting out the features of a mechanism balancing the rights of landlords and tenants and criteria for what might be considered a 'basic rent', 'economically justified rent' or 'decent rent'."

The Court was marching along its own prudent lines, but it nevertheless introduced originality by way of reference to the law part of the judgment, where the Court addressed the issue of substance of measures of redress in a more specific way.

9.4 Expanding Pilot Judgments

In a number of cases the Court has followed the pattern of the "old style" or, to borrow the expression from Philip Leach and his colleagues, "full" pilot judgments. This trend is evident in several cases of 2009. Let me mention them here without going into details of each and every case. They are: *Burdov v. Russia (no. 2)*, *Olaru and Others v. Moldova*, *Yuriy Nikolayevich Ivanov v. Ukraine* and *Suljagic v. Bosnia and Hercegovina.*[18] An overall examination of these judgments should show that the Court has become more specific in spelling out the duties of the state, and has indeed started prescribing the substance of the

18 *Burdov v. Russia (no. 2)*, app. no. 33509/04, judgment of 4 May 2009; *Yuriy Nikolayevich Ivanov v. Ukraine*, app. no. 40450/04, judgment of 15 October 2009; *Olaru and Others v. Moldova*, app. nos. 476/07, 22539/05, 17911/08, 13136/07, judgment of 28 October 2009; *Suljagic v. Bosnia and Hercegovina*, app. no. 27912/06, judgment of 3 November 2009; for comments see Leach et al. (fn. 8), 18-22.

measures of redress in the operative parts of judgments. What was hinted at in *Hutten-Czapska* became a rule by 2009. There is however a background to this stance of the Court's where I will begin.

The story begins with a somewhat peculiar case in which the Court seems to have expanded its powers to prescribe general measures of redress to such an extent that it was reminiscent of an attempt to limit the sovereign power of a member state, contracting party to the Convention. The case was *L. v. Lithuania* and judgment was given in 2007.[19] The case concerned reassignment of sex and the issue before the Court was whether the applicant had the right to have a state funded sex change operation. The key element of the case consisted of the fact that Lithuanian legislation granted such a right, but its enjoyment was subject to the terms posed by secondary legislation, which has never been adopted. The Court went so far as to order the respondent state to pass a piece of legislation within a specified period.

The Court's prescription of a general measure of redress, consisting of the adoption of a statute, was far-reaching. It required a national parliament to adopt an act within a short period, despite all possible complications susceptible to show up in the parliamentary procedure. In other words, the measure prescribed seemed to be surprisingly rigid. However the Court's way out of the problem was the introduction of the alternative, enabling the respondent state to comply with the judgment by paying a sum of money specified in the operative part of the judgment, along with the general measure of redress prescribed. The operative part of the judgment, under items 4 and 5 read as follows:

> [The Court]
> 5. *Holds* by five votes to two that the respondent State, in order to satisfy the applicant's claim for pecuniary damage, is to pass the required subsidiary legislation to Article 2.27 of its Civil Code on gender reassignment of transsexuals, within three months of the present judgment becoming final, in accordance with Article 44 § 2 of the Convention;
> 6. *Holds* by six votes to one that alternatively, should those legislative measures prove impossible to adopt within three months of the present judgment becoming final in accordance with Article 44 § 2 of the Convention, the respondent State is to pay the applicant EUR 40,000 (forty thousand Euros) in respect of pecuniary damage.

This was a real innovation, which did not find support from all the judges sitting on the bench. One of the judges was against the admissibility of the application on the grounds

19 *L. v. Lithuania,* app. no. 27527/03, judgment of 11 September 2007.

of non-exhaustion of domestic remedies. Another judge dissented, being of opinion that "by adopting such a solution, the Court risks acting *ultra vires*".[20]

This opinion of the dissenting judge is quite significant, because it clearly shows the state of mind within the sitting judges of the Court. Not all of them were ready to adopt such a bold step as to prescribe a specified general measure of redress.[21] It seemed at first that the case of *L. v. Lithuania* was not to make echoes in the Court's case-law, for the prudent approach towards prescribing general measures of redress prevailed.

Let me point out that the judgment, given in *L. v. Lithuania*, was not a pilot judgment, despite that fact the Committee of Ministers in its supervisory role proceeded as if it were. This was done in an atmosphere in which pilot judgments gained grounds to such an extent that we can actually speak of their expansion.

The turning point came in 2009 with a series of pilot judgments, all of them belonging to the old style and mentioning the measures of redress for systemic violations of human rights in their operative parts.[22] These were all chamber judgments and in each and every one of them the Court, following the technique of pilot judgments, made specific prescriptions to the respondent states in respect of the general measures they were to adopt in order to comply with the Court's rulings.

It was the case of *Burdov (no. 2)* that opened the series. The applicant, who had succeeded in a previous case before the ECHR, was entitled to certain benefits because of his illness, provoked by the Chernobyl disaster. He repeatedly sued the authorities on a domestic level, but the judgments obtained in his favour remained unenforced. When he filed another complaint with the ECHR the Court found a systemic violation of Article 6 of the Convention. The Court stated in the operative part of the judgment under item 6 as follows:

> "[The] respondent State must set up, within six months from the date on which the judgment becomes final ... An effective domestic remedy or combination of such remedies which secures adequate and sufficient redress for non-enforcement or delayed enforcement of domestic judgments in line with the Convention principles as established in the Court's case-law."

Commentators have remarked that the Court "did not specify that the general measures required a legislative response as such", but it however "laid down a specific timetable"

20 See the separate opinion of Judge Fura-Sandstrom attached to the judgment.

21 Cf. my comments on the case: D. Popovic, "Prevailing of Judicial Activism over Self-Restraint in the Jurisprudence of the European Court of Human Rights", *Creighton Law Review* Vol. 42, no. 3 (2009), 389-390.

22 See footnote 18.

for the adoption of those.[23] There are commentators who praise the Court's approach in *Burdov (no. 2)* as "a final way to put pressure on the respondent state".[24] This is basically true and that is what makes the difference between this judgment and the one rendered in *L. v. Lithuania*, where the Court referred to the passing of subsidiary legislation in the operative part of the judgment. However, although the measures required by the Court were not specified, one could hardly imagine the introducing of a new domestic remedy in a different way from legislation. Substantially the Court's approaches in the two judgments, mentioned here, are the same. The Lithuanian authorities were given the possibility of opting to pay a sum of money to the applicant, which they chose, whereas the Russian authorities submitted a bill to the parliament in order to comply with the Court's judgment.[25] What is more, the Committee of Ministers acted as if the judgment given in the Lithuanian case offered no possibility of option for the respondent government.

In the case of *Yuriy Nikolayevich Ivanov v. Ukraine* the problem was similar to the one in *Burdov*. The systemic problem consisted of non-enforcement of judgments on a domestic level. The Court followed the same avenue of pilot judgments and used almost the same formula in item 5 of the operative part of the judgment, which read:

> "[The] respondent State must set up without delay, and at the latest within one year from the date on which the judgment becomes final ... an effective remedy or a combination of such remedies which secures adequate and sufficient redress for non-enforcement or delayed enforcement of domestic judgments in line with the Convention principles as established in the Court's case-law."

The Court was marching on along the same lines. In *Olaru and Others v. Moldova* the problem was the non-implementation of legislation granting provisions for public employees. Therefore the Court slightly adapted the wording of the operative part of its judgment, stating in item 4:

> "[The] respondent State must set up, within six months from the date on which the judgment becomes final ... an effective domestic remedy which secures adequate and sufficient redress for non-enforcement or delayed enforcement

23 Leach et al. (fn. 8), 19.

24 A. Buyse, "The Pilot Judgment Procedure at the European Court of Human Rights: Possibilities and Challenges", in: *Nomiko Vima – European Court of Human Rights, 50 Years*, Athens 2010, 84.

25 For Lithuania cf. D. Jociene, "The Subsidiary Character of the System of the European Convention on Human Rights with Reference to Cases against Lithuania", *Baltic Yearbook of International Law*, Vol. 9/2009, 33-35. For Russia cf. Leach et al. (fn. 8), 144; see also Council of Europe – Committee of Ministers, Supervision of the execution of judgments of the European Court of Human Rights, 3rd annual report 2009, 136-137.

> of final domestic judgments concerning social housing in line with the Convention principles as established in the Court's case-law."

Moreover, the Court added in the next item 5 of the operative part:

> "[The] respondent State must grant such redress within one year from the date on which the judgment becomes final, to all victims of non-enforcement or unreasonably delayed enforcement of social housing final judgments in cases lodged with the Court before the delivery of the present judgment."

If we compare the judgment in *Olaru and Others* to the two cases mentioned above, *Burdov (no. 2)* and *Yuriy Nikolayevich Ivanov*, it is to be noted that the Court went a step further in *Olaru*, because it specified the substance of the measures to be taken. That judgment marks a slow evolution in the Court's attitude towards prescribing general measures of redress.

The evolution was evident in the judgment that followed. In *Suljagic* the respondent state was Bosnia and Hercegovina and the issue at stake were foreign currency savings, which could not be withdrawn from the banks. The Court held that Article 1 of the First Protocol was violated on the case. In the operative part of the judgment the respondent state was given a time-limit of six months to comply with the judgment by (a) issuing government bonds in the Federation of Bosnia and Hercegovina, (b) paying instalments and (c) undertaking to pay the default interest.[26]

The peculiarity of the *Suljagic* judgment consists in the fact that it was indeed one of the two entities constituting the state of Bosnia and Hercegovina, which was to adopt the general measures of redress, for it was only in that entity that the systemic problem occurred. This is however not specifically significant for the purpose of this book. On the contrary, it is to be noted that the Court specified the substance of the general measure, thus following the pattern offered by the *Olaru* judgment.

The Court has been constantly evolving its attitude towards prescribing general measures of redress for violations of human rights. Their prescription has almost become a practice when applying the pilot judgment procedure. At the same time the Court has become more specific in posing duties upon member states in the sense that the Court is more precise about what measures are to be taken by a respondent state to comply with a judgment of the Court.

---

26 *Suljagic v. Bosnia and Hercegovina*, app. no. 27912/02, judgment of 3 November 2009, operative part, item 5. For comments on the case see: A. Grgic et al., *The right to property under the European Convention on Human Rights*, Strasbourg 2007, 42 (referring only to the admissibility decision taken in 2006).

What was exceptional in *L. v. Lithuania* does not seem to be such any more. A recent example can be quite illustrative in this respect, showing how the Court's judgments constitute new and rather specific obligations to member states. In the case of *Greens and M.T. v. The United Kingdom* the Court took its own previous judgment as a starting point.[27] The previous case was *Hirst v. The United Kingdom (no. 2)* in which the Grand Chamber found a violation of Article 3 First Protocol because of disenfranchisement of convicted prisoners under domestic legislation. Persons being convicted and serving a prison sentence were excluded from voting in local and parliamentary elections in the United Kingdom.[28] The Court used in *Hirst (no.2)* in paragraph 83 of the judgment its usual formula:

> "[The] Court notes that its function is in principle to rule on the compatibility with the Convention of the existing measures. It is primarily for the State concerned to choose, subject to supervision by the Committee of Ministers, the means to be used in its domestic legal order to discharge its obligation under Article 46 of the Convention."

Five years elapsed before one of the Court's chambers had to face the same issue in respect of the same member state. In *Greens and M.T. v. the United Kingdom* the issue of voting in prison was also at stake. The Court therefore made a reference to the judgment in *Hirst (no. 2)*. The Court's main finding was, as expressed in paragraph 77 of the judgment, that the British relevant legislation had not been amended since the judgment of the Court's in *Hirst (no. 2)*. The member state had failed to comply with its obligations stemming from a previous judgment of the Court. Moreover there had meanwhile been a large number of follow-up applications filed with the Court, concerning the same issue.

The situation I have just described in respect of non-complying with the judgment in *Hirst (no. 2)* gave the Court a pretext for altering its approach slightly and reintroducing the pattern of the old type pilot judgments. While the obligation to comply with a judgment of the Court had been put outside the operative part, as we have seen above, the Court expressed its stance more resolutely in *Greens and M.T. v. The United Kingdom*. Item 6 of the operative part in the latter judgment provided as follows:

> "[The] respondent State must bring forward, within six months of the date upon which the present judgment becomes final, legislative proposal intended to amend the 1983 Act and, if appropriate, the 2002 Act in a manner which is Convention-compliant."

27 *Greens and M.T. v. The United Kingdom*, app. nos. 60041/08 and 60054/08, judgment of 23 November 2010.
28 *Hirst v. The United Kingdom (No. 2)*, ECHR 2005-IX.

The approach the Court made in this case shows a line of development, if compared to the judgment in *L. v. Lithuania*. What once upon a time was an exception tends to become a rule. The Court demands the introduction of a new and Convention-compliant piece of legislation. However the approach in *Greens and M.T.* seems to be more realistic because it insists only on introducing a bill into the parliamentary procedure within a specified time-limit. This does not change the substance. By issuing pilot judgments the Court imposes obligations to amend and improve domestic legislation, which would have hardly been imaginable at the time when the Convention was drafted.

It should also be pointed out that, as far as the handling of pilot judgments is concerned, the Court has enjoyed an increased amount of support from the Committee of Ministers. This body has turned out to be very efficient and industrious in fulfilling its task consisting of the supervision of the execution of judgments. Such an attitude by the Committee of Ministers has led to the expansion of pilot judgments. These judgments, representing a new tool for the protection of human rights, have been labelled by commentators in two ways. Some insist on the fact that pilot judgments enhance the approach which brings the ECHR closer to the pattern of work practised by the constitutional courts of the member states, contracting parties to the Convention.[29] Others are of opinion that the mode of handling pilot judgments, especially while supervising their execution, serves the purpose of returning the protection of human rights to a national level, where it actually belongs.[30]

29 Garlicki (fn. 12), 192. I expressed the same view, cf. Popovic (fn. 7), 121. See also Buyse (fn. 24), 83 (with a reference to Sadurski, whose paper was published in 2008)

30 Buyse (fn. 24), 85 (with a reference to an article published in 2008 by Costas Paraskeva).

Conclusion of Part Three

At the end of this part of the book a question may arise, whether the Court has predominantly tended to develop the law of the Convention, by introducing innovations or to restrain itself, while performing its activity in the process of the emergence of the European human rights law.

This is a point of discussion that I have recently covered in academic papers. The question was thoroughly researched by Paul Mahoney, currently chief justice of the Administrative Tribunal of the European Union, who was previously the registrar of the ECHR for many years. He addressed the topic at the beginning of the 1990s and concluded that the Court's activism and self-restraint were, as he put it, "two sides of the same coin". Neither of the two tendencies or techniques that have just been mentioned prevailed in his view.[1]

Nineteen years later I addressed the same topic in a lecture given in an American university.[2] My conclusion was different from Mahoney's, for it seemed to me that a tendency to develop the law and bring in innovations had prevailed in the Court's approach to cases. It is difficult to know whether this was due to the amount of time which had elapsed between the two articles during which the Court had slowly altered its attitude, or maybe to some other reason.

While my first conclusion concerning this part of the book is the mere existence of legal developments, which finally resulted in completing the emergence of the whole corpus of European human rights law, my second conclusion will attempt to complete this. It is obvious that the Court, throughout the developments I have just referred to, has slightly shifted from the application of Article 41 of the Convention to a way of practice in which the application of that provision goes in parallel with the one of Article 46.[3] The latter served for the most part the purpose of evolving remedies of redress for violations of human rights. This was a spontaneous process and I very much doubt that it was ever a proper plan by the judges sitting on the bench of the ECHR to achieve such an outcome. On the

1 P. Mahoney, "Judicial Activism and Self-Restraint in the European Court of Human Rights: Two Sides of the Same Coin", *Human Rights Law Journal*, 11 (1990). Cf. substantially the same opinion as Judge Malinverni, prefacing the thesis of E. Kastanas, *Unité et diversité: notions autonomes et marge d'appréciation des Etats dans la jurisprudence de la Cour européenne des droits de 'homme*, Bruxelles 1996, ix.

2 D. Popovic, "Prevailing of Judicial Activism over Self-Restraint in the Jurisprudence of the European Court of Human Rights", *Creighton Law Review* Vol. 42, no. 3 (2009), 361-396.

3 My esteemed colleague, Judge Birsan, also stressed the fact of parallel application of the articles of the Convention in one of his recent academic papers; cf. C. Birsan, "Les aspects nouveaux de l'application des articles 41 et 46 de la Convention dans la jurisprudence de la Cour européenne des droits de l'homme"; in: H. Hartig (ed.), *Trente ans de droit européen des droits de l'homme -études à la mémoire de Wolfgang Strasser*, Bruxelles 2007, 43.

contrary, the judges were guided by necessity and they mostly faced the challenges they had to deal with when rendering justice in particular cases.

Finally, if we were to analyse the Court's powers after having highlighted the developments, which were based on those powers and represent the outcome of their use, it occurs to me that it is necessary to introduce a slight rectification to a conclusion one might make at first glance. Namely, the Court's powers are basically to interpret the Convention and to afford remedies for violations of human rights. However, these powers seem to be threefold, rather than twofold, if we consider the substance of the legal developments set out in this part.

While affording remedies to repair violations of human rights, the Court has made use of adjudicating just satisfaction, but it went beyond, so as to develop measures of redress, under Article 46 of the Convention. By developing measures of redress the Court diversified its approach to the protection of human rights and accordingly effectually exercised the power to recommend, as well as the one to prescribe a remedy. This is what makes the Court's powers threefold, for the ECHR is competent to interpret the Convention, but also to recommend a measure of redress and finally to even prescribe one. As time goes on the latter becomes more and more frequent in the Court's jurisprudence. In the course of development marked by evolving remedies aiming at redressing of violations of human rights, the pilot judgments turned out to be an important lever to enhance this evolution. It has been used by the Court with a considerable amount of support coming from the Committee of Ministers of the Council of Europe based on the power to supervise the execution of Court's judgments vested with that body.

Part 4
Redefining the Fundamental Approach to the Protection of Human Rights

INTRODUCTION

The fundamental approach of the founding fathers of the Convention to the idea of the protection of human rights was that the state should refrain from interfering with human rights of individuals, guaranteed by the Convention. Such a starting point did not need any particular explanation; on the contrary it was comprehensive *per se*. The state is a subtle and sophisticated mechanism by far superior in strength, if compared to individuals. For that reason the latter need protection when they have to face that potentially harmful machinery capable of interfering with their rights. The ECHR was founded and vested with a mission to provide such protection to individuals.

The fundamental idea of the founding fathers was expressed in a picturesque way in the Consultative Assembly of the Council of Europe at the time of adopting the draft of the future Convention. It was Philip MP, whose words, as translated for the official minutes, were the following:

> "[W]hen a fundamental freedom has been violated, an individual, even the most humble, even the weakest, may be able to come before the Court as an equal of the greatest State or the most powerful Government."[1]

The Convention and the Court were to create a realm of security for individuals, by providing them equality before the law. They were to prevent the state from interfering with human rights. It was therefore evident that the primordial obligation of a state, contracting party to the Convention, was construed to be negative. Namely, the state must not interfere with human rights, and in abstaining from such interference it would basically satisfy the requirements of the Convention.

Several articles of the Convention were drafted in such a way as to confirm and illustrate this basic approach of the founding fathers. For instance, the wording of Article 8(2) is quite significant in this respect:

> "There shall be no interference by a public authority with the exercise of this right..."

Similar wording was used in Articles 9, 10 and 11 of the Convention. Limitations and conditions of exercise of freedoms can only be prescribed by law and they must be such

1 Collected Edition of the "Travaux Préparatoires" of the European Convention on Human Rights, Volume II, The Hague 1975, 262.

that are necessary in a democratic society. In these provisions the concept of a negative obligation of the state *i.e.* the obligation to abstain from interfering with individuals' rights, is expressed in the clearest and most evident way.

The rights contained in the articles of the Convention, that I have mentioned, are called freedoms, a fact which reflects the idea of a private sphere free from interference by the State, which is not allowed to interfere with the rights guaranteed by respective provisions. It is therefore worth noting that the founding fathers of the Convention used the same expression of freedom for no less than seven fundamental rights, out of ten, originally envisaged by the draft.[2]

The main concern of the founding fathers of the Convention was to provide on "what a state must not do", rather than to what it must do.[3] In other words, the founding fathers took the negative obligation of a state as the main concept and a starting point in the construction of the European mechanism of the protection of human rights.

It is also to be noted that the text of the Convention provides on some positive obligations of the states, contracting parties to the Convention.[4] Above all this is the case in Article 1 of the Convention, which provides a general obligation to respect human rights. The same applies to Article 46, providing on obligation to abide by the final judgment of the Court, but also to some others. An example can be found for instance in Article 6, which creates the obligation of a member state to organise the administration of justice on a national level in such a way as to enable a fair trial for everyone. The same also applies to Article 3 First Protocol, under which the states are to hold free elections regularly etc.

However, positive obligations were for the most part, to borrow an expression from Harris, O'Boyle and Warbrick, "read into" the Convention by the Court.[5] The topic of this part of the book is to show how the Court, by the evolution of its jurisprudence, slowly transformed the main standpoint of the founding fathers. The Court has on many occasions developed the Convention in such a way as to favour the rise of positive obligations of member states. By doing so it has, to a considerable extent, redefined the basic approach of the founding fathers of the Convention to the protection of human rights, which relied on perceiving the obligations of member states as primordially negative.

This part of the book is composed of two chapters. One deals with a general approach to the concept of state obligations and their various types, as well as definitions of these

2 Collected Edition (fn. 1), 276.

3 I am borrowing the expression from Professor Merrills, as quoted by Alastair Mowbray; see A. Mowbray, *The Development of Positive Obligations under the European Convention on Human Rights by the European Court of Human Rights*, Oxford – Portland Oregon 2004, 3.

4 D.J. Harris, M. O'Boyle & C. Warbrick, *Law of the European Convention on Human Rights*, Oxford – New York 2009, 19.

5 Ibid.

(Chapter X). The other considers the rise of positive obligations in the Court's jurisprudence (Chapter XI).

X A General Approach to the Concept of State Obligations

There is some discrepancy among academics concerning the types of state obligations in respect of the protection of human rights. Although usually perceived by most of the writers in this field to be twofold, there are some who expose on three different types of state obligations.

State obligations lack definition in the text of the Convention and they should be properly defined and classified by the scholars. The origin of positive obligations in the Court's case-law merits special attention.

10.1 A Threefold Typology

The usual division of state obligations under the Convention is twofold. Along with the situations in which member states are to refrain from interfering with the rights guaranteed by the Convention, there are others, in which the state is to properly act in fulfilling its mission to protect human rights. In order to define the second sort of obligations just mentioned German literature on the subject has developed the notion of a "duty to protect" (*Schutzpflicht*).[1] What's more, the Germans have developed an overall concept of a "duty to perform" (*Gewährleistungspflicht*), which is considered to represent a starting point in understanding what in English is called positive obligations under the Convention.[2]

The French authors also make the basic distinction between the two main types of state obligations. Let me take Sudre as an example. He adopts the usual dichotomy of *droits de* and *droits à* or in other words the dichotomy of *abstantion/prestation* in respect of state obligations to protect human rights.[3] However, the same author underlines the fact that the usual dichotomy has been called into question by the practice of the ECHR, because some state obligations can be considered to be mixed in character. They actually stand between the two types of obligations universally accepted by the scholars.[4]

The dichotomy of state obligations has its origin in the distinction between two types of rights, namely civil and political on the one hand, and social and economic on the other.[5]

1 Ch. Grabenwarter, *Europäische Menschenrechtskonvention*, München – Wien 2003, 140.
2 Ibid. 139.
3 F. Sudre, *Droit européen et international des droits de l'homme*, Paris 2005, 234-235.
4 Ibid.
5 Sudre (fn. 3), 235.

It has been remarked that civil and political rights are generally referred to as protecting individuals against intrusion by the state, whereas "socio-economic rights are rights to protection by the state against want or need."[6] The distinction of two types based on the substance of the rights is however mostly doctrinal, for as it has been rightly observed that there are civil and political rights that also demand state action. One example is the obligation to organise the system of justice in such a way as to provide a fair trial in each and every legal suit.[7]

There are legal authors who have chosen to divide state obligations in respect of human rights into three different groups, instead of only two. One version of the tripartite typology is to be found in Harris, O'Boyle and Warbrick, who refer to three different types of obligations, namely the obligations to respect, protect and fulfil human rights.[8] Slightly different names given to the various types of obligations by another author do not introduce any substantial change. Akandji-Kombe speaks of obligations to respect, to protect and to implement.[9]

This rather short review of the doctrine well shows the efforts made by many authors to fit the developments of the Court's case-law into a comprehensive system. To close the heading I shall agree with Renucci, who insists on the fact that the ECHR has never been in favour of elaborating a general theory of positive obligations.[10] This being true, a remark should be added that developing theories has never been a task for the Court. Its rulings have formed the foundations for the fruitful efforts of legal scholars, who have developed the doctrine of state obligations in respect of human rights protection and the various types of obligations.

10.2 Positive and Negative Obligations

There is no proper and clear-cut definition of positive obligations in the Court's case-law. It should be added at once that there is no definition of negative obligations either. However, as I have already stated in the Introduction to this part of the book, a negative obligation is somehow comprehensive *per se*. The state should not interfere with individual rights and it should therefore refrain from action. In other words, the negative obligations can

6 S. Fredman, *Human Rights transformed – positive rights and positive duties*, Oxford – New York 2008, 66.
7 Sudre (fn. 3), 235-236.
8 D.J. Harris, M. O'Boyle & C. Warbrick, *Law of the European Convention on Human Rights,* Oxford – New York 2009, 19.
9 J.-F. Akandji-Kombe, *Positive Obligations under the European Convention on Human Rights*, Strasbourg 2007, 5.
10 J.-F. Renucci, *Droit européen des droits de l'homme*, Paris 2002, 518.

well be perceived as *obligations to respect* human rights.[11] This is a conclusion one can draw from a brief analysis of the literature on this subject.

A positive obligation of the state, says Mowbray, is an obligation, which creates for the state a "duty to undertake specific affirmative tasks".[12] This general approach to the definition of positive obligations varies among authors, while preserving its core substance. Thus, for instance, Grabenwarter says that in a presence of a positive obligation the state is constrained to enable and ensure the exercise of fundamental rights by positive measures.[13] Sudre defines positive obligations as those calling for state performance.[14] This goes along with Renucci's opinion, who also insists on positive measures by the state, as a main element of a definition of positive obligations.[15]

As the scholars are unanimous in substance, as far as the definition of positive and negative obligations is concerned, let me give the final word to Akandji-Kombe who has somehow synthesised the common approach made by different authors:

> "What distinguishes positive obligations from negative obligations is that the former require positive intervention by the state, whereas the latter require it to refrain from interference."[16]

Another part of the endeavour to define positive obligations may begin at this point. It concerns different kinds of positive obligations, as perceived and understood by scholars. The legal authors contributing to this area of research speak of procedural and substantive, as well as of express and implied positive obligations.

10.3 Types of Positive Obligations

There are two different criteria to classify the positive obligations of a state in respect of human rights. One tends to distinguish between two types of obligations by taking their substance into account, whereas the other is based on the origin of the obligations. Both typologies find their roots in the Court's case-law.

11 Cf. Harris, O'Boyle & Warbrick (fn. 8), 19; Akandji-Kombe (fn. 9), 5, 10-11.

12 A. Mowbray, *The Development of Positive Obligations under the European Convention on Human Rights by the European Court of Human Rights*, Oxford – Portland Oregon 2004, 2.

13 Grabenwarter (fn. 1), 139-140: "Hier ist der Staat gefordert, durch positive Maßnahmen … Grundrechtsausübung erst zu ermöglichen und sicherzustellen."

14 Sudre (fn. 3), 235: "réclamant des prestations de l'État."

15 Renucci (fn. 10), 518.

16 Akandji-Kombe (fn. 9), 11.

10.3.1 Procedural and Substantive Obligations

The criterion for distinguishing procedural and substantive positive obligations lies in the substance of the action expected of the state.[17] Substantive positive obligations are those which require measures to be provided by the state in order to enable the individuals to enjoy their fundamental rights, guaranteed by the Convention. An example of this kind can be found in the case of *Öneryildiz v. Turkey*, where the question was whether it was incumbent upon the public authorities to introduce measures preventing a gas explosion in a slum quarter. The Grand Chamber of the Court held in paragraph 101 of the judgment:

> "[The authorities] consequently had a positive obligation under Article 2 of the Convention to take such preventive operational measures as were necessary and sufficient to protect individuals."[18]

Another example of a substantive positive obligation can be found in *Hurtado v. Switzerland*. The issue was whether detained persons were entitled to prompt medical treatment.[19] The Court was in a position to pronounce a friendly settlement between the parties, but it is the opinion of the old Commission of Human Rights, acting at that time, which deserves our attention. The Commission stated in paragraph 79 of its opinion on the case:

> "Article 3 of the Convention requires the State authorities to adopt measures to safeguard the physical well-being of a person placed in the charge of the police, judicial or prison authorities.
> Under Article 3 of the Convention the State has a specific positive obligation to protect the physical well-being of persons deprived of their liberty."

In both examples taken at random the substantive character of the positive obligation incumbent on state authorities is clearly visible. The authorities were supposed to take action and introduce measures, the outcome of which would have been to avoid the violation of a particular provision contained in the Convention, guaranteeing human rights of individuals. By failing to act and take the respective measures the authorities breached their positive obligations, which resulted in violating the Convention. The measures that should have been taken by the authorities did not concern judiciary proceedings. On the

---

17 Akandji-Kombe (fn. 9), 16.

18 *Öneryildiz v. Turkey*, ECHR 2004-XII; on the case see P. van Dijk et al. (eds.), *Theory and Practice of the European Convention on Human Rights*, Antwerpen – Oxford 2006, 363; F. Sudre et al., *Les grands arrêts de la Cour européenne des droits de l'homme*, Paris 2003, 497-505.

19 *Hurtado v. Switzerland*, Judgments and Decisions A 280 (1994). See the Commission's opinion attached to the Court's striking out judgment, paragraph 79; on the case see Mowbray (fn. 12), 52.

contrary they fell within the scope of state administrative action. It is quite different if we turn to the other kind of positive obligations belonging to this typology, namely the procedural ones.

A procedural positive obligation of the state exists in situations in which a procedural action is required of the state.[20] This can be, for instance, the case when the State is under an obligation to conduct a proper investigation in a criminal matter. One of the cases in which the Court held that such obligation existed was *Nachova v. Bulgaria.*[21] The case concerned the shooting, by a police officer, of two Roma conscripts, who were allegedly trying to escape. The domestic judiciary ruled that the officer had acted in accordance with the regulations. The Grand Chamber of the Court held unanimously that there had been a violation of Article 2 of the Convention, on the grounds that the respondent state had failed to comply with its positive obligation to conduct an effective official investigation. The Grand Chamber expressed its view in paragraph 110 of the judgment in the following manner:

> "The obligation to protect the right to life under Article 2 of the Convention, read in conjunction with the State's general duty under Article 1 of the Convention to 'secure to everyone within [its] jurisdiction the rights and freedoms defined in [the] Convention' requires by implication that there should be some form of effective official investigation when individuals have been killed as a result of the use of force."

In the following paragraphs (111-113) the Court made it clear what effective investigation actually meant. It covers the fact that the authorities must act of their own motion once the matter has come to their attention. The persons responsible for and carrying out the investigation must be independent and impartial in law and in practice. Finally, the investigation must also be effective in the sense of leading to a determination of whether the force used was justified or not in the circumstances and to the identification and punishment of those responsible. To fulfil all these requirements was the positive obligation of the state. As it referred to the elements of a judicial procedure, in which state action was required, it is perceived and defined as procedural.[22]

In the case of *Ramsahai v. The Netherlands* the Grand Chamber invoked its own ruling in *Nachova* and went further by introducing details in order to make the procedural obligation of conducting an independent investigation more precise.[23] The case was similar

20 Cf. Akandji-Kombe (fn. 9), 17.

21 *Nachova v. Bulgaria,* ECHR 2005-VII; for bibliography see V. Berger, *Jurisprudence de la Cour européenne des droits de l'homme,* Paris 2009, 29.

22 Harris, O'Boyle & Warbrick (fn. 8), 49.

23 *Ramsahai v. The Netherlands,* ECHR 2007-.

to *Nachova*. It concerned the tragic event of a shooting of a young man by police officers. The Grand Chamber held in paragraph 356 of the judgment that there was on the side of the respondent state "[a] failure to comply with the procedural obligation imposed by Article 2 of the Convention".

This was based on the Grand Chamber findings that the investigation, which took place in the Netherlands, was inadequate and that it lacked independence. The starting point was the authority of the *Nachova* judgment, which was invoked in paragraph 321 of the judgment.[24] As to the inadequacy of the investigation, the Court found in paragraph 332 in *Ramsahai* that the investigation had not clarified the inconsistency of the statements of the police officers involved, which was crucial for establishing the truth on the event. The lack of independence in the investigation was rooted, in the Court's view, in the fact that the same police unit conducted the forensic examination and the questioning of witnesses. This was not sufficient to ensure the full independence of the investigation, as the Court stated in paragraph 296 of the judgment, despite the existence of the supervision of independent body.

The Court's ruling in *Ramsahai* was thus developing the approach made in *Nachova*. The example well illustrates the way the Court handles the positive obligations of the state. The general trend reflected in the two cases just mentioned was to introduce details and make a positive obligation more precise.

10.3.2 Express and Implied Obligations

It has already been mentioned in this chapter that some of the positive obligations of the state in respect of human rights are to be found in the text of the Convention. Two examples immediately spring to mind. Firstly, it is the overall obligation of Article 1 to secure to everyone within State jurisdiction the rights and freedoms guaranteed by the Convention, and secondly, the obligation of Article 46 (1) is to abide by the final judgment of the ECHR.

There are other positive obligations belonging to this group, provided for by several articles of the Convention. However, it is not always easy to identify the existence of such positive obligations, if merely considering the text of the Convention. If we take the examples offered by Harris, O'Boyle and Warbrick, the difficulty will become obvious.[25] The positive obligations mentioned by the authors at the relevant point in their book are those envisaged in Articles 2(1), 3 and 6 of the Convention, as well as the one in Article 3 First Protocol. The wording of the respective provisions poses problems. It is clear that Article 2(1) contains a positive obligation for the state, because it reads:

---

24 *Ramsahai v. The Netherlands,* ECHR 2007, paragraph 321. Paragraphs 110-113 of the judgment in *Nachova* were cited.

25 Cf. Harris, O'Boyle & Warbrick (fn. 8), 19.

> "Everyone's right to life shall be protected by law. No one shall be deprived of his life intentionally save in the execution of a sentence of a court following his conviction of a crime for which this penalty is provided by law."[26]

It is much less easy to identify a state positive obligation in Article 3 of the Convention. The eminent authors I have cited above understand the provision of that article of the Convention to mean that the state must provide prison conditions that are not inhuman.[27] It needs a bit more interpretation effort to reach such a conclusion, to which of course I agree, when reading the text of Article 3 of the Convention, where it is provided:

> "No one shall be subject to torture or to inhuman or degrading punishment".

The same applies to Article 6 of the Convention, guaranteeing the right to a fair trial. The eminent authors understand the provision so as to create an obligation upon the state "to provide courts, legal aid and translators in connection with the right to a fair trial". It is true that courts, free assistance and interpreters are mentioned in the text, but the wording is such that does not directly express the obligation of the state.

On the contrary, the wording of Article 3 First protocol is quite clear in this respect, because it says:

> "The High Contracting Parties undertake to hold free elections..."

The mode and scope of interpretation enables one to identify the existence of a positive obligation incumbent on the state. Therefore it might be dubious in some cases whether the text of the Convention and its additional Protocols actually provides for a positive obligation or not. Express positive obligations are not always undisputedly formulated. Besides, they are less numerous than those belonging to the other group of positive obligations mentioned in the heading.

By contrast to the express obligations, most of the state positive obligations are, to borrow the expression from Alastair Mowbray, "*judicial creations*".[28] Or in other words, they have been "*read into the Convention by the Court*".[29]

The two kinds of positive obligations differ insofar as their legal basis is concerned. The express positive obligations find their legal bases in the text of the Convention itself.

---

26 It should nevertheless be noted that this text no longer represents a valid provision of European law of human rights. It was abolished by Article 1 Sixth Protocol, which reads: "The death penalty shall be abolished. No one shall be condemned to such penalty or executed".

27 See footnote 25.

28 Mowbray (fn. 12), 2.

29 The expression used by Harris, O'Boyle & Warbrick (fn. 8), 19.

Those that are implied are more problematic and rather complex in this respect. The Court has developed positive obligations taking the Convention as a starting point, despite the fact that its text lacked an express wording on the subject. Therefore questions of justification, methodology of the Court's approach, scope and even the mere existence of an implied positive obligation generally arise.[30]

Implied positive obligations of the state are by far more numerous that those being express in origin. As they are creations of the Court's jurisprudence they must be adequately treated and properly researched. The latter task has been performed by scholars.

10.4 Origins of Positive Obligations

It is to be concluded from the previous heading that implied positive obligations were more numerous than those that were express. At the same time it was exactly this kind of obligations which mostly contributed to the development of the whole concept of positive obligations, as well as to redefining the fundamental approach by the Court to the protection of human rights. It is therefore of interest to turn to the origins of positive obligations, with a special reference to the roots of those among them which are implied.

At this point I agree with Frédéric Sudre. In his opinion the origins of positive obligations are basically to be found in the effective character of the rights guaranteed by the Convention. As guaranteed rights must necessarily be effective, state positive obligations are inherent in those rights.[31] In his view it is the positive obligation which completes, in a certain way, the right, as guaranteed under the Convention. Without such an obligation there would have been no rights for individuals.

However, it was the ECHR that formulated this kind of approach to the protection of human rights and Sudre invokes the Court's ruling in *Airey v. Ireland* in support of his thesis.[32] As early as in 1979 the question was raised in this case. The issue was the impact of the Convention on the realisation of social and economic rights within states parties. The Court held in paragraph 26 of the judgment in *Airey* as follows:

> "[The Convention] is designed to safeguard the individual in a real and practical way as regards those areas with which it deals. Whilst the Convention sets forth what are essentially civil and political rights, many of them have implications of a social and economic nature…There is no water-tight division separating that sphere from the field covered by the Convention."

30 Mowbray (fn. 12), 2.

31 Sudre (fn. 3), 236-237.

32 *Airey v. Ireland,* Judgments and Decisions A 32 (1979).

In *Airey* free assistance was at stake, but the Court nevertheless took a broader stand towards the problem in the paragraph cited above. It was evident to the judges that the whole sphere of social and economic issues would have to be tackled by the Court's jurisprudence, if the Convention was to guarantee fundamental rights in a proper manner. This was a deviation from the ideas of the founding fathers of the Convention, as expressed for instance by Lord Layton MP, who took the floor during the first session of the Consultative Assembly in 1949 to pronounce the following words:

> "What we are proposing to do is to define and guarantee the political basis of this association of European nations. What the members of this association are saying, if this proposal materializes, is that the maintenance of certain basic democratic rights in any one of our countries is not the concern of that country alone, but it is the concern of the whole group."[33]

Three decades elapsed between the moment at which those words were pronounced and the adoption of the judgment in *Airey*, in which the Court held that it was insufficient to stick exclusively to civil and political rights. If these were to be made effective the state had to act in order to enable individuals to make proper use of their rights. Therefore it was the social and economic sphere of state action that led to the introduction and rise of state positive obligations. Their rise represented the process of profoundly transforming and actually redefining the fundamental approach to the protection of human rights. If the state fails to act and take proper measures providing for its positive obligations, inherent in the rights guaranteed by the Convention, the State is to be held liable for violations of human rights.[34] Public authorities are quite simply not allowed to remain passive when human rights are at stake; on the contrary, they are under an obligation to perform their duties in this regard.

33 *Collected Edition of the "Travaux Préparatoires" of the European Convention on Human Rights,* Volume III, The Hague 1975, 50.

34 F. Sudre (fn. 3), 238.

XI The Rise of Positive Obligations

11.1 Addressing the Issue

It has been underlined by an eminent scholar that the ECHR refuses to elaborate a general theory of state positive obligations, originating in the Convention, while at the same time it almost systematically uses the technique of positive obligations in its own jurisprudence.[1] I must say I agree with Sudre on this point, with the only remark that developing legal theory does not fall within the Court's role. This is the mission of the scholars and academic researchers. As to the achievements of the latter it is indispensable to mention some valuable contributions, which resulted in well known publications. At least two titles deserve to be put forward here, and both of them have already been cited in this part of the book. One is Mowbray's monograph, which appeared in 2004 and the other is Akandji-Kombe's handbook of 2007, published in the Council of Europe series of Human rights handbooks.[2] The former has more data and more profound analysis of relevant cases, whereas the latter has a somewhat broader approach to general issues and theory.

As an illustration of the state of mind in academic circles, in which state positive obligations have been gaining ever more ground, one could take the example of a well reputed manual on European Human Rights Law. While I was preparing the manuscript of this book the 5th edition of the manual, by Jacobs & White appeared.[3] It is worth noting that, as far as the positive obligations are concerned, the authors made efforts to complete and make the text of their book up-to-date by adding passages concerning positive obligations in respect of several articles of the Convention. That was the case for protection from slavery and forced labour, private life, home and correspondence, freedom of thought, conscience and religion, freedom of expression, as well as for freedom of assembly and association.[4] Such an effort to expose on positive obligations on points where it had not been done so previously clearly shows the progress of the concept of positive obligations in various fields of European human rights law. The development of the Court's case-law

1 F. Sudre, *Droit européen et international des droits de l'homme*, Paris 2005, 238.

2 See footnotes 3, A. Mowbray, *The Development of Positive Obligations under the European Convention on Human Rights by the European Court of Human Rights,* Oxford – Portland Oregon 2004; J-F. Akandji-Kombe, *Positive Obligations under the European Convention on Human Rights,* Strasbourg 2007.

3 Now I am referring to Jacobs, White & Ovey, *The European Convention on Human Rights*, Oxford – New York 2010. I shall use the most recent edition in this part of the book. In previous parts of the book I used the third edition of the manual, which appeared in 2002.

4 Cf. Jacobs, White & Owey (fn. 3), 198; 358-361; 422-423; 449-450; 452-453.

lay behind the attitude of the learned authors, who wanted to get in line with the evolution of the concept of positive obligations.

One more remark seems to be necessary under this heading. Its purpose is to address the issue of the rise of positive obligations in general. In the lines to follow in this chapter I intend to expand on state positive obligations in respect of various articles of the Convention. The approach does not tend to be exhaustive and embrace the phenomenon as a whole, *i.e.* all possible types of state positive obligations under the Convention. Quite the contrary, my intention is to take those examples which best demonstrate the topic of Part 4 of this book, namely to display the shift in the general approach to the protection of human rights and the way of redefining that approach by developing positive obligations.

11.2 Outstanding Examples of State Positive Obligations in Respect of Guaranteed Rights

11.2.1 *Difficulty to Systemise*

It is not easy to introduce a proper systemic pattern when dealing with state positive obligations to respect human rights. Most of these have emerged in the Court's jurisprudence, a fact which at least to some extent calls for a case to case approach to the phenomenon.

If positive obligations are not easy to systemise and expose in a clearly comprehensive survey, they are certainly tokens of the shift in the general approach to the protection of human rights, as performed by the Court. The way in which human rights law operates today substantially differs from the original ideas of state inactivity and non-interference in the sphere of guaranteed fundamental rights, prevailing at the time of the founding fathers of the Convention. Positive obligations, for the most part, merit to be considered as one of the main sources of such a significant difference.

11.2.2 *Duty to Protect and to Investigate (Article 2 of the Convention)*

Duty to Protect Life

The relevant provision of Article 2 of the Convention states that:

> "Everyone's right to life shall be protected by law."

At the beginning this was supposed to mean that the state must refrain from intentional and unlawful taking of one's life. The preparatory work shows that the origin of this provision is to be found in Article 3 of the Universal Declaration of Human Rights of the United Nations of 1948.[5]

It was in the 1990s that several of the Court's judgments heralded the idea of the existence of a positive obligation implied in Article 2 of the Convention. The right to life, as guaranteed by that provision, found its corollary concept in the duty of the state to protect human life.

The first case in which the Court tackled the issue of a positive obligation implied in Article 2 of the Convention was *McCann and Others v. United Kingdom.*[6] The case concerned events which took place in Gibraltar, where the British Army was deployed in order to prevent anti-British action by the illegal Irish Republican Army (IRA). The outcome was fatal for Mr. McCann, Ms. Farrell and Mr. Savage. The applicants alleged that the killing of these three persons by the security forces constituted a violation of Article 2 of the Convention.

The Court firstly agreed with the Commission of Human Rights and stated in paragraph 161 of the judgment:

> "[A] general legal prohibition of arbitrary killing by the agents of the State would be ineffective, in practice, if there existed no procedure for reviewing the lawfulness of the use of lethal force by State authorities."

However, the Court did not find a violation of Article 2 (1) of the Convention on these grounds.[7] The Court did not find the killings to have been premeditated either.[8] The applicants submitted before the Court, as expressed in paragraph 186 of the judgment, *in fine* that:

> "[T]he killings came about as a result of incompetence and negligence in the planning and conduct of the antiterrorist operation to arrest the suspects as well as a failure to maintain a proper balance between the need to meet the threat posed and the right to life of the suspects."

The investigation of the events established that the suspects, who lost their lives, had been unarmed and that they had not had a detonator device, as well as that there had been no bomb in the car, as the security forces had suspected. The soldiers who shot the three

5 *Collected Edition of the "Travaux Préparatoires" of the European Convention on Human Rights,* Volume III, The Hague 1975, 44; 276.

6 *McCann and Others v. United Kingdom*, Judgments and Decisions A 324 (1995); for bibliography see V. Berger, *Jurisprudence de la Cour européenne des droits de l'homme,* Paris 2009, 23.

7 See paragraphs 162-164 of the *McCann* judgment.

8 Cf. paragraphs 174-184 of the judgment.

persons admitted that they shot to kill.[9] The question before the Court, as formulated in paragraph 201 of the judgment, therefore was:

> "[W]hether the anti-terrorist operation as a whole was controlled and organised in a manner which respected requirements of Article 2 and whether the information and instructions given to the soldiers which, in effect, rendered inevitable the use of lethal force, took adequately into consideration the right to life of the three suspects."

The Court gave a response to this question in its findings contained in paragraphs 212-213 of the judgment. The Court concluded that it remained unclear whether the soldiers participating in the operation had been properly trained and instructed to use their firearms so as to only wound their targets in the specific circumstances. The Court also found that it could not be proved that the use of force by the soldiers was no more than absolutely necessary in the defence of persons from unlawful violence within the meaning of Article 2(2) of the Convention. On these grounds the Court held in paragraph 214 of the judgment that there was a breach of Article 2 of the Convention.

The judgment in *McCann* was rendered by ten votes to nine. The nine dissenting judges were of opinion that the Court did not have sufficient reason to conclude that another different and more suitable form of training should have been given to the soldiers. They also expressed the view that the reproaches made concerning the control and organisation of the arrest operation were not justified.[10]

The most important point of disagreement between the majority and the minority of judges consisted, in the opinion of the latter, of the fact that

> "[No] failings have been shown in the organisation and control of the operation by the authorities which could justify a conclusion that force was used against the suspects disproportionately to the purpose of defending innocent persons from unlawful violence... [The] use of lethal force in this case, however regrettable the need to resort to such force may be, did not exceed what was, in the circumstances as known at the time, 'absolutely necessary' for that purpose and did not amount to a breach by the United Kingdom of its obligations under the Convention."[11]

9 Cf. paragraphs 198-199 of the judgment.
10 See the joint dissenting opinion of the nine judges, attached to the *McCann* judgment, paragraph 24.
11 Joint dissenting opinion, paragraph 25.

It was the standard of the use of force when absolutely necessary, provided for in Article 2(2) of the Convention that was at the origin of the development. On the one hand, as we have seen above, the Court ruled in favour of the right of individuals to challenge the use of force first before domestic courts and then also before the ECHR. On the other hand, such use of force was clearly subject to the ECHR scrutiny.

It has been remarked by Mowbray that the Court did not adopt the applicants' attitude towards a positive obligation arising from Article 2 of the Convention, but it nevertheless assessed and scrutinised for the first time the conduct of public authorities' armed forces in the course of their operation.[12] There are legal writers who, like Baumgartner, go a bit further, so as to interpret the judgment in *McCann* as introducing a special positive obligation of the state. This author is of opinion that such an obligation is based on what is called "organisational fault".[13]

Another example of the Court's approach to positive obligations under Article 2 of the Convention can be found in the case of *L.C.B. v. United Kingdom.*[14] The case concerned the atmospheric test of nuclear weapons carried out by the British in the Pacific Ocean, more specifically on Christmas Island. During such tests, service personnel were ordered to line up in the open and to face away from the explosions with their eyes closed and covered until twenty seconds after the blast. The applicant alleged that the purpose of this procedure was to expose servicemen to radiation for experimental purposes. The Government denied such allegations.

The applicant's father was present on Christmas Island during tests in 1957 and 1958. The applicant, who was born in 1966, was in about 1970 diagnosed with leukaemia. The applicant's hospital records stated "Father – Radiation exposure" among positive causative factors of her disease. She received chemotherapy treatment until the age of ten, missed half of her primary school education and was unable to participate in sport and other normal childhood activities. At the time in which the Court gave judgment on her case the applicant still had regular medical check-ups and was afraid to have children, because of a genetic predisposition to leukaemia.[15]

The applicant's complaint before the ECHR, as stated in paragraph 25 of the judgment, was that

> "[The] State's failure to warn her parents of the possible risk to her health caused by her father's participation in the nuclear tests, and its earlier failure

12 Mowbray (fn. 2), 9.

13 Ch. Grabenwarter, *Europäische Menschenrechtskonvention*, München – Wien 2003, 157. The German expression is *Organisationsverschulden*.

14 *L.C.B. v. United Kingdom*, Reports 1998-III.

15 *L.C.B. v. United Kingdom*, paragraphs 10-16 (As to the facts).

> to monitor her father's radiation dose levels, gave rise to violations of Article 2 of the Convention."

In this judgment the Court attempted for the first time to take a stand on the scope of Article 2 of the Convention from the standpoint of the state's positive obligations.[16] Before giving the floor to the Court and citing its holding it is worth mentioning that the Court found no violation in the case. The Court held that it had no jurisdiction to consider the applicant's complaint concerning the state's failure to monitor the extent of her father's exposure to radiation, because the complaint had not been raised before the Commission. The Court also found no violation of Article 2 of the Convention in relation to the state's failure to advise the applicant's parents and monitor her health prior to her diagnosis with leukaemia.

Despite such a verdict on the merits, one of the Court's *dicta* deserves attention, because it put the Court's stance towards positive obligations under Article 2 of the Convention in clear wording. The Court stated in paragraph 36 of the *L.C.B.* judgment:

> "[The] Court considers that the first sentence of Article 2 (1) of the Convention enjoins the State not only to refrain from the intentional and unlawful taking of life, but also to take appropriate steps to safeguard the lives of those within its jurisdiction."

Three years after the ruling in *McCann* this was a breakthrough. The Court recognised that there was a positive obligation incumbent on the state under Article 2 of the Convention. It did not limit itself to scrutinising the state's conduct, a fact from which originated a positive obligation in respect of the right to life.

The academics are almost unanimous in evaluating the meaning of the Court's *dictum* in *L.C.B.* Thus, Renucci for instance, interprets the Court's ruling as a general enlargement of the field of application of Article 2 of the Convention, in the sense that it could apply to the State's dangerous activities, menacing the lives of individuals.[17] Sudre refers to the above-mentioned *dictum* as grounds for the overall obligation of the state to protect life by law.[18]

Mowbray appears to have a slightly different approach from the authors mentioned so far, for he insists that the Court's ruling in another case is primordial. He cites the Court's holding in *Osman v. United Kingdom*, a case from the same year as *L.C.B.* in which

---

16 Cf. Akandji-Kombe (fn. 2), 21. It is to be noted that the Court cited an authority from its own case-law, but it concerned Article 8 of the Convention.

17 J.-F. Renucci, *Droit européenne des droits de l'homme,* Paris 2002, 79.

18 Sudre (fn. 1), 275.

the Court actually invoked its own holding in *L.C.B.* as authority.[19] However, despite the difference in sources the wording remains the same, for the *Osman* judgment only reproduced the respective rule of *L.C.B.* which puts Mowbray in line with all the other authors I have cited above. The implied positive obligation of the state has emerged in the wording, if not in the final holding on the two cases mentioned above, no matter which of the two judgments of 1998 we take as the milestone.

In two Turkish cases the Court developed its approach to the positive obligation to protect life under Article 2 of the Convention. Both cases were judged in 2000. They were the cases of *Mahmut Kaya* and *Kilic.*[20] The cases were given judgments by the same chamber and on the same date. In both cases the applicants alleged that their brothers were assassinated by state security forces, which however could not be proved. One of the persons who lost their lives was a medical doctor and the other was a journalist. They had been associated with the PKK, an illegal organisation, favouring Kurdish separatism.[21]

In *Mahmut Kaya* the Court took a precise stance on the existence of a positive obligation to protect life under Article 2 of the Convention, by putting in paragraph 86 the following reasoning:

> "[Not] every claimed risk to life can entail for the authorities a Convention requirement to take operational measures to prevent that risk from materializing. For a positive obligation to arise it must be established that the authorities knew or ought to have known at the time of the existence of a real and immediate risk to the life of an identified individual or individuals from the criminal acts of a third party and they failed to take measures within the scope of their powers which, judged reasonably, might have been expected to avoid that risk."

That is why the Court, even though it was not established beyond reasonable doubt that any State agent had been involved in the killing of doctor Hasan Kaya, held the Turkish State liable on the grounds that it had failed to protect his life.[22]

In *Kilic v. Turkey* the applicant's brother, Kemal Kilic, who lost his life under unclarified circumstances, was a journalist in south-eastern Turkey. He had informed the province governor of the death threats he had received and requested protection. The governor's office refused him protection. A month later Kemal Kilic was found dead. The Court ruled that there had been a violation of Article 2 of the Convention on the grounds of the state's

19 Cf. Mowbray (fn. 2), 15-16 and *Osman v. United Kingdom*, Reports 1998-VIII, paragraph 115, where paragraph 36 of the *L.C.B.* judgment is cited. The Court found no violation of Article 2 of the Convention in *Osman*, as was also the case in the previous authority.

20 *Mahmut Kaya v. Turkey*, ECHR 2000-III; *Kilic v. Turkey*, ECHR 2000-III.

21 For analysis and comments see Jacobs, White & Ovey (fn. 3), 152-153.

22 *Mahmut Kaya v. Turkey*, item 1 of the operative part of the judgment.

failure to protect life.[23] The Court's ruling used an identical formula to the one we have seen in *Mahmut Kaya*.[24]

The rule was clear and it set a positive obligation to protect life under Article 2 of the Convention based on the fact that the state authorities "knew or ought to have known" that there had been an immediate risk to the life of an individual. It is also to be noted that the victim in *Kilic* had complained to the authorities of the existence of such a risk.

In a recent case before the Court the question was raised on the excessive character of the burden put on the state. The case was *Dink v. Turkey*.[25] The Court applied the test that it had already developed in its previous jurisprudence. Although the victim, a journalist, who had been murdered by an ultranationalist, had not demanded protection, the authorities were actually aware of the threat to the journalist's life, or at least they ought to have been aware. This is why the Court held there was a violation of Article 2 of the Convention.[26]

Duty to Investigate Killings and Suspicious Deaths

The origin of a positive obligation implied in Article 2 of the Convention and consisting of a duty to investigate a killing, incumbent on a member state, contracting party to the Convention, is to be found in the rule of paragraph 161 of the *McCann* judgment. As the rule has already been cited above, let me only rephrase it in order to repeat its essential elements. Arbitrary killing by state agents is prohibited. Such a prohibition would nevertheless turn out to be ineffective in the absence of a procedure for reviewing the lawfulness of the use of lethal force by state authorities.

In *McKerr v. United* Kingdom the Court provided justification for its stance on the State's duty to investigate a killing.[27] The case concerned the killing of suspected terrorists by the British security forces in Northern Ireland in 1982. The Court delivered judgments in three similar cases on the same date. These were followed by a series of judgments concerning killings by the security forces in Northern Ireland.[28] In all cases the Court found violations of Article 2 of the Convention on the grounds of an implied procedural positive obligation. The insufficiencies of the investigation provided grounds for the Court's holdings.

Substantially, the Court reiterated in *McKerr* its own standpoint as expressed in *McCann*, but the Court developed its approach and made it more detailed in respect of justifying

23 *Kilic v. Turkey*, item 1 of the operative part of the judgment.

24 Cf. paragraph 63 of the judgment in *Kilic* to the paragraph 86 of *Mahmut Kaya* judgment, cited in the text above.

25 *Dink v. Turkey*, app. nos. 2668/07, 6102/08, 7072/09 and 7124/09, judgment of 14 September 2010.

26 *Dink v. Turkey*, app. nos. 2668/07, 6102/08, 7072/09 and 7124/09, paragraph 74.

27 *McKerr v. United Kingdom*, Reports 2001-III.

28 Jacobs, White & Owey (fn. 3), 160.

the rule on the state's positive obligation. It was in paragraph 111 of the *McKerr* judgment that the Court, beginning with the most general duty incumbent on the State to secure the rights and freedoms under the Convention, stated as follows:

> "The essential purpose of such an investigation is to secure the effective implementation of the domestic laws which protect the right to life and, in those cases involving State agents or bodies, to ensure their accountability for deaths occurring under their responsibility."

The effective character of guaranteed rights was at the origin of the duty to investigate. The state was to implement its own law to protect human rights and in order to make this effective it was necessary to investigate the killings. This was an element already contained in the rule of *McCann*. However, the formula of the *McKerr* judgment seems to have broadened the approach in the sense that it widened the scope of the obligation to investigate to encompass killings both by state agents and private persons.[29]

The Court did not limit itself to discovering the positive obligation to investigate killings. Its jurisprudence set certain requirements that such investigations had to fulfil, if they were to comply with the state's obligations under the Convention. In short, the investigation of a killing of a person must be carried out by an independent body, it must be prompt and also, it must lead to the identification and punishment of the responsible persons.[30]

In *Šilih v. Slovenia* the Court developed its jurisprudence on procedural obligations arising from Article 2 of the Convention.[31] The case concerned the death of the applicants' son, who lost his life subsequent to an allergic reaction to a medical treatment he had been subject to.

The operation of national law was at stake. The domestic legal rules provided for procedures to investigate, but these were too slow by far and did not meet the demand of reasonable expedition.[32] The Court found a violation of the state's duty to investigate and ruled in paragraph 154 of the judgment:

> "The Court notes the State's obligation to carry out an effective investigation or to provide for the possibility of bringing civil or criminal proceedings as may be appropriate to the case has in the Court's case-law been considered as an obligation inherent in Article 2 which requires, *inter alia*, that the right to life be 'protected by law'. Although the failure to comply with such an obligation

---

29 Thus, Mowbray (fn. 2), 30.

30 Cf. a short and clear exposé of the three requirements by Akandji-Kombe (fn. 2), 34-35.

31 *Šilih v. Slovenia*, ECHR 2009-.

32 For comments on the case see Jacobs, White & Ovey (fn. 3) 161; D.J. Harris, M. O'Boyle & C. Warbrick, *Law of the European Convention on Human Rights*, Oxford – New York 2009, 51.

> may have consequences for the right protected under Article 13, the procedural obligation of Article 2 is seen as a distinct obligation."

The Court thus reiterated its own stance on the duty to investigate, even in those circumstances in which, as the Court stated in paragraph 156 of the same judgment, the state was not ultimately found responsible for the death of a person. Its positive obligation was to conduct the investigation promptly and with reasonable expedition. The proceedings in the Slovenian case that I have just cited lasted for more than a decade, which led the Court to find a violation of the state's positive obligation and give its ruling accordingly.

11.2.3 From Prohibiting Torture to Introducing Safeguards (Article 3 of the Convention)

Drafters' Intentions

Article 3 of the Convention is a rather short text. It provides:

> "No one shall be subject to torture or to inhuman or degrading treatment or punishment."

The idea that was at the origin of inserting this provision into the Convention was to prevent state organs from continuing with practices which were considered to be irreconcilable with the rule of law and human civilization. A British MP to the Consultative Assembly, Cocks, expressed the grounds for introducing such a provision in an almost poetical way, saying:

> "I feel that this is occasion when this Assembly should condemn in the most forthright and absolute fashion this retrogression into barbarism. I say that to take the straight beautiful bodies of men and women and to maim and mutilate them by torture is a crime against high heaven and the holy spirit of man. I say that it is a sin against the Holy Ghost for which there is no forgiveness. I declare that it is incompatible with the civilization."[33]

Mr. Cocks insisted further on in his speech that torture should be "absolutely condemned" and that "no cause whatever" could be deemed sufficient to "justify its use or existence". It was evident from the words I have just quoted that the state was prohibited from using a certain conduct, consisting of torture, inhuman or degrading treatment of an individual.

33 *Collected Edition* (fn. 5), 40.

Thus, the main idea of the drafters of the text of the Convention was clearly brought to light – the substance of the provision of Article 3 was prohibitive. The states parties to the Convention were not allowed to use a certain conduct, considered to be uncivilized. However, the Court's jurisprudence introduced novelties, consisting of positive obligations, based on the Court's subtle approach to the problems and questions raised in its day-to-day practice of implementing this particular provision of the Convention.

Controversial Comments

If one wants today, after decades of evolution of the Court's case-law, to make an inventory of the positive obligations arising from Article 3 of the Convention, the first and maybe most striking feature will be to establish that the commentators are not unanimous on the types of positive obligations existing within the realm of that article. Three examples can illustrate well the state of mind in this respect.

Jacobs, White and Ovey are of opinion that positive obligations under Article 3 of the Convention involve two elements. The first one is that measures of the Contracting Party must "constitute effective deterrence". The second element is the "requirement for an effective investigation capable of leading to prosecution of well-founded allegations of ill-treatment".[34] The authors thus seem to be tending towards the classification of positive obligations under Article 3 into two different types. Some of these are substantial and the others procedural.

Mowbray for his part also admits the existence of procedural positive obligations within the scope of Article 3 of the Convention. At the same time he does not find any common denominator for the non-procedural positive obligations. He therefore seems to be inclined to a method consisting of enumeration, while displaying such obligations. This author exposes on "protective measures", "acceptable conditions of detention", "adequate medical treatment for detainees" and the "duty to investigate" as positive obligations of the State under Article 3 of the Convention.[35]

Akandji-Kombe also provides an example of the enumerative method in his approach to the same problem. However, he finds different positive obligations under Article 3 of the Convention, if compared to the authors I have quoted above. He classifies among these "the protection of minors", then "the protection of persons deprived of their liberty", as well as "the protection of close relatives of persons who have disappeared".[36]

The situation in regard of positive obligations originating in Article 3 of the Convention is not an exception. Quite the contrary, it could rather be perceived as a rule. The positive

34 Jacobs, White & Ovey (fn. 3), 176.

35 Mowbray (fn. 2), 43-65.

36 Akandji-Kombe (fn. 2), 28-32.

obligations are of jurisprudential origin. They are complex in character, not necessarily easy to define and there might be even some doubt as to their scope and their very existence.

The Court has not always been sufficiently clear in spelling out these obligations. That is why there are controversial comments and discrepancies of approach to the phenomenon among legal writers. I shall therefore once again allow myself, for the purposes of this book, to deal with only those positive obligations, which seem to be the most illustrative of the subject I am treating – redefining the fundamental approach of the Court's to the protection of human rights.

Ill-Treatment by Private Individuals

It was clear from the text of the Convention that state agents had to refrain from performing torture or degrading or inhuman treatment. Nevertheless the text left the door open for interpretation. Its wording did not exclude the possibility of construing the provision of Article 3 as generally prohibiting certain patterns of behaviour, irrespective of whether its perpetrator was a state agent or not. It was in the 1980s that the question of whether the rule of Article 3 could apply in a case when inhuman treatment was perpetrated by someone who was not a state agent was raised before the Court.

The Court responded in the negative in the case of *Campbell and Cosans v. United Kingdom.*[37] The issue at stake was the use of corporal punishment as a disciplinary measure in the state schools in Scotland. The Court refused to follow *Tyrer* and unanimously found no violation of Article 3 on the case.

The Court repeated its stance in another British case. It was *Costello-Roberts v. United Kingdom*, a case dating from 1993, in which the Court held that the corporal punishment, inflicted on the applicant, who was seven years of age, in a boarding school did not constitute a violation of Article 3 of the Convention.[38] This judgment was given by a majority vote of five to four. The minority of judges expressed the opinion that "the ritualised character of the corporal punishment [was] striking".[39] More important than this was the attitude of the dissenters that:

> "Article 3 is the first point of reference for examining a case concerning disciplinary measures at school."

---

37 *Campbell and Cosans v. United Kingdom,* Judgments and Decisions A 48 (1982); for bibliography see Berger (fn. 6), 642-43.

38 *Costello-Roberts v. United Kingdom,* Judgments and Decisions A 247 C (1993); for comments on the case see Jacobs, White & Ovey (fn. 3), 177; Harris, O'Boyle & Warbrick (fn. 32), 107; Akandji-Kombe (fn. 2), 28; A. Reidy, *The prohibition of torture*, Strasbourg 2003, 17. For bibliography see Berger (fn. 6), 88-89.

39 Cf. Joint Partly Dissenting Opinion of Judges Ryssdal, Thor Vilhjalmsson, Matscher and Wildhaber, attached to the judgment.

The position taken by the dissenting judges in *Costello-Roberts* heralded a tendency towards a shift in the Court's stance towards the scope of applicability of Article 3 of the Convention. The boarding school in which the events of the case occurred was an independent one and received no financial support from the government.[40] The headmaster of the school, who administered the corporal punishment, could therefore by no means be perceived as a state agent. Some of the sitting judges, although representing the minority in this affair, were in favour of the applicability of Article 3 of the Convention to the case. However, their opinion could not prevail in the early 1990s.

The landmark case came five years later, towards the end of the 1990s. It was *A. v. United Kingdom*.[41] The issue in this case was whether a beating of a nine-year old boy with a garden cane, given by the boy's stepfather, should be awarded protection under Article 3 of the Convention. The Court held that there was a violation of Article 3, putting it clearly in paragraph 22 of the judgment:

> "[The] obligation on the High Contracting Parties under Article 1 of the Convention to secure to everyone within their jurisdiction the rights and freedoms defined in the Convention, taken together with Article 3, requires States to take measures designed to ensure that individuals within their jurisdiction are not subjected to torture or inhuman or degrading treatment or punishment, including such ill-treatment administered by private individuals."

The main contribution to the interpretation of Article 3 of the Convention consisted of introducing its extended meaning, which granted protection against ill-treatment of individuals performed by private persons. At the same time the Court advanced its reasoning by making reference to taking "measures designed to ensure" that no one within the jurisdiction of a member state, contracting party to the Convention is submitted to ill-treatment. This clearly referred to a positive obligation of the state.

In the present case the respondent state actually failed to provide adequate protection against inhuman treatment, which constituted a violation of Article 3 of the Convention.

It was not only the extension of the meaning of the provision of Article 3 which was the outcome of the Court's ruling in *A. v. United Kingdom*; it was indeed the recognition of a positive obligation of the state to prevent private persons from performing ill-treatment. An extensive interpretation of Article 3 of the Convention was however at the origin of the developments described under this heading.

---

40 *Costello-Roberts v. United Kingdom*, Judgments and Decisions A 247 C (1993) paragraph 7.

41 *A. v. United Kingdom*, Reports 1998-VI; for comments on this case and further developments of the Court's case-law see Harris, O'Boyle & Warbrick (fn. 32), 107; Mowbray (fn. 2), 44-47; Reidy (fn. 38), 37.

Medical Treatment of Detainees

The Court's jurisprudence has developed an overall positive obligation of the state to create acceptable conditions of detention for persons deprived of liberty.[42] One of the important aspects of such an obligation consists of the provision of adequate medical treatment to detained persons.[43]

We have seen above that the Court held in *Hurtado v. Switzerland* that the state authorities were required to provide safeguards for the well-being of a detained person.[44] The Commission for Human Rights found in that case in favour of the applicant. The Court struck the case from the list, because the government of Switzerland had reached a friendly settlement with the applicant, who was a Colombian national and had to wait eight days after the arrest to be examined by a medical practitioner. The applicant suffered a fracture of a rib.[45] The Commission's view, expressed in paragraph 79 of its opinion was that:

> "Article 3 of the Convention requires the State authorities to adopt measures to safeguard the physical well-being of a person placed in the charge of the police, judicial or prison authorities."

The idea of a positive obligation incumbent on the state was thus quite evident. The authorities were not to refrain from action, but on the contrary, they had to perform activity, which was to result in the physical well-being of the detained person.

One of the frequently discussed, although somewhat peculiar, cases concerning the positive obligation to provide medical care to persons deprived of liberty was *Kudla v. Poland.*[46] The applicant in that case was a detainee suffering from depression and with suicidal tendencies. The adequacy of the psychiatric care of the applicant was at issue.[47] The Grand Chamber of the Court found no violation of Article 3 of the Convention, for as stated in paragraph 96 of the judgment:

> "during his detention the applicant regularly sought, and obtained, medical attention".

---

42 Cf. Mowbray (fn. 2), 48-52; Akandji-Kombe 29-31 (fn. 2); Sudre (fn. 1), 294-298; P. van Dijk et al. (eds), *Theory and Practice of the European Convention on Human Rights*, Antwerpen – Oxford 2006, 420-425; Reidy (fn. 38), 26 who describes the evolution of the Commission's and Court's positions in respect of the conditions of detention.

43 Mowbray (fn. 2), 52-59; Van Dijk et al. (fn. 42), 440.

44 *Hurtado v. Switzerland*, Judgments and Decisions A 280 (1994); see footnote 24.

45 Mowbray (fn. 2), 52; Van Dijk et al. (fn. 42), 424.

46 *Kudla v. Poland,* ECHR 2000-XI; for bibliography see Berger (fn. 6), 403-404; see also F. Sudre et al., *Les grands arrêts de la Cour européenne des droits de l'homme*, Paris 2003, 110-118.

47 For the Court's stance on positive obligations in cases of mentally ill persons see Reidy (fn. 38), 29-31.

It has been observed by some commentators that the ruling in *Kudla* confirmed an implied guarantee of respectful treatment of detainees.[48] Others went as far as to interpret the Court's stance in the judgment as putting an obligation upon the state to "provide detainees with 'requisite medical assistance'".[49] *Kudla* certainly reaffirmed the existence of a state positive obligation to supply medical treatment to detainees, despite the fact that there had been no violation of Article 3 found in the case.

In *Keenan v. United Kingdom* the duty of the state authorities to protect a prisoner suffering from mental illness was again at stake.[50] The applicant's son committed suicide in prison. He had had psychiatric treatment for a personality disorder, while serving a prison sentence. However, effective medical monitoring was lacking, which resulted in significant defects in the medical care provided to a mentally disturbed person held in custody.

The Court started its reasoning on the Article 3 issue by invoking its general stance in paragraph 111 of the judgment:

> "[The] authorities are under obligation to protect the health of persons deprived of liberty. The lack of appropriate medical care may amount to treatment contrary to Article 3."

The Court went further and held that there was a violation of Article 3 of the Convention on the case. The Court expressed the grounds for its holding in paragraph 116 of the judgment, saying:

> "The lack of effective monitoring of Mark Keenan's condition and the lack of informed psychiatric input into his assessment and treatment disclose significant defects in the medical care provided to a mentally ill person known to be a suicide risk."

This judgment was given on the merits in respect of Article 3 of the Convention by a majority of five votes to two. The dissenting judges, Fuhrmann and Kuris, invoked the Court's holding in *Kudla* as a general rule, that they were supportive of.[51] The reason for

48 Sudre et al. (fn. 46), 112.
49 Mowbray (fn. 2), 55.
50 *Keenan v. United Kingdom*, ECHR 2001-III; for comments on the case see Mowbray (fn. 2), 56-59; Reidy (fn. 38), 29.
51 See the Joint partly dissenting opinion of Judges Fuhrmann and Kuris attached to the judgment in *Keenan*, paragraph 2.

their dissent was on factual grounds, for in their opinion "[The] prison authorities did all that could reasonably be expected from them".[52]

There was indeed no dispute between the majority and the minority of judges, sitting in this case, as far as the existence of a positive obligation to provide medical care to detainees was concerned. The Court's ruling in *Keenan* followed the line of well-established jurisprudence, recognising such an obligation.

A specific issue concerning a positive obligation to provide medical care appeared in the case of *Stojanovic v. Serbia*.[53] The question was whether a belated compliance of state authorities with the positive obligation to provide medical care to a detained person constituted a breach of Article 3 of the Convention.

The majority took the stand that there was no violation of Article 3 in the case. The facts were quite simple. A medical dentistry specialist proposed on 5 May 2004 that the applicant, who was serving a prison sentence at the time, should be provided with dentures. More than three years elapsed before the applicant was actually provided with dentures on 25 June 2007.[54]

The Court only took note of the fact that the applicant had been provided with dentures and struck out that part of the application, on the grounds that the applicant had been provided with the relevant medical care.[55]

Judge Zagrebelsky dissented on the issue.[56] In his opinion there had been a violation of Article 3 of the Convention in this case, and he expressed himself in the following way:

> "The Court, to my knowledge, has never found the matter to have been resolved in a case under Article 3 of the Convention such as the present one. …The Government's action was taken after a long period of three years and four months (nearly three years after the application had been lodged). No redress has been granted in respect of the violation complained of (still less have the Government taken action to fulfil their procedural obligations under Article 3 of the Convention)…I am unable to see how it can be said that the issue of the case has been resolved by the sole fact that a possible violation of Article 3 has finally ended and I am deeply worried by a judgment that sets such a precedent in the Court's Article 3 case-law."

52 Ibid., paragraph 3.

53 *Stojanovic v. Serbia*, app. no. 34425/04, judgment of 19 May 2009. Although I was elected to the Court as the national judge of Serbia, I did not sit on the bench in this case; there was an *ad hoc* judge appointed by the Government of Serbia.

54 *Stojanovic v. Serbia*, app. no. 34425/04, paragraphs 14 and 15.

55 Ibid., paragraphs 80 and 81.

56 See dissenting opinion of Judge Zagrebelsky attached to the judgment in *Stojanovic v. Serbia*.

The reason for dissent in this case shows how the Court's case-law is developing in respect of positive obligations. The dissenting judge looked for a violation in a situation in which the respondent government complied with the state positive obligation to provide medical care to detainees only after a significant delay. The idea was that belated compliance with a positive obligation could not absolve the state from its specific duty. Although rejected by the majority of judges sitting on the bench, this avenue tried to introduce a more refined understanding of a particular positive obligation. It attempted to develop a positive obligation by introducing a more detailed approach to its substance. The effect of such an approach would have been to widen the scope of a positive obligation by refinement of its character. It has been said that a dissent of yesterday may become a rule of tomorrow. That is how positive obligations develop and become more subtle in nature.

Duty to Investigate

We have seen in Judge Zagrebelsky's dissenting opinion in *Stojanovic* that he referred *inter alia* to procedural obligations under Article 3 of the Convention. The procedural obligations consist of the duty incumbent on the state to investigate allegations of serious ill-treatment committed by state agents.[57]

The obligation to investigate emerged in *Aksoy*, the case in which the Court found a violation of Article 3 of the Convention, but it did not say precisely that this was on procedural grounds.[58] The applicant in *Aksoy* complained of having been ill-treated, while in police custody, in different ways, such as having water thrown over him, being beaten, submitted to electric shocks and "Palestinian hanging".[59] The Court could not clearly establish the existence of all the forms of mistreatment which the applicant complained of, although there was relevant medical evidence to support the applicant's allegations. The Court however set a general rule in paragraph 61 of the judgment:

> "[Where] an individual is taken into police custody in good health but is found to be injured at the time of release, it is incumbent on the State to provide a plausible explanation as to the causing of the injury, failing which a clear issue arises under Article 3 of the Convention."

It was thus made clear that there was an issue under Article 3 but the question remained open as to the substance of the positive obligation incumbent on the respondent state. This was spelt out in a more refined way less than two years later in a Bulgarian case.

---

57 See Mowbray (fn. 2), 59-64; Akandji-Kombe (fn. 2), 32-35; Reidy (fn. 38), 36-43.

58 *Aksoy v. Turkey*, Judgments and Decisions 1996-VI; for bibliography see Berger (fn. 6), 40.

59 *Aksoy v. Turkey*, paragraph 60.

The question of a duty to investigate ill-treatment, falling within the scope of Article 3 of the Convention, seems to be fully and thoroughly entrenched for the first time in *Assenov and Others v. Bulgaria.*[60] The applicants, who had been arrested by the police, claimed to have been mistreated by police officers. The Court found that the claim was valid, because it was based on medical evidence. The Court held that there had been a violation of Article 3 of the Convention in this case based on the respondent state's failure to carry out an effective official investigation of the alleged ill-treatment by the police. The Court expressed its stance in paragraph 102 of the judgment, which reads as follows:

> "[Where] an individual raises an arguable claim that has been seriously ill-treated by the police or other such agents of the State unlawfully and in breach of Article 3, that provision, read in conjunction with the State's general duty under Article 1 of the Convention to 'secure to everyone within their jurisdiction the rights and freedoms defined in ... [the] Convention' requires by implication that there should be an effective official investigation."

It has been remarked that the duty to investigate under Article 3 of the Convention runs parallel to the procedural obligation under its Article 2.[61] A failure to investigate serious allegations of torture runs the risk of finding a violation according to both Articles 3 and 2 of the Convention. Procedural positive obligations incumbent on member states arise from both provisions.

In *Labita v. Italy* the Court also found a violation of Article 3 of the Convention on the grounds that no effective official investigation had been held into allegations of ill-treatment of a prisoner.[62] The applicant complained of various forms of mistreatment, such as being beaten, his testicles being squeezed, being handcuffed during medical examinations, as well as being transferred from the prison to the courts' premises in inhuman conditions.[63] The applicant's allegations were supported by evidence consisting of relevant medical certificates.[64]

The Court compared the duties of investigation under Article 3 with the ones from Article 2 of the Convention and found these identical in nature. At this point it should be noted that the academic writers hold the obligation to investigate under Article 3 of the Convention to be narrower than the procedural obligation under Article 2, for the latter requires the investigation of the killing irrespective of the status of the perpetrator.[65]

---

60 *Assenov and Others v. Bulgaria*, Judgments and Decisions 1998-VIII.
61 Mowbray (fn. 2), 61; Akandji-Kombe (fn. 2), 33.
62 *Labita v. Italy*, ECHR 2000-IV.
63 *Labita v. Italy*, paragraphs 29-30.
64 *Labita v. Italy*, paragraphs 31-35.
65 Cf. Mowbray (fn. 2), 65.

The Court's further finding in *Labita* was that the investigation of the alleged ill-treatment that the applicant complained of was "very slow" and therefore ineffective, because of the regrettable "inactivity of Italian authorities".[66]

This made the Court conclude in paragraph 136 of the judgment:

> "[Having] regard to the lack of a thorough and effective investigation into the credible allegation made by the applicant that he had been ill-treated by warders when detained... the Court holds that there has been a violation of Article 3 of the Convention."

The *Labita* judgment shows a pattern in the Court's finding of violations of human rights on the grounds of the positive obligation to investigate under Article 3. There must be allegations of ill-treatment; those allegations must be credible, *e.g.* confirmed by medical evidence and the investigation of such allegations must prove to be effective, if the state is to escape responsibility based on its duty to investigate.

11.2.4 Positive Obligations in Respect of Length of Proceedings (Article 6)

The obligation incumbent on a member state, contracting party to the Convention concerning the length of proceedings falls within the broader scope of such obligations. They arise from Article 6 of the Convention, which grants the right to a fair trial to everyone. Granting a fair trial calls for state action. It means that each and every member state, contracting party to the Convention must set up its own judiciary in such a way as to enable fair proceedings in civil and criminal cases. That is what the German scholars call *Organisationsgarantie* and it has to be laid down in terms of domestic law under the Court's own and rather strict scrutiny.[67] Therefore it has been rightly remarked by commentators that to meet its obligation to grant a fair trial the state must legislate.[68]

Setting up a system of judiciary does not only refer to the organisation, but furthermore to the functioning of courts-of-law at member state level. The good functioning of the judiciary is also required under Article 6 of the Convention and one of the issues which are most often raised in respect of the proper functioning of the judiciary on a national level is the so-called reasonable time requirement. It is indeed "the single most common complaint received by the Strasbourg Court".[69]

---

66 *Labita v. Italy*, paragraphs 131-135.

67 Grabenwarter (fn. 13), 341.

68 Akandji-Kombe (fn. 2), 61.

69 Jacobs, White & Ovey (fn. 3), 272.

Proceedings on a national level must be completed within a reasonable time, for otherwise the whole system of administration of justice would loose its purpose and substance. Various member states have had problems arising from the length of proceedings and have faced applications alleging a breach of the reasonable time requirement. One of those is Italy. In the case of *Bottazzi v. Italy* the Grand Chamber stated in paragraph 22 of the judgment as follows:

> "Article 6, paragraph 1 of the Convention imposes on the Contracting States the duty to organise their judicial systems in such a way that their courts can meet the requirements of this provision."[70]

That was the announcement of principle, given in a situation which had provided the Court with a motive to formulate it. The Court stated in the same paragraph of the judgment that since 1987 it had already rendered 65 judgments in which a breach of Article 6 of the Convention had been found on the grounds of exceeding reasonable time in domestic proceedings.

The government of Italy reacted and a bill was presented to parliament in order to adopt new legislation, which was to improve the situation. The act of parliament adopted was the well known *Pinto law.*[71] It introduced the possibility of claiming damages before domestic courts in case of extended proceedings. The remedy was thus compensatory in character.

Other countries having the same problem either followed the example of Italy, by introducing a compensatory remedy or the one of Austria, which had introduced a preventive remedy. The latter consisted of filing a special request under the Courts Act (*Gerichtsorganisationsgesetz*) aiming at making the proceedings underway more expedient.[72] Let me only mention two examples, among many in this respect. Poland adopted the Austrian system, whereas Serbia followed the Italian pattern. There were also countries that combined the two approaches[73]

The essential point in all the examples I have invoked is that the member states had to legislate in order to meet their duties under the Convention. These duties represented their

70 *Bottazzi v. Italy,* ECHR 1999-V.

71 For more information on the subject see M. Fabri, "The Italian Maze Towards Trials Within Reasonable Time", in: *The right to trial within a reasonable time and short-term reform of the European Court of Human Rights,* Bled, Slovenia 2009, 10-21.

72 See *Holzinger v. Austria*, ECHR 2001-I, paragraph 16 (Relevant Domestic Law).

73 For Poland see K. Kowalska, "Effective Remedies for Excessive Length of Proceedings", *in: Pilot Judgments Procedure in the European Court of Human Rights,* 3rd Informal Seminar for Government Agents and other Institutions, Warsaw 2009, 164-168; for Serbia see S. Caric, *Pravo na sudjenje u razumnom roku*, Beograd 2008, 59-73. For countries that combined the approaches see also S. Caric, 42-52.

positive obligations. Such obligations induced member states to pass legislation in order to bring their national legal systems into conformity with the Convention.

11.2.5 *From the Protection of the Home to the Protection of the Environment (Article 8)*

The Court's jurisprudence under Article 8 of the Convention can well illustrate the switch in the approach to the protection of human rights made by the ECHR. Article 8 provides for the protection of private and family life, correspondence and the home. The concept of the home has evolved. On the one hand it developed in such a way as to include business premises as well as the place of one's dwelling.[74] On the other hand the concept faced evolution because the Court took a stand leading to the conclusion that the respect of the home called for positive measures by a member state in order to meet its duties under the Convention.

In *Moreno Gomez v. Spain* the Court laid down a definition of the home.[75] Paragraph 53 of that judgment reads *inter alia*:

> "A home will usually be the place, the physically defined area, where private and family life develops. The individual has a right to respect for home, meaning not just the right to the actual physical area, but also to the quiet enjoyment of that area."[76]

The complaint in *Moreno Gomez* was filed with the ECHR because of the excessive noise that the applicant suffered from numerous nightclubs in the vicinity of her flat in a residential area of Valencia.

The Court found a violation of Article 8 of the Convention, stating in paragraph 62 of the judgment:

> "[T]he respondent State has failed to discharge its positive obligation to guarantee the applicant's right to respect for her home."

The Court thus put forward its stance that the concept of the home was subject to positive obligations by the state, which meant that it should be understood in such a way as to cause

74 See D. Popovic, "Protection Of Business Premises Under The European Convention On Human Rights", *Constitutional Law Review* 2009/1 Batumi (Georgia) 41-48.

75 *Moreno Gomez v. Spain*, ECHR 2004-X.

76 For a definition of the concept of "home", according to the Court's case-law preceding *Moreno Gomez* cf. U. Kikelly, *The right to respect for private and family life*, Strasbourg 2003, 19; for its delimitation see Popovic (fn. 74), 45-46.

state activity. Although there was no direct interference by state authorities with the applicant's home in this case, a violation of Article 8 was found because of the lack of positive action on the side of the respondent state.[77]

The judgment in *Moreno Gomez* followed the Court's landmark ruling made in another Spanish case. It was the case of *Lopez Ostra*.[78] The applicant in that case was a lady who lived in the city of Lorca, where a heavy concentration of leather industries provoked excessive pollution. The applicant had requested environmental protection from the domestic authorities, but eventually failed to obtain protection from the nuisance caused by the industrial plant, which had caused the pollution.

The Court's main finding in respect of the pollution, as affecting the applicant's home in respect of Article 8 of the Convention was expressed in paragraph 51 of the judgment. The Court was of the opinion that a person's health did not necessarily need to be damaged for the protection of the home under Article 8 to come into play. The Court stated:

> "[Severe] environmental pollution may affect individuals' well-being and prevent them their homes in such a way as to affect their private and family life adversely, without, however, seriously endangering their health."

The Court took a stand in the same paragraph that it was not of primordial importance whether the approach to the issue would be the one of interference by a public authority, under paragraph 2 of Article 8 of the Convention or the one of a positive obligation incumbent on the state under paragraph 1 of the same provision. This was crucial for the Court's interpretation, because as far as the text of Article 8 is concerned, one might regard its first paragraph as a mere proclamation of a right, regardless of any positive duty on the side of the state ("*everyone has the right*"). It is the wording of paragraph 2 of the same article which is actually prescriptive and forbids the state to interfere with the proclaimed right ("*there shall be no interference by a public authority with the exercise of this right*").

The Court's interpretation of Article 8 in *Lopez Ostra* made a shift from a negative obligation not to interfere with a certain right to a positive obligation, containing a duty to act in a certain manner, which was considered to be incumbent on the state. The Court stated later in the same paragraph of the judgment that the two approaches I have just mentioned were "broadly similar". This was due to the fact that:

> "In both contexts regard must be had to the fair balance that has to be struck between the competing interests of the individual and of the community as a whole, and in any case the State enjoys a certain margin of appreciation."

77 For comments on the case see Akandji-Kombe (fn. 2), 46; Harris, O'Boyle & Warbrick (fn. 32), 390-391.
78 *Lopez Ostra v. Spain*, Judgments and Decisions A 303 C (1994); for bibliography see Berger (fn. 6), 503.

The ECHR found that in the case at stake the authorities had indeed taken certain steps, fulfilling the functions assigned to them under domestic law, but it was essential to establish whether

> "[the] national authorities took the measures necessary for protection of the applicant's right for her home and for her private and family life under Article 8."[79]

The Court's final finding therefore was expressed in paragraph 58 of the judgment with the following words:

> "[The] Court considers that the State did not succeed in striking a fair balance between the interest of the town's economic well-being... and the applicant's effective enjoyment of her right to respect for her home."

By introducing such an interpretation of Article 8 of the Convention, the Court made room for environmental protection, which was not mentioned in the text of the Convention, to take its place among the values granted protection in terms of European Human Rights Law. *Lopez Ostra* was the first case in which the Court upheld an environmental complaint.[80]

Some commentators are inclined to speak of "the right to a healthy environment".[81] However, the Court's position on the subject remains somewhat indecisive because of the intervention of the margin of appreciation. The latter was mentioned in paragraph 51 of the judgment in *Lopez Ostra*, as we have seen above, and the issue of delimitation of its scope re-emerged in a British case, that was given a Grand Chamber judgment in 2003. It was the *Hatton* case.[82]

The issue in *Hatton* was the incidence of the level of noise from aircraft taking off and landing at the Heathrow Airport in London on the enjoyment of applicants' rights under Article 8 of the Convention. The Chamber judgment was in favour of the applicants finding a violation by five votes to two and the case was presented to the Grand Chamber of the Court.[83]

The Grand Chamber held in paragraph 96 of the judgment, as follows:

---

79 *Lopez Ostra v. Spain*, paragraph 55.

80 Mowbray (fn. 2), 183.

81 Akandji-Kombe (fn. 2), 47.

82 *Hatton and Others v. United Kingdom*, ECHR 2003-VIII; for bibliography see Berger (fn. 6), 506.

83 For comments on the Chamber judgment in *Hatton* see Mowbray (fn. 2), 184-186.

> "There is no explicit right in the Convention to a clean and quiet environment, but where an individual is directly and seriously affected by noise or other pollution, an issue may arise under Article 8."

This language of the Court's deserves reflection. Although there is no explicit right, an issue may arise under a certain provision of the Convention. This leads to the conclusion that aside from explicit rights, there may be others, which are not explicit. Or in other words, the Court seems to be ready to recognise certain rights that are not found in the text of the Convention. In making such a statement the Court invoked its ruling in *Lopez Ostra* as authority.

The Grand Chamber also expressed the view that the Convention was applicable in environmental cases both when the state directly caused pollution, and when its responsibility arose from its failure to properly regulate private industry. At this point the Court reiterated its previous stance, expressed in *Lopez Ostra*. In both situations state responsibility could be analysed either in terms of a positive duty under paragraph 1 of Article 8 of the Convention, or in terms of interference by a public authority, under paragraph 2 of the same provision.[84]

The Grand Chamber held in *Hatton* that a margin of appreciation should prevail over the Court's scrutiny of the measures taken by the domestic authorities in order to prevent pollution. The real issue for the Court was in this case whether the margin of appreciation should be wide or narrow. In this respect it must be noted that the Grand Chamber interpreted the ruling in *Lopez Ostra* as being based on a "failure by the national authorities to comply with some aspect of the domestic regime".[85] Considering the flight regime at Heathrow Airport from the standpoint of noise, creating a nuisance to the applicants, who all lived in the vicinity of the airport, the Court found several reasons to justify the state's policy. This led to the conclusion that the action of the respondent government fell within the margin of appreciation accorded to a member state.[86] The main ruling was given in paragraph 129 of the judgment, where the Grand Chamber stated:

> "[The] Court does not find that, in substance, the authorities overstepped their margin of appreciation by failing to strike a fair balance between the right of the individuals affected by those regulations to respect for their private life and home and the conflicting interests of others and of the community as a whole."

84 *Hatton and Others v. United Kingdom,* paragraph 98; cf. *Lopez Ostra v. Spain,* paragraph 51.
85 *Hatton and Others v. United Kingdom,* paragraph 120.
86 *Hatton and Others v. United Kingdom,* paragraphs 124-129.

The Court's judgment was rendered at this point by twelve votes to five. The dissenting judges insisted on the positive obligation of the state. Admitting that it was not easy to determine "the extent of permissible direct State interference and of the State positive obligation" they stressed the Court's supervisory function. Although subsidiary in character, that function of the Court should by all means apply, according to the dissenters, in cases in which "a positive duty on the State to ensure as far as possible that ordinary people enjoy normal seeping conditions" is at stake.[87]

The majority in *Hatton* seem to have understood the positive obligation incumbent on the state as the one of striking the fair balance between conflicting interests, whereas the minority were in favour of the existence of a specific positive obligation, arising from Article 8 in respect of the home.

Despite the dilemma provoked by the interpretation of the rule in *Hatton*, the positive obligation of the state in respect of the home seems to be quite clear. Moreover, it has been developing towards a new phenomenon, consisting of the protection of environment.

The protection of the environment has emerged in the Court's jurisprudence, but its scope and contents have remained undefined. It has been remarked by commentators that the two texts under Article 8 of the Convention, which applied in paragraph 51 of the judgment in *Lopez Ostra*, and concerning the first and second paragraphs of the said provision of the Convention have not merged into one.[88] Protecting home under Article 8 led to the introduction of the protection of the environment, but this process is still taking shape. It is based on the positive obligation of the state, a concept which once again has served as a tool in the development of the Court's case-law.

11.2.6 From Restraining from Interference with Property to the Protection of Property (Article 1 First Protocol)

Transforming the peaceful enjoyment of property in the course of the creation of European human rights law has been one of the significant contributions to its development and slowly taking shape.[89] Positive obligations of member states have emerged throughout the evolution of the Court's case-law. It is worth noting at this point that the most recent manuals on European Human Rights Law have basically the same approach to the issue. They start with the developments that have recently taken place, mostly beginning with the *Öneryildiz* judgment.[90] This is the case with the book by Jacobs, White and Ovey, but

87 *Hatton and Others v. United Kingdom*, Joint dissenting opinion of Judges Costa, Ress, Türmen, Zupancic and Steiner, paragraphs 6 and 12.

88 Harris, O'Boyle & Warbrick (fn. 32), 391.

89 I have consecrated a separate study, to this particular process of development; see D. Popovic, *Protecting Property in European Human Rights Law*, Utrecht 2009, especially 145-147 (summarised conclusions)

90 *Öneryildiz v. Turkey*, ECHR 2004-XII.

also with the one by Harris, O'Boyle and Warbrick.[91] These two manuals however cover positive obligations concerning Article 1 First Protocol under a separate heading, which seems to be a novelty if compared to another manual of the same calibre, dating from 2006, where there was no such heading.[92]

On the other hand there are authors who delve deeper into the past to research the emergence of positive obligations under Article 1 First Protocol. One of these is Akandji-Kombe, who uses the word "discover" in order to describe the emergence of positive obligations in respect of the protection of property. According to this author the first positive obligation "discovered" in this context was the obligation to compensate victims who had been deprived of their possessions in the public interest.[93] He finds support for his theory in paragraph 54 of the judgment in *James and Others.*[94] The Court stated in that paragraph that

> "the protection of the right of property…would be largely illusory and ineffective in the absence of any equivalent principle".

The relevant equivalent principle that the Court referred to was the payment of compensation, which had been mentioned earlier in the same paragraph. To my mind it may be somewhat doubtful whether this particular positive obligation of the member state was of jurisprudential origin. The reason for that is to be found in the text of the Article 1 First Protocol, which reads:

> "No one shall be deprived of his possessions except in the public interest and subject to the conditions provided for by law and by the general principles of international law".

It is especially the fact that reference is made to the general principles of international law, which raises some doubts. The Court itself has stated in *Lithgow and Others* that "the obligation to pay compensation derives from an implicit condition in Article 1 of Protocol no 1".[95]

It is however true that the judgment in *James and Others* was rendered more than five months before the one in *Lithgow and Others* and that fact speaks in favour of the theory

91 See Jacobs, White & Ovey (fn. 3), 479-481; Harris, O'Boyle & Warbrick (fn. 32), 664-666. The latter book however mentions older cases quite briefly.

92 Cf. Van Dijk et al. (fn. 42), 863-893.

93 Akandji-Kombe (fn. 2), 53.

94 *James and Others v. United Kingdom*, Judgments and Decisions A 98 (1986); for bibliography see Berger (fn. 6), 739-740; for comments see Sudre et al. (fn. 46), 515-521.

95 *Lithgow and Others v. United Kingdom*, Judgments and Decisions A 102 (1986), paragraph 109.

put forward by Akandji-Kombe that is mentioned above.[96] One gets the impression that the Court was eager to underline its fidelity to the text of the Convention in the latter judgment after having taken a bolder approach in the previous one. This however seems to be a matter of technique. The approach to each of the cases does not seem to fall within the wide interpretation of the Convention provisions that some of the commentators are nowadays complaining of, especially in the context of the protection of property.[97] It is therefore doubtful whether the ECHR wanted to overstep the limits of the text of the Convention in *James* and return to it in *Lithgow*. Even if that were the case, Akandji-Kombe may be right, but the question remains open.

Positive obligations of member states in respect of the protection of property under Article 1 First Protocol emerged in the case-law of the ECHR in the clearest manner with the case of *Öneryildiz v. Turkey*.[98] The applicant in that case was a man who lived with his family in a slum quarter in Istanbul. The place where he lived had been built illegally on a piece of land, which belonged to the Treasury. The applicant's construction as well as the occupation of the slum was not authorized by the authorities. The Court held nevertheless that the applicant had possessions in terms of Article 1 First Protocol.[99]

A methane explosion occurred in the slum quarter, provoking the eruption of a mountain of waste. This led to the destruction of slums, including the one belonging to the applicant. There were also thirty-nine casualties in the accident. The applicant invoked Article 1 First Protocol before the ECHR, demanding protection of his property. The Court, as I said earlier, first held that the applicant had possessions, but then it went further by tackling the issue of whether there had been interference with the applicant's property.

It was clear that there was by no means interference with the property in the sense that an action of the state had provoked the loss of applicant's possessions. However, the Court made its approach to the issue more refined than ever before, stating in paragraph 134 of the judgment and referring to Article 1 First Protocol:

> "Genuine, effective exercise of the right protected by that provision does not depend merely on the State's duty not to interfere, but may require positive measures of protection, particularly where there is a direct link between the measures an applicant may legitimately expect from the authorities and his effective enjoyment of his possessions."

96 See footnote 93.

97 Cf. M. Bossuyt, "Should the Strasbourg Court Exercise More Self-Restraint?", *Human Rights Law Journal*, Vol. 28, No. 9-12 (2007), 327-328.

98 *Öneryildiz v. Turkey*, ECHR 2004-XII; for comments on the case see Sudre et al. (fn. 46), 497-505.

99 Popovic (fn. 89), 126-127.

In the following paragraph the Court went on along the same lines and held:

> "In the Court's view, the resulting infringement amounts not to 'interference' but to the breach of a positive obligation, since the State officials and authorities did not do everything within their power to protect the applicant's proprietary interests."

On those grounds the Court found a violation of Article 1 First Protocol on the case.[100] It is worth noting that the Court's reasoning deliberately rejected a concept that had been adopted in its previous and rather firm jurisprudence ("interference") in order to introduce another one ("positive obligation"). However, neither of the two was mentioned in the text of the Convention itself. The state was considered responsible for failing to protect the property instead of being discharged on the grounds that it did not interfere with the applicant's possessions at all. This was a decisive switch in the Court's approach to the issue of the protection of property.

In a subsequent case the Court was faced with the question of the extension and the real scope of the state's obligation to protect property. Therefore it held in the case of *Budayeva and others* that the state could not be held liable to compensate the full market value of the property destroyed in a disastrous event.[101]

It was in a case in which Poland was the respondent state that the ECHR laid down its principle stance concerning a specific positive obligation of a member state in respect of Article 1 First Protocol. The positive obligation in question could be labelled as the one of ensuring legal and practical conditions for the implementation of domestic legislation. The case was *Broniowski v. Poland.*[102] It was rather complex and originated in a claim that an heir had to demand from the State compensation for the estate which had been left outside the Polish borders at the time when they were drawn, back in 1944. The claim was justified in terms of domestic law, but the state never met its obligation to compensate. The Court found that the behaviour of the state authorities ran counter to a positive obligation and stated in paragraph 184 of the judgment:

> "The rule of law underlying the Convention and the principle of lawfulness in Article 1 Protocol No. 1 require States not only to respect and apply in a consistent manner, the laws they have enacted, but also, as a corollary to this duty, to ensure the legal and practical conditions for their implementation."

100 *Öneryildiz v. Turkey,* ECHR 2004-XII, operative part, item 3.

101 *Budayeva and Others v. Russia*, app. nos. 15339/02, 21166/02, 20058/02, 11673/02, 15343/02, judgment of 20 March 2008; for comments see Jacobs, White & Ovey (fn. 3), 479-480; Popovic (fn. 89), 128-129.

102 *Broniowski v. Poland,* ECHR 2004-V; for bibliography see Berger (fn. 6), 735-736.

The interpretation of the Convention as applied to the set of facts in this case deserves attention, because the ECHR held in paragraph 187 of the judgment that there had been a violation of Article 1 First Protocol on the grounds of proportionality. Namely, the Court found that the applicant had had to bear a disproportionate and excessive burden, unjustified "in terms of the legitimate general community interest pursued by the authorities". The failure to meet a state positive obligation violated the applicant's right to the peaceful enjoyment of property.[103]

The Court further developed its approach to the positive obligations in respect of Article 1 First Protocol in a judgment against Romania. It was in the *Paduraru* case of 2005.[104] The issue in *Paduraru* was to some extent similar to the one in *Broniowski*. The fundamental difference between the two consisted in the fact that it was incumbent on the state to compensate for the property lost outside the new borders in the Polish case, whereas in the Romanian case the state had to recover in kind a piece of property nationalised under the communist regime.

The Romanian state was reluctant to restore the property in spite of the existence of a final judgment rendered on a domestic level, stating that the applicant had remained its rightful owner. What the ECHR found in paragraph 105 of the judgment in *Paduraru* went very much along with the Court's attitude expressed in *Broniowski*:

> "[Each] State must equip itself with an adequate and sufficient legal arsenal to ensure compliance with the positive obligations imposed on it by the Convention."

The ECHR seems to have departed from the idea of a positive obligation to respect domestic law and judicial decisions, which we saw earlier in *Broniowski*.[105] However, it went a step further so as to make the positive obligation at stake more precise. According to the Court's statement given in paragraph 112 of the judgment it occurs to me that the Court's genuine motive in *Paduraru* was to introduce the obligation to recover property. Let me quote the Court:

> "[The] Court notes that the State has failed to discharge its positive obligation to take timely and consistent action to address the issue of general interest raised by the return or sale of property transferred to State ownership under nationalisation decrees."

---

103 Cf. Akandji-Kombe (fn. 2) 54-55.

104 *Paduraru v. Romania*, ECHR 2005-XII; for comments see Akandji-Kombe (fn. 2), 55; Popovic (fn. 89), 129-130.

105 Thus: Akandji-Kombe (fn. 2), 55.

This paragraph is colourful as it shows the Court's effort to make a positive obligation more precise on one hand, but also, on the other hand, to affirm what a positive obligation consists of in general. The latter was done by defining a state positive obligation as one consisting of a "timely and consistent action" by the authorities.[106]

Two more types of positive obligations in respect of Article 1 First Protocol deserve to be mentioned. They are both connected to issues concerning Article 6 of the Convention. One of them is related to the right of access to court and the other to the right to execution of a final judgment rendered on a domestic level.

In the case of *Sovtransavto v. Ukraine* the Court had to decide on the issue of whether the state was responsible for legal certainty in general and especially in a situation in which the protection of property was at stake. The Court held that it was incumbent on the state to "secure the effective exercise of the rights" envisaged by the Convention.[107] The Court also found in paragraph 96 of the judgment:

> "Positive obligations may entail certain measures necessary to protect the right of property."

As the ECHR found that there had been serious procedural shortcomings throughout the litigation between private parties on a national level, it went further by concluding in paragraph 98 of the judgment, as follows:

> "[The] State failed to comply with its obligation to secure to the applicant company the effective enjoyment of its right to property."

It should be underlined that this positive obligation applies "both to disputes between individuals and to those between individuals and the state".[108]

The second of the two positive obligations I have mentioned above consists of the duty of the state to provide execution of a final judgment given on an internal level. The landmark case in this respect was *Burdov v. Russia*.[109] In that case the applicant had two final court's decisions rendered in his favour on a domestic level that he was unable to bring to enforcement. The ECHR held in paragraph 40 of the judgment:

106 Thus: Popovic (fn. 89), 129-130,

107 *Sovtransavto v. Ukraine*, ECHR 2002-VII, paragraph 96.

108 Akandji-Kombe (fn. 2), 56; for the limits of this positive obligation cf. Grgic et al., *The right to property under the European Convention of Human Rights*, Strasbourg 2007, 17-18.

109 *Burdov v. Russia*, ECHR 2002-III.

> "[The] impossibility for the applicant to obtain the execution of these judgments constituted an interference with his right to peaceful enjoyment of his possessions."

A line of the Court's jurisprudence followed this ruling, so it has become clear that the positive obligation of a member state consists of enforcement of domestic judgments. The authorities were at the same time not allowed to cite a lack of funds as an obstacle to the execution of a judgment rendered against the state.[110]

---

110 *Burdov v. Russia*, ECHR 2002-III, paragraph 41; for comments see Grgic et al. (fn. 108), 18; Akandji-Kombe (fn. 2), 56, who makes reference to the ECHR judgments following *Burdov* in this respect.

Conclusion of Part Four

To conclude this part it suffices to underline the fact that state positive obligations under European human rights law are fairly numerous nowadays. Some of them are rooted in the text of the Convention itself, but many of them are of jurisprudential origin. This is due to the fact that, throughout its evolution, the ECHR has considerably altered its technique, as well as its main approach to the protection of human rights. The old-fashioned approach of the Court, which was to be satisfied with the fact that a member state restrained from interference with individuals' rights has been overtaken in the Court's jurisprudence. It has been largely replaced by a doctrine of the existence of the state's duty to intervene and take positive action, aiming at enabling individuals to effectively enjoy their rights. One of the most recent scholarly definitions of positive obligations can illustrate the stage of development achieved very well. Let me quote:

> "The Court's case-law in respect of a number of provisions of the Convention states that public authorities should not only refrain from interfering arbitrarily with individuals' rights as protected expressly by the Articles of the Convention, they should also take active steps to safeguard them. These additional obligations are usually referred to as positive obligations as the authorities are required to act so as to prevent violations of the rights encompassed in the Convention or punish those responsible."[1]

This stage of evolution has been achieved by the rise of positive obligations and their frequent use as a tool in reaching the Court's judgments. Positive obligations therefore have been one of the most significant recent developments in European human rights law and have contributed to the enlargement of the field of protection of human rights in general.

1 M.D. Evans and A. Weber, Manuals on the wearing of religious symbols in public areas and on hate speech, published as *Yearbook of the European Convention on Human Rights* 51A, Leiden – Boston 2008, 129, 227 (Glossary).

Overall Concluding Remarks

The overall concluding remarks of this book will try to summarise what the main objective of the research was, in order to highlight the crucial elements of the study.

My starting point is that the judicial activity as such is a creative process. The courts of law, while rendering justice to the parties in a lawsuit, perform an extraordinary function, which consists of completing enacted legal rules. By that particular activity of the courts, the law is properly set in motion. They indeed complete a body of law by making it a coherent system. What applies to the law and the courts of law in general also applies to the ECHR and European human rights law. The latter has emerged as a body of law, being the outcome of the activity of the former.

As the creative character of the judiciary serves legal developments, it should be underlined that the role of precedent is one of the most important factors, if not actually decisive, in the evolution of law. Sticking to the rules of previous judgments in subsequent cases does not hinder the evolution of law. On the contrary, it can be seen as its tool and the example of the ECHR and its role in developing European human rights law is quite significant in that respect.

The ECHR is not formally bound by its previous rulings, but it nevertheless follows its own precedents, unless it finds cogent reasons to depart from these. This attitude of the Court has greatly contributed to the legal developments that have occurred in respect of the protection of human rights and the shaping of European human rights law as a coherent body of law.

If one perceives the legal developments I have just mentioned in the way they have been described here, a question will inevitably arise on the scope and significance of activist approach to cases, as performed by the ECHR within the process of the emergence of European human rights law. It seems that such an approach has been preponderant if compared to the self-restraint of the Court. At least two arguments speak in favour of such a theory.

One of these consists in the fact that the ECHR has used constantly evolving remedies, besides just satisfaction, to redress violations of human rights. This has been done under Article 46 of the Convention and by way of applying its provisions.

Another contribution to this particular evolution, leading to the emergence of the European human rights law, was even a bolder step forward than the one just mentioned. It consisted in the development by the Court's jurisprudence of various positive obligations of the state under different articles of the Convention. That process led to a substantial transformation of the Court's attitude towards the protection of human rights. Instead of being satisfied with a finding that the state did not interfere with an individual's human rights, the Court has started demanding that the State perform a positive action. This has been done in order to make the state comply with its positive obligations, as understood by the Court's interpretation of the Convention and its own precedents. In following this path the ECHR has not only enlarged the scope of protection of human rights, but it has also showed a considerable amount of judicial creativity.

Bibliography

J-F. Akandji-Kombe, *Positive Obligations under the European Convention on Human Rights*, Strasbourg 2007.

J. Allard & A. Garapon, *Les juges dans la mondialisation*, Paris 2005.

P. Ardent, *Institutions politiques et droit constitutionnel*, Paris 2003.

J.H. Baker, *An Introduction to English Legal History*, London 1979.

E. Bates, "Supervising the Execution of Judgments Delivered by the European Court of Human Rights: The Challenges Facing the Committee of Ministers", in: Th. Christou and J.P. Raymond (eds.), *European Court of Human Rights – Remedies and Execution of Judgments*, London 2005.

V. Berger, *Jurisprudence de la Cour européenne des droits de l'homme*, Paris 2009.

C. Birsan, "Les aspects nouveaux de l'application des articles 41 et 46 de la Convention dans la jurisprudence de la Cour européenne des droits de l'homme", in : H. Hartig (ed.), *Trente ans de droit européen des droits de l'homme – études à la mémoire de Wolfgang Strasser*, Bruxelles 2007.

M. Bossuyt, "Should Strasbourg Court Exercise More Self-Restraint?", *Human Rights Law Journal* Vol. 28, No. 9-12 (2007).

M. Boumghar, *Une approche de la notion de principe dans le système de la Convention européenne des droits de l'homme*, Paris 2010.

A. Buyse, "The Pilot Judgment Procedure at the European Court of Human Rights: Possibilities and Challenges", in: *Nomiko Vima – European Court of Human Rights*, 50 Years, Athens 2010.

S.G. Calabresi (ed.), *Originalism – A Quarter-Century Debate*, Washington DC 2007.

G. Canivet, "La pratique du droit comparé par les cours suprêmes", *Tulane Law Review* 80 – 1/2005.

M. Cappelletti, *Le pouvoir des juges*, Paris – Aix-en-Provence 1990.

S. Caric, *Pravo na sudjenje u razumnom roku /Right to a Trial Within Reasonable Time*, Belgrade 2008.

M.A. Cohendet, *Droit constitutionnel*, Paris 2006.

Collected Edition of the "Travaux Préparatoires" of the European Convention on Human Rights, Volume II, The Hague 1975.

G. Cuniberti, *Grands systèmes de droit contemporains*, Paris 2007.

J.P. Costa, "The Evolution and Current Challenges of the European Court of Human Rights", *Regent Journal of Law & Public Policy* 1/2009.

Council of Europe, *Yearbook of the European Convention on Human Rights*, Leiden – Boston 51/2008.

R. David & C. Jauffret Spinosi, *Les grands systèmes de droit contemporains*, Paris 2002.

M.B. Dembour, *Who Believes in Human Rights? Reflections on the European Convention*, Cambridge 2006.

R. Deneger and P. Mahoney, "The Prospects for a Test Case Procedure in the European Court of Human Rights", in: H. Hartig (ed.), *Trente ans de droit européen des droits de l'homme – études à la mémoire de Wolfgang Strasser*, Bruxelles 2007.

Lord Denning, *The Discipline of Law*, London 1979.

P. van Dijk e.a. (eds.), *Theory and Practice of the European Convention on Human Rights*, Antwerpen – Oxford 2006.

N. Dongois, *La justice est-elle juste?*, Grolley 2006.

A. Drzemczewski, "The internal organisation of the European Court of Human Rights: the composition of chambers and the Grand Chamber", *European Human Rights Law Review* 3/2000.

R. Dworkin, *Taking Rights Seriously*, London 1987.

A. Dyevre, *L'activisme juridictionnel en droit constitutionnel comparé: France, États-Unis, Allemagne*, thèse de doctorat à l'Université Paris I, 2007.

R. Ergec, *Protection européenne et internationale des droits de l'homme*, Bruxelles 2006.

M.D. Evans and A. Weber, Manuals on the wearing of religious symbols in public areas and on hate speech, published as *Yearbook of the European Convention on Human Rights* 51A, Leiden – Boston 2008.

M. Fabri, "The Italian Maze Towards Trials Within Reasonable Time", in: *The right to trial within a reasonable time and short-term reform of the European Court of Human Rights*, Bled, Slovenia 2009.

J.F. Flauss, "Du droit international comparé des droits de l'homme dans la jurisprudence de la Cour européenne des droits de l'homme", in: *Publications of the Swiss Institute of Comparative Law 43 – The Role of Comparative Law in the Emergence of European Law*, Lausanne – Zürich, 2000

Th. Fleiner & L. Basta-Fleiner, *Allgemeine Staatslehre*, Oxford – New York 2004

Th. Fleiner & L. Basta-Fleiner, Constitutional Democracy in a Multicultural and Globalised World, Springer 2009.

N. Frangakis, "Systemic Human Rights Violations in the Jurisprudence of the European Court of Human Rights", in: *Nomiko Vima – European Court of Human Rights 50 Years*, Athens 2010.

S. Fredman, *Human Rights transformed – positive rights and positive duties*, Oxford – New York 2008.

D. Frison, *Introduction au droit anglais et aux institutions britanniques*, Paris 2005.

M. Fromont, *Droit administratif des états européens*, Paris 2006.

M. Fromont, *Grands systèmes de droit étrangers*, Paris 2001.

L. Garlicki, "Broniowski and After: On the Dual Nature of Pilot Judgments", in: L. Caflisch e.a. (eds.), *Liber Amicorum Luzius Wildhaber, Human Rights– Strasbourg Views*, Kehl –Strasbourg – Arlington 2007.

Y. Gaudemet, *Droit administratif*, Paris 2005.

M.D. Goldhaber, *A People's History of the European Court of Human Rights*, New Brunswick – New Jersey – London 2007.

D. Gomien, *Short guide to the European Convention on Human Rights*, Strasbourg 2005.

S. Goyard-Fabre, "Loi", in: Ph. Raynaud & S. Rials, *Dictionnaire de philosophie politique*, Paris 2003.

Ch. Grabenwarter, *Europäische Menschenrechtskonvention*, München – Wien 2003.

S. Greer, *The European Convention on Human Rights – Achievements, Problems and Prospects*, Cambridge 2006.

A. Grgic e.a., *The right to property under the European Convention on Human Rights*, Strasbourg 2007.

P. Grossi, *L'Europa del diritto*, Roma – Bari 2007.

W. Haller & A. Költz, *Allgemeines Staatsrecht*, Basel – Genf – München 1999.

D.J. Harris, M. O'Boyle & C. Warbrick, *Law of the European Convention on Human Rights*, Oxford – New York 2009.

M. Hunt, "State Obligations Following from a Judgment of the European Court of Human Rights", in: Th. Christou and J.P. Raymond (eds.), *European Court of Human Rights – Remedies and Execution of Judgments*, London 2005.

Jacobs, White & Owey, *The European Convention on Human Rights*, Oxford – New York 2010.

Jacobs and White (C. Ovey and R. White), European Convention on Human Rights, Oxford – New York, 2002.

M.W. Janis, R.S. Kay, A.W. Bradley, *European Human Rights Law – texts and materials*, Oxford – New York 2008.

Ph. Jestaz, *Les sources du droit*, Paris 2005.

D. Jociene, "The Subsidiary Character of the System of the European Convention on Human Rights with Reference to Cases against Lithuania", *Baltic Yearbook of International Law*, Vol. 9, 2009.

S. Jovanović, *O državi (On the State)*, Beograd 1922.

E. Kastanas, *Unité et diversité : notions autonomes et marge d'appréciation des Etats dans la jurisprudence de la Cour européenne des droits de l'homme*, Bruxelles 1996.

J.M. Kelly, *A Short History of Western Legal Theory*, Oxford - New York 1999.

U. Kikelly, *The right to respect for private and family life*, Strasbourg 2003.

M. Kirby, "Precedent - Report on Australia", in: E. Hondius (ed.), *Precedent and the law*, Bruxelles 2007.

M. Kirby, *Judicial Activism - Authority, Principle and Policy in the Judicial Method*, London 2004.

K. Kowalska, "Effective Remedies for Excessive Length of Proceedings", in: *Pilot Judgments Procedure in the European Court of Human Rights*, 3rd Informal Seminar for Government Agents and other Institutions, Warsaw 2009.

Ph. Leach, *Taking a Case to the European Court of Human Rights*, Oxford 2005.

Ph. Leach, H. Hardman, S. Stephenson & B.K. Blitz, *Responding to Systemic Human Rights Violations*, Antwerp - Oxford - Portland 2010.

P. Legrand & G.Samuel, *Introduction au common law*, Paris 2008.

G. Letsas, *A Theory of Interpretation of the European Convention on Human Rights*, Oxford - New York 2007.

M. Levinet, *Théorie générale des droits et libertés*, Bruxelles 2006.

D. Lochak, *Les droits de l'homme*, Paris 2002.

K. Lucas-Alberni, *Le revirement de jurisprudence de la Court européenne des droits de l'homme*, Bruxelles 2008.

P. Mahoney, "The Comparative Method of the European Court of Human Rights: Reference Back to National Law", in: *Publications of the Swiss Institute of Comparative Law, 43 – The Role of Comparative Law in the Emergence of European Law*, Lausanne – Zürich, 2000.

P. Mahoney, "Judicial Activism and Self-Restraint in the European Court of Human Rights: Two Sides of the Same Coin", *Human Rights Law Journal*, 11 (1990).

E. Meese, III, "Speech Before the American Bar Association" on July 9, 1985", in: S.G. Calabresi (ed.), *Originalism – A Quarter-Century Debate*, Washington DC 2007.

J.G. Merrills & A.H. Robertson, *Human Rights in Europe*, Manchester 2001.

E.A. Morse, "Reflections on the Rule of Law and 'Clear Reflection of Income': what constrains Discretion?", *Cornell Journal of Law and Public Policy*, 8 1998/9.

A. Mowbray, *The Development of Positive Obligations under the European Convention on Human Rights by the European Court of Human Rights*, Oxford – Portland Oregon 2004.

P. Pactet, *Institutions politiques – Droit constitutionnel*, Paris 2002.

D. Popovic, "Autonomous Concepts of the European Human Rights Law", in: M. Jovanovic & I. Krstic (eds.), *Human Rights Today – 60 years of the Universal Declaration,* Utrecht 2010

D. Popovic, "Prevailing of Judicial Activism over Self-Restraint in the Jurisprudence of the European Court of Human Rights", *Creighton Law Review* Vol. 42, no. 3 (2009).

D. Popovic, "Protection Of Business Premises Under The European Convention On Human Rights", *Constitutional Law Review* 2009/1 Batumi (Georgia).

D. Popović, "European Court of Human Rights and the Concept of Separation of Powers", in: M. Prabhakar (ed.), *Separation of Powers – Global Perspectives*, Hyderabad 2008.

D. Popovic, "Pilot Judgments of the European Court of Human Rights", in: *Council of Europe, The role of the Supreme Courts in the Domestic Implementation of the European Convention on Human Rights* (Proceedings of the Regional Conference Belgrade 20-21 September 2007) Strasbourg 2008.

D. Popović, "La raison comparatiste et la liberté", *Mélanges en honneur de Slobodan Milacic*, Bruxelles 2007.

D. Popovic, "Le droit comparé dans l'accomplissement des tâches de la Cour européenne des droits de l'homme", in: L. Caflisch e.a. (eds.), *LiberAmicorumLuziusWildhaber – Human Rights – StrasbourgViews*, Kehl – Strasbourg – Arlington 2007.

D. Popovic, *Protecting Property in European Human Rights Law*, Utrecht 2009.

D. Popovic, *Evropski sud za ljudska prava /European Court of Human Rights*, Belgrade 2008.

D. Popović, *Uvod u uporedno pravo/Introduction to Comparative Law*, Belgrade 2007.

K. Reid, *A Practitioner's Guide to the European Convention on Human Rights*, London 2008.

A. Reidy, *The prohibition of torture*, Strasbourg 2003.

J-F. Renucci, *Droit européen des droits de l'homme*, Paris 2002.

M-L. Rouquette, *La créativité*, Paris 2007.

Ch. Rozakis, "Is the Case-Law of the European Court of Human Rights a Procrustean Bed? Or is it a Contribution to the Creation of a European Public Order? A Modest Reply to Lord Hoffmann's Criticisms", *UCL Human Rights Review* 2/2009,

Ch. Rozakis, "The European Judge as Comparatist", *Tulane Law Review*, 80 – 1/2005.

A. Scalia, "Foreword to Part I", in: S.G. Calabresi (ed.), *Originalism – A Quarter-Century Debate*, Washington DC 2007.

D. Shelton, *Remedies in International Human Rights Law*, Oxford – New York 2006.

H. Simon & G. Funk-Baker, *Einfürung in das deutsche Recht und die deutsche Rechtssprache*, München – Paris – Kopenhagen – Athen – Bern 2006.

B. Stirn, D. Fairgrave & M. Guyomar, *Droits et libertés en France et au Royaume-Uni*, Paris 2006.

F. Sudre e.a., *Les grands arrêts de la Cour européenne des droits de l'homme*, Paris 2003.

F. Sudre, *Droit européen et international des droits de l'homme*, Paris 2005.

F. Terré, "Un juge créateur de droit? Non merci ! ", *Archives de philosophie du droit*, tome 50/2007.

J.L. Thireau, *Introduction historique au droit*, Paris 2009.

M. Troper, *La philosophie du droit*, Paris 2008.

F. Tulkens, "The Right to a Trial Within a Reasonable Time: Problems and Solutions", in: Venice Commission (ed.), *Can excessive length of proceedings be remedied?*, Strasbourg 2007.

L. Wildhaber, "Precedent in the European Court of Human Rights", in: L. Wildhaber, *The European Court of Human Rights 1998-2006 – History, Achievements, Reform*, Kehl – Strasbourg – Arlington 2006.

S. Whittaker, "Precedent in English Law: A View from the Citadel", in: E. Hondius (ed.), *Precedent and the law*, Bruxelles 2007.

V. Zagrebelsky, "Questions autour de Broniowski", in: L. Caflisch e.a. (eds.), *Liber Amicorum Luzius Wildhaber – Human Rights – Strasbourg Views*, Kehl – Strasbourg – Arlington 2007.

B. Zupančič, *O tumačenju prethodnih odluka (presedana) i presuda Evropskog suda za ljudska prava / On the Interpretation of Precedents and Judgments of the European Court of Human Rights*, manuscript 2004.

K. Zweigert & H. Kötz, *An Introduction to Comparative Law* (translated by T. Weir), Oxford – New York 1998.

Index

Table of Cases